PHI BETA POGO

BY WALT KELLY

Edited by

Mrs. Walt Kelly and Bill Crouch, Jr.

Introduction by Doug Marlette

Cartoons, photos, articles and special drawings of Pogo Possum and his pals from the pages of the Okefenokee Star *offer the knowledge needed to pass Basic Possum.*

F A Fireside Book
Published by Simon & Schuster Inc.
New York   London   Toronto   Sydney   Tokyo

To Lucy Shelton Casell

 Fireside
Simon & Schuster Building
Rockefeller Center, 1230 Avenue of the Americas
New York, New York   10020

ACKNOWLEDGMENTS

Grateful acknowledgment is made to the authors and publishers
of the following pieces reprinted with permission.

"Some Thoughts on Pogo and Comic Strips Today" by Bill Watterson, copyright © 1988 by Bill Watterson.
"Possum Pastoral" by Edward Mendelson, copyright © 1988 by Edward Mendelson.
"Two Mavericks at the Disney Studio: Ward Kimball Remembers Walt Kelly" by Thomas Andrae and Geoffrey Blum,
    copyright © 1988 by Thomas Andrae and Geoffrey Blum.
Art Afterpieces by Ward Kimball, copyright © 1964 by Ward Kimball.
"Walt Kelly" by George J. Lockwood, copyright © 1985 by Cartoonist PROfiles, Inc.
"Walt Kelly–Selby Kelly" by Nancy Beiman, copyright © 1984 by Cartoonist PROfiles, Inc.
"Selby Kelly" by Jud Hurd, copyright © 1974 by Cartoonist PROfiles, Inc.
Turning the Pages by Peter Schwed, copyright © 1984 by Peter Schwed.
"Pogofest in Georgia" by Bill Maher, copyright © 1987 by Waycross (GA) *Journal-Herald*.
"Tales of Pogo's Campaign Trail in 1988," "Milton Caniff Talks on Walt Kelly," and "An Interview with Selby
    Kelly," copyright © 1988 by Bill Crouch, Jr.

Library of Congress Cataloging-in-Publication Data
Phi beta Pogo.
"A Fireside book."
    1. Kelly, Walt. Pogo. I. Kelly, Selby. II. Crouch,
Bill. 1945-   . III. Kelly, Walt. Pogo. Selections. 1989.
PN6728.P57P46 1989   741.5'092 [B]   89-11334
ISBN 0-671-67782-9

Designed by Helen Barrow
Manufactured in the United States of America
10 8 6 4 2 1 3 5 7 9

CONTENTS

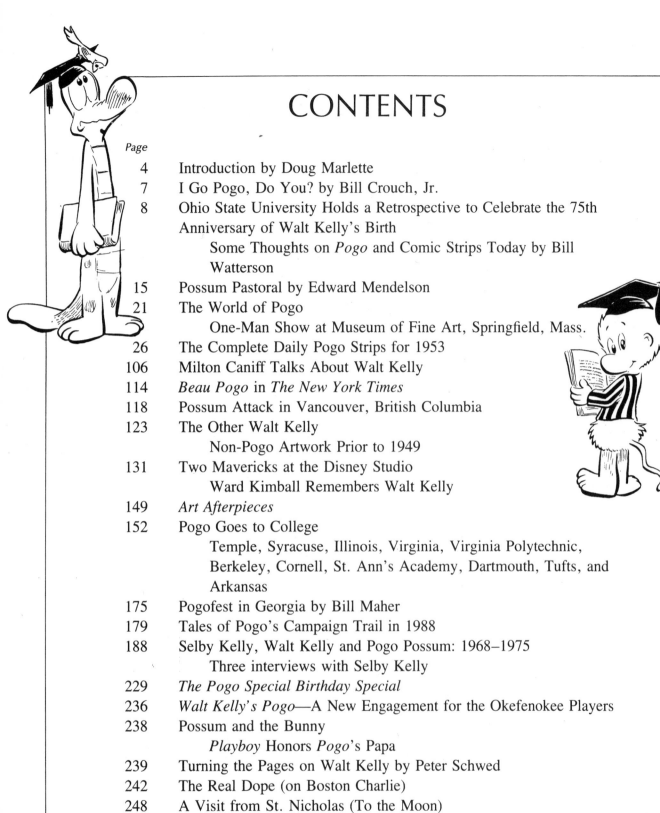

INTRODUCTION

WALT KELLY was the truth, the whole truth, and nothing but the truth.

Great cartoonists are like great athletes. Their talent dominates you. They get around and through your defenses and force you to play their game—to see through their eyes. Walt Kelly inspired us all. The giants of the trade today sing hymns of praise to the wonder of his wit and the glory of his artwork. In fact, and this is the highest compliment one cartoonist can pay another, he was the kind of cartoonist who made other cartoonists want to talk shop.

There is nothing professional cartoonists, especially neophytes, like better than to talk shop. Because we are so few in number and far between geographically we glom onto each other pathetically whenever we meet and talk shop endlessly. It's our way of bonding. We can spend hours discussing pen points, brushes and Zipatone—not to mention copiers and fax machines. But it's all shoptalk. Probably nobody has inspired more of those discussions of the rudiments of our craft than Walt Kelly. His perfect mastery and love of craft radiates from his work and has always generated much speculation among those of us trying to unravel the secrets of the cartoon cosmos.

How did he get that line, that zip, that flexibility and control in his brush? How did he put such rambunctious three-dimensional life into those two-dimensional characters? If we could just use the same tools or learn something of his work habits, maybe that's the source of his magic.

When I was an apprentice cartoonist of eighteen or so and learning my trade I fell under the spell of the legendary Kelly lettering. Although to look at my work now you wouldn't know it, I was a devoted disciple. Being lefthanded to such an awkward extent that I was allowed to park in handicapped spaces, I struggled with my lettering. My handwriting was, and still is, a wretched, indecipherable scrawl. Thus, I was enchanted by Pogo.

Never mind Kelly's much-heralded ornate Old English script, as spoken by Deacon Mushrat, or the circus-poster-style pontifications of P.T. Bridgeport—those were calligraphic accomplishments beyond my crippled and limited aspiration. I worshipped Kelly's simple straightforward balloon lettering. I lusted after that look of uniform liveliness in his lettering. I studied it. Committed it to memory. Painstakingly, I copied and recopied the Kelly alphabet, breaking it down into its component stylistic parts. His vertical strokes always leaned slightly at an angle, like the leaning tower of Pisa. His horizontals were . . . well, perfectly horizontal. His line was unfailingly thin vertically, thick horizontally. I dutifully bought the exact penpoints he used (an obscure brand no longer manufactured, according to one of his former assistants, who revealed this to me as though it were a Russian military secret). I sandpapered the point down to the proper angle for my hand—just as the master was said to have done. I practiced and practiced and practiced. It was no use. My lettering looked like it was done by a blind speed freak in a hurricane. To paraphrase Walt, I had met the enemy and it was me.

Of course, it was many years later before I figured out that it wasn't Kelly's juicy brush strokes or hysterical folk poetry or even his gorgeous lettering that created the Kelly magic. Walt Kelly had learned the true secret—the secret of all cartooning, the secret of all art. He had learned how to transmute himself, his essential soul, out of the confines of his protoplasm—his flesh, bones, and tissue—and onto the page. He learned to do it naturally—without interference, obstruction or contrivance—so that what we saw on the page was an extension of his essential spirit.

That's the secret. Pogo was Walt's daily meditation—Walt Kelly communing with himself like some Zen Master of the comic pages—and we get a ringside seat at the ashram. This book is chock-full of that secret—that man, that spirit, and that magic.

Walt Kelly's Pogo—the truth, the whole truth, and nothing but the truth.

Doug Marlette
Atlanta, 1989

This self-portrait of Walt Kelly appeared in a 1952 promotional folder filled with clippings about *Pogo*'s first years of syndicated triumphs. It was titled "Thank you, Mr. Editor. YOU made me what I is today!" When the deluxe 11-by-15½-inch folder was sent out to prospective newspapers, *Pogo* was already in 273 papers with a potential readership of 37 million people.

I GO POGO, DO YOU?

Welcome to the fifth anthology of the fanzine Okefenokee Star, a name derived from Pogo's residence in Georgia's Okefenokee Swamp and his first appearance in newspaper comic strip form in the New York Star, a short-lived tabloid published from June 23, 1948, through January 28, 1949.

By the time this latest book appears, Pogo Possum and his fellow swamp critters will have been seen again cavorting across newspaper pages from San Diego to Boston, Miami to Seattle, with many stops along the way. Although Pogo never retired, his resyndication by the Los Angeles Times Syndicate on January 8, 1989, has made a big splash. Pogo's sabbatical from syndication was a full 13½ years. This means that almost an entire generation of Pogophiles has been lost.

Phi Beta Pogo, as the title implies, sheds some light on Walt Kelly's extensive touring of college and university campuses both to lecture and to do special Pogo artwork. It is fitting that this volume begins with a report on the Pogo party held August 25, 1988, at Ohio State University the day prior to what would have been Walt Kelly's seventy-fifth birthday.

Primary research has always been one of the strengths of the Okefenokee Star. This tradition is continued with new information on Kelly's years at the Disney studio, several interviews with Selby Kelly, and a review of what Pogo did between engagements from July 1975 until January 1989.

I Go Pogo. Do you?

BILL CROUCH, Jr.

Ohio State University
Holds a Retrospective Exhibit
and Birthday Party to Celebrate the
75th Anniversary of Walt Kelly's Birth

ABOUT three hundred Pogophiles and friends of the late Walt Kelly gathered on August 25, 1988, at Ohio State University's Library for Communication and Graphic Arts to have a Pogo party. The event took place the day prior to what would have been Kelly's seventy-fifth birthday.

The party coincided with a major retrospective exhibition of Walt Kelly's work at the Philip Sills Exhibit Hall of the Ohio State University Libraries. The display was on view from August 1 through September 9, 1988. An extremely informative catalog of the show was published in an edition of only 750 copies.

Calvin and Hobbes creator Bill Watterson of Universal Press Syndicate, a former Ohioan, made a rare public appearance and gave the keynote address, which is reprinted, with his permission, immediately following this synopsis of events.

During the afternoon of August 25, Selby Kelly presented a slide show titled ''The Other Side of Walt Kelly,'' which featured her late husband's non-*Pogo* work. That evening she also made the welcome announcement that *Pogo* would be returning to newspapers around the country.

The evening program began with a welcome from Lucy Shelton Caswell, curator of OSU's Library for Communication and Graphic Arts. Life-size full-color foamboard cutouts of Pogo and his pals, lovingly constructed by herself and her staff, were also present.

Having Bill Watterson as keynote speaker was a major accomplishment. The thirty-year-old cartoonist does not like to be photographed or interviewed. He explained that when his face and name become better known, his privacy suffers.

Following Watterson's speech, the large assembly was led in numerous tunes from ''Songs of the Pogo.'' True to its birthday party format, the evening ended with ice cream and cake.

It was a joyous event. The sound of happy voices singing ''Go, Go Pogo'' and ''Deck Us All With Boston Charlie'' was enough to give any Pogophile goosebumps.

A picture being worth a thousand words, these photographs give a fair indication of the quality of the exhibition and the fun of the party.

The sellout crowd at the Pogo Party made this button a sellout. Only 275 were manufactured, instantly making it a rare collector's item. Party participants also received "Pogo for President" posters while the supply lasted. Campaign Headquarters had sent only two hundred of them.

Hail, hail, the gang's all here! Lucy Shelton Caswell of Ohio State University (left) and Selby Kelly (right) are happily surrounded by Pogo and the swamp critters.

An overview of the installation of the exhibit.

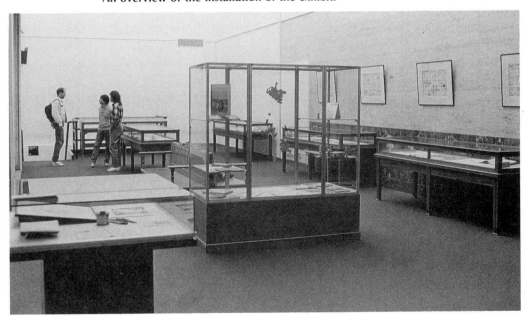

Some Thoughts on Pogo and Comic Strips Today by Bill Watterson

I was six or seven years old when it became obvious that I would never have the brains or the physique to be an astronaut, and I decided to become the next best thing, a cartoonist. As I grew up, my two favorite comic strips were *Peanuts* and *Pogo*. In hindsight, I find this somewhat interesting, because *Peanuts* and *Pogo* used the cartoon medium in very different ways. Whereas *Peanuts* eliminates detail and line with deceptive sophistication, *Pogo* is one of the most beautifully lush strips ever drawn. *Peanuts* explores the inner world of private insecurities and alienation, whereas *Pogo* explores the boisterous outer world of politics and interaction. Reading these two strips as a kid, I learned a lot about the flexibility of the comic strip, and its potential for personal expression. Obviously, one could do just about anything with this medium. As I draw *Calvin and Hobbes,* that realization impresses me more and more strongly all the time.

* * *

I discovered *Pogo* when I was in fifth or sixth grade. I found a copy of *The Pogo Papers* at a library book sale. Flipping through it, I was struck by how dense and black the drawings were—which I interpreted as meaning this was for grown-ups, not kids—and I asked my mom if she'd ever seen the work. She said my dad used to read *Pogo*, and had always liked it. After some inner debate, I decided Dad was worth the 25 cents, so I asked my mom for a quarter and bought the book for him. When I got home I started to read it . . . and Dad never got the book.

This was when I was twelve, and Walt Kelly died three years later. It is somewhat strange to be giving a talk about a strip that was largely before my time. I know virtually nothing about Walt Kelly, and what I know about *Pogo* comes only from reading the book collections of it I own. I am no authority on the man or his work, so the time to ask for a refund is now.

Still, *Pogo* was one of the biggest cartoon influences on me, so I'll talk about why, and maybe in the process reveal a thing or two about comic strips as a medium.

My goal tonight is not so much to provide great insight into the strip, as to share my enthusiasm for it. Comic strips have changed a great deal since *Pogo*, and not always for the better. What I want to do is encourage you to reintroduce yourself to the strip. Take a good long look at *Pogo,* and I think you'll gain a greater appreciation for what comic strips are all about.

* * *

Most of the original *Pogo* books are long out of print. Over the years, with the help of a friend or two, I've been able to acquire most of them. It has not been easy. I've had a dream several times where I walk into a book store, and am astounded to find row after row of *Pogo* books that I've never seen before. Twenty or thirty books no one has ever heard of. Obviously they would complete my collection. With typical dream perversity, I discovered I have just five dollars in my wallet, enough to buy only one book. I know that if I run home to get more money, someone else will buy all the other books before I get back. So, with a horrible mixture of excitement and despair, I flip through the books trying to decide which one to get. I wake up clammy with sweat every time. And now I take a charge card everywhere I go.

It is a shame that these books are so rare. They are the last glimpse we have of the comic art form at its peak. There have been a few fine and imaginative strips since *Pogo*, of course, but none has taken such complete advantage of the cartoon medium. *Pogo* shows what a comic strip can really be.

Cartoons are words and pictures. Comic strips are not generally regarded as fine art, but if you think about it, words and pictures are the two most powerful

© Universal Press Syndicate

tools of communication we have. With words and pictures, there is little in the way of human thought we cannot express. The significance and sophistication of the commentary is limited only by the ability of the cartoonist. I was fortunate to discover fairly early with *Pogo* just how much impact a comic strip can have. With the exception of *Krazy Kat*, I can think of no other strip that has used words and pictures so effectively or so powerfully.

The standard cartoon wisdom is that "a good drawing will not save a bad idea," and it has come to be accepted that a bad drawing will not hurt a good idea. This is generally true enough. What many people have forgotten, though, is that a good drawing can send a good idea to the moon and back. *Pogo*'s writing was funny, but the drawings made the characters come alive. It is certainly likely that Kelly's experience as a Disney animator taught him the comic potential of visual liveliness. Whatever its source, Kelly certainly had a wonderful gift for letting his characters reveal themselves through expression, gesture and action. This is something one rarely sees any more in either animation or in comics. A blinking profile head does nothing to establish the character. The viewer must rely entirely on the words the character says. Some cartoonists are good enough writers that they can make characters who never move interesting and likeable. Even so, they miss the great potential of this visual medium. *Pogo*, like older animation, shows how much drawings can say about the character without any words at all. A foreigner could get a pretty fair idea of what Albert Alligator was like, just by looking at the pictures of him. More to the point, Kelly used his artwork to enhance the story, not just to prop it. Porkypine's secret softheartedness is all the more tender for his perpetual scowl. Pogo's nervous romance with Hepzibah is made all the more ridiculous for the skunk's shaded eyes and curvaceous figure. The drawings were integral to the strip's charm.

There are certain little technical feats that I've always admired about the drawings in *Pogo* as well. The next time you look at the strip, notice the characters' weight. I get a kick out of seeing small details like the back of a bear's neck bulging out over his collar, or the way a character's cheeks squish up when he puts his head in his hands. This stuff is by no means essential to a cartoon, but again it brings life to the drawings. These animals have flesh and solidity. It's a very subtle, and I think very funny, form of realism.

Kelly took the power of drawings to the nth degree by making the dialogue balloons artwork as well. P. T. Bridgeport spoke in circus posters, or even in newspaper headlines with accompanying photos of himself. Deacon Mushrat spoke in Gothic typeface. These characters were defined not only by what their words said, but also by the way their words *looked*. This is brilliant. Kelly's art did more work than almost any other cartoonist's. *Pogo* was never a strip a friend could tell you about. You had to *see* it to appreciate it, and the more you looked at it, the better it got. The drawings were fun all by themselves. *Pogo* was a comic strip to look at. . . . How far we've fallen since then!

I think the most important part of any comic strip is characterization. The characters need to have unique, rounded personalities to make the strip believable and engrossing. Developing this is tough work. Many cartoonists rely on stereotypes as an easier way around the problem. Rather than unfold personalities through time, they cast their strips with immediately recognizable cliches: the henpecked father; the liberated, confident careerwoman; the precocious child; the rebellious teenager . . . and so on. These are characters who are identified and defined entirely by their social circumstances. Take them out of their roles and they have no reason to exist. These characters are not individuals who happen to be in certain societal roles, they are roles incarnate. Flat characters like these are the death of spontaneity and surprise—two things on which all humor depends. A cartooning rule of thumb it took me a long time to learn is this: if you can sum up who your characters are in a sentence or two, you're in trouble. People are complicated, and cartoon characters need to reflect that complexity to be intriguing to the reader. One reason *Pogo* is fun to read and reread is that the core characters are many-sided. They react differently in different circumstances. They all have good sides and bad that reveal themselves gradually. The characters are full of life and unpredictability.

Like the level of draftmanship I mentioned earlier, the writing in Pogo is also quite different from what you see in comics now. I once called *Pogo* ''the last of the Enjoy the Ride strips.'' If you look at *Krazy Kat* or *Little Nemo in Slumberland*, two very early comic strips, you'll see an approach to humor that is unlike that of current comic strips. Both *Krazy Kat* and *Little Nemo* are essentially one-gag strips, endlessly varied. *Krazy Kat* revolved around the throwing of the brick, and the story in *Little Nemo* was always a dream where the kid wakes up in a heap on the floor in the last panel. The destination of these strips was always pretty much the same, but the cartoonist took us on a different road to get there each time. In comics nowadays, we want to go somewhere new every day, and we just want the shortest road. We tell our cartoonists to get us to the punchline as quickly as possible. This is a shame for those of us who like to meander around and see the sights on the back lanes. *Pogo* was not a one-gag strip, but it was an Enjoy the

Ride strip. In fact, Kelly often took so many detours that he seemed to forget where he was taking us anyway. It didn't matter. The fun was in the trip.

All this is a roundabout way of saying *Pogo* celebrated conversation and dialogue for its own sake. The strip rarely had a punchline per se. Somehow I can't imagine people cutting out one day's strip and putting it on the refrigerator: it wasn't the kind of strip with a snappy saying in the last panel that makes Mom think of little Junior. Instead, it was a strip where characters talked and talked, inevitably misunderstood each other, and argued. It was a wonderful, rich parody of what passes for communication between human beings. The word balloons were filled with puns, obscure references, inside jokes, utter nonsense, and once in a while, quiet wisdom. If the drawings in *Pogo* get better with each rereading, so do the words.

Another aspect of the words worth reflection is the dialect. Comic characters don't talk in dialect any more, either. Most of the characters in *Pogo* that didn't speak in some elaborate typeface talked in a pidgin Southern that twisted words into pretzels and gave them new meaning and cadence. It gave the swamp a cohesiveness, and made it a world all its own. The swamp was not just an exotic backdrop for cute animals. The swamp was a place, a locale. You could tell it was a real place because the creatures there talked differently from us. The swamp language had a rhythm to it, and had its own internally consistent way of mangling the meaning of ordinary words. Unlike the simple phonetic renderings of hick pronunciation in *Li'l Abner*, the language in *Pogo* was a type of punning poetry, similar in spirit to *Krazy Kat*'s, although worlds apart in look and sound. It provided the characters with a unique voice that was part of us, and part making fun of us.

How the politics in *Pogo* must have affected readers is difficult for me to imagine. Apparently Kelly sometimes drew substitute strips for squeamish editors, so they would have an alternative to running his political commentary. It is a sad fact that a substantial part of newspaper readers still think the so-called ''funnies'' are meant exclusively for the entertainment of prepubescents and that newspapers have an obligation to protect young, innocent minds from the sinister influence of actual thought. We still seem to have trouble accepting that comic strips are legitimate vehicles for comment, satire, and criticism. This is unfortunate because it's one of the things cartoons do best. Despite the daily bombardment of images we face each day, pictures still have a visceral power over us. Rather than call someone a pig, you will offend him more if you draw him as one. This is because the drawing will tell the person exactly what *kind* of pig you mean. A picture is indeed worth a thousand words, and the best cartoons are often fueled by rage.

I had a job for six months as an editorial cartoonist in Cincinnati. The brevity of my employment there gives you some idea of my skills as a political analyst. Having disgraced myself once, I will not attempt to bluff my way through a discussion of *Pogo*'s politics, despite its significance to the strip. I will say that, in my opinion, *Pogo*'s commentary in the fifties holds up the best. I think the suspicion and demagoguery of the McCarthy years focused Kelly and sharpened his attacks to a degree unmatched later, even with [Spiro] Agnew and [J. Edgar] Hoover. One thing, anyway, is clear: Pogo's swamp had true evil in

it. Most cartoonists ridicule prominent politicians by making them look foolish and stupid. Kelly, of course, did this often. With Simple J. Malarkey, though, Kelly introduced a fearsome character. This caricature of Senator McCarthy was not so much a buffoon as a monster. His eyes were black with white pupils, which gave him an appearance of soulless menace. Malarkey was dangerous. I remember my surprise as a kid reading the sequence where Molester Mole, hardly a sympathetic character in his own right, runs into a swamp to flee a tarred, but not yet feathered Malarkey. The swamp water is thick, black, sludge, and the twisted, vine-covered trees are so dense that no light comes in from above. Malarkey, with only the whites of his eyes showing through the tar, wades in after him with an axe. Suddenly the mole was sympathetic, and the creepy atmosphere of this scene was quite unlike anything I'd ever read in a comic strip before. Other bad guys could be made into buffoons, but Malarkey was evil and scary.

* * *

Pogo showed me in a very concrete way how powerful a comic strip can be. This has been Kelly's most lasting influence on me. Over the years, I have learned from dozens of other artists as well, but I still enjoy coming back to *Pogo*. The humor and the artwork were what first attracted me to *Pogo*, but those things are the colorful sugar coating on the medicine. The medicine is that *Pogo* is *about* something. There is a message and a unique sensibility that permeates the work, and this is what makes it endure.

Pogo talked about the quiet dignity and common sense of the average man. It talked about the shortcomings of human nature and human behavior—"we have met the enemy and he is us." It talked about suspicion and prejudice, pollution, and the bomb. It also celebrated silliness, nonsense, and the simple pleasure of a big picnic. It talked about friendship and love, our strange political system, baseball, and hundreds of other things great and small. The artwork and humor were wonderful in themselves, but they were ultimately tools to a greater end. This is what sets *Pogo* so far beyond most other comic strips.

A comic strip can be more than just an illustrated gag a day. It can be commentary. It can be art. *Pogo* was one man's overview and opinion of our species and the world we've created for ourselves. Like all the very best cartoonists, Kelly humbles us by holding up a magical mirror that distorts and exaggerates our physical presence, but reveals our inner selves with unblinking objectivity. In Pogo, you and I appear as ludicrous animals; as naive and silly as Churchy la Femme, as loud and full of ill-formed reasoning as Albert Alligator, as pompous and smuggly self-righteous as Deacon Mushrat, as sinister and blind as Molester Mole . . . and as simple and virtuous as Pogo Possum. Walt Kelly produced this world with as much style, energy, and sophistication as the comics have ever seen. He brought to the comics page a beauty and intelligence one rarely sees in this sadly despised medium. In short, although *Pogo* ended years before I ever had a drawing published, Kelly gave me a standard to apply to myself and to cartooning as a whole. Kelly opened the door for me to the limitless potential of cartoon art. The challenge I face as a cartoonist now myself, is to try to build on what Kelly and the one or two others of his rank have established. It is, quite honestly, very hard work and not a little intimidating.

* * *

Finally, I cannot resist going off on two nasty tangents of my own, since it is not often I have a large group of people more or less held captive before me.

First, it interests me that for all the appeal of those cute animals in *Pogo*, Kelly did very little in the way of licensing. I vaguely remember seeing an animated *Pogo* TV special, and I have a rather poor plastic sculpture of Churchy that came with soap or something. To venture my own opinion, I think the comic strip world is much more fragile than most people realize, and that wonderful, lifelike characters are easily corrupted and cheapened by having them appear on every drugstore shelf and rack. Whatever Kelly's reasoning for refusing the glut of merchandising that was undoubtedly available to him, he set little precedent by his decision, which I think is a shame. Several fine strips have turned themselves into shameless advertisements for products. I, for one, am glad it didn't happen to *Pogo*.

Second, I mentioned several characteristics of *Pogo* that we no longer see in comics any more. We don't see much dialogue. We don't see much animation. We don't see exotic settings. We don't see dialect, and so on. There are two reasons for this. One is that artists and writers of Walt Kelly's caliber come along infrequently. They do come, but not as often as one might like. For that, we simply have to be patient. The other reason is this: the size newspapers have been printing comics have been reduced over the last twenty years to the point where a strip like *Pogo* cannot be done now. If Walt Kelly was just starting out today, there would be no *Pogo* as we know it. Everything that made *Pogo* one of the greatest comic strips ever drawn is a virtual impossibility in today's newspaper market. *Pogo* would simply be illegible.

The newspaper business has changed. Afternoon papers are largely gone, and comics are no longer used as weapons to draw readers away from the competition. There is no competition—or rather, the competition is television. In one of the great ironies of the business, newspapers everywhere are trying to duplicate the visual appeal of TV by adding color graphics, charts, and photographs to their pages. But, to save space and cut costs, newspapers have reduced the comics—the one truly visual part of the newspaper that television cannot imitate.

The effect on comics has been disastrous. Comics today have fewer panels, fewer words, and simpler drawings than ever before. White space attracts the eye, and when twenty comics are printed down to two columns on one newspaper page, the comic with the least [substance] there is the most attractive. Adventure strips are in their death throes because there is no longer any room to tell a decent story. Characters cannot converse unless we see only the tops of their heads. Can they go to a jungle or a futuristic city? Can they be shown in shadow, or viewed from above? No, all comic characters can do now is sit in a blank room with a diagonal wedge of Zipatone behind them. The comic strip is a restrictive medium to begin with, but the restrictions have become absurd.

With few exceptions, comics today are vapid and lifeless. They have no room to do what they do best. Cartoons are words and pictures, but there is no space for either. Newspaper comics have been deprived of their ability to entertain.

Imagine a Sunday cartoon taking up an entire newspaper page, as comics used to in the thirties. As a cartoonist, it boggles my mind to think what I would do with that much space. Or even half that much space. Clearly Spaceman Spiff will never get to wander across a planet that big, though.

If newspapers were ever to print comics bigger, it is generally assumed that they would simply keep the same amount of newspaper space and drop all but the most popular strips. This cowers syndicates and cartoonists alike into accepting most any reduction. Nobody wants to lose his job over a few little picas. Garry Trudeau is the only cartoonist so far who has managed to hold his work at an older size, and his circumstances were unique. Without a radical change in the way newspapers print comics, it seems to me that the future of cartooning will lie in some other form of publication.

The one unmentioned factor in all this is you, the newspaper reader. You are the ones being shortchanged. Look at *Pogo* and see what you're being cheated of today. I urge you to complain to your newspaper about the amount of space it devotes to the comics. Newspapers are in the business of serving you. Make them do it.

And on that grim note, I'll open up the floor for any questions.

BILL WATTERSON
Ohio State University
August 25, 1988

Possum Pastoral
by Edward Mendelson

Edward Mendelson is the literary executor of the poet W. H. Auden's estate and has taught English at Columbia, Harvard, and Yale. His "Possum Pastoral" piece was published under "Letters and Comment" in the spring 1978 issue of the Yale Review.

Other articles in that issue included "Freud, Orwell, and the Bourgeois Interior"; "Death of the 'Kenyon Review.' A Story"; and "Blake's 'Song of Innocence.' "

It is a testament to Kelly's talent that although he never went on to college from high school, Pogo Possum has continually captivated academics around the country.

FEW spectacles are more grim than that of an academic explaining a joke. Freud found courage to write about jokes through reading Theodor Lipps's *Komik und Humor*; others may find the polysyllabic Lipps less emboldening. In writing about the wit in *Pogo* it is best to say no more than what almost everyone knows already: that Walt Kelly was equally the master of paradox and farce, that he could produce trilingual puns and pie-in-the-face buffoonery, and, what is more impressive, he seemed able to do both simultaneously. It is easier to write about the self-consciousness of his art—the word is not too strong—and the seriousness of his craft. Though Kelly himself avoided any explicit claims to the high esthetic line—not surprisingly, considering the state of the comic pages when he began, and the incongruity of sounding at all serious in that company—his readers knew better. *Pogo* analysis, though in decline of late, is a discipline that dates back almost to the first days of *Pogo* itself.

The critics missed the point, though, when, as Kelly grumbled twenty years ago, they wrote that *Pogo*'s roots lay in "Joyce, Malthus, Socrates, and a lot of other dead people known to stalwart, quick-striking little bands of thinkers and students." Kelly responded, with only seeming modesty, that his sources were not in the literary, sociological, or philosophical traditions, but in the whole range of experience: in *Pogo*, he said, "everything that is here is owed to everybody." Claims like this one are made only by artists or charlatans, and Kelly was no charlatan. His inclusive claims hide his esthetic self-consciousness. The history of the comic strip conforms to the broad pattern found in all the arts, through which the strongest and most innovative artists tend both to recapitulate and to undermine their predecessors. Kelly parodied or adapted, not his literary predecessors, but the likes of *Krazy Kat* (a giant to be toppled) and *Little Orphan Annie* (a pretender to be exposed). His borrowings from other comic strips often amounted to outright theft—as Eliot, who had all the *Pogo* books sent from America, said that a great writer is not influenced, but steals—and Kelly likewise described himself to a compiler of potted biographies as a "member of the Independent Order of Purse Snatchers."

While he would often pay homage to *Krazy Kat* by quoting it, he was more interested in proving that *Pogo* was more "like life" than its rivals. This he effected by taking over his rivals' conventions and then demonstrating how inadequate those conventions were. Whenever, on any of the slightest or more unlikely pretexts, the Houn' Dog and Pogo Possum disguised themselves as "Li'l Arf an' Nonny," the one with a vocabulary limited to "Arf," the other wearing a curly wig and speaking lines limited to interjections like "Jeeping whilkers," the two would constantly find themselves—as who would not?—in situations that demanded somewhat greater complexity of language and gesture. Behind the joke is Kelly's insistence, in plainfolks manner, that his strip mirrors the plenitude of life, while all those others on the comics page limit themselves to formal conventions and stylized situations. When the dog closes his eyes so that, blanked out, they look like Li'l Arf's, he remarks, "My word, it's difficult to see this way, ain't it?" Pogo, disguised as Nonny, replies, "It evident don't matter much"—referring to the eyesight and insight of the model.

Critical parody of this kind tends to be a hallmark of high art in its playful moments, especially when critical parody is linked, as it is in *Pogo*, to an almost obsessive interest in producing effects that are possible only in the medium of that art. To shift levels for a moment: in *Shakespeare and the Idea of the Play*, Anne Righter notes that "from the beginning, Shakespeare seems to have been concerned with the play metaphor to a degree unusual even among his contemporaries." Kelly is as aware of his speech balloons and the borders of his panels as any playwright could ever be aware of scene divisions and proscenium arch. Albert Alligator constantly strikes his matches on the panel border, and when the verbal nonsense in the strip gets especially dizzying, characters lean against the border for support from the most reliably solid surface in the strip's world—a solid that exists only in the form of the strip, not as a representation of anything in the world outside. Seminole Sam, the shyster fox, tries to sell the dog a team of trained gnats who spell out speech balloons over the dog's head; they eventually commit the dog to writing a check in payment for their services. In one strip in which Albert and the dog immovably stare at each other over a table, through four panels, Kelly enlivens the sequence with what might be called pseudo-action: in each panel he changes the pattern of the tablecloth. When a character loses his voice he "speaks" in empty speech balloons (in which a wasp gets trapped at one point). The mouse is sometimes so garrulous that he has to push against his own speech-balloon to keep from being squashed in the corner of the panel. In the world of *Pogo* if you happen to be upside down you speak in upside-down lettering, incomprehensible to the upright. And when Kelly is not parodying Li'l Arf an' Nonny (or later, Lulu Arfin' Nanny), he runs rings around the one other form that shares the comics' pattern of brief daily episodes: the soap opera. Howland Owl at one point provides a daily script service, transcribed from the soaps, for Albert and the turtle Churchy La Femme. The scripts, despite lines as useful as "Don't kiss me, Sam, you'll catch my hangnails," scarcely make life as easy as they were meant to do.

Whoever finally writes *Kelly and the Idea of the Comic Strip* will no doubt observe that the most thoroughly self-aware sequence in all of *Pogo* appeared only a few months after the strip began. In the strip of February 28, 1950, Howland Owl, as an editor of a newspaper to which Porkypine has submitted some incomprehensible comic strips, guides Porky through "one of these rigadoons," that is, through the strip itself. Gesturing with a pointer, Owl explains in the opening panel that "the first bit of convulsive waggery is the date" (Porky: "Indisputably droll"); while, in the second panel, "the next merriment pops up when you see the copyright notice" ("a true guffaw there, possibly a boffola"). Prodding a speech balloon in the third panel, Owl says it is "glutted, as you see, with attic wit." And in the fourth panel Owl gestures at the box in which Kelly's name would normally appear, and says, "The *last* laugh is the *first* thing a artist got to git. So he *must* learn to sign his name, big and black with a box 'round her . . . then he's free to see can he find a idea for his strip." In the box is the name "Otempora O'Mores." As Porky remarks, "This boy don't spell so good." Had McLuhan seen this strip, *Understanding Media* could have appeared ten years sooner than it did, and might have been a lot more lucid.

Kelly seems to have bamboozled reporters by hinting that he picked up the "southern" dialect of *Pogo* while working in the Army's foreign language unit during the war. Kelly worked in the unit, but the dialect of *Pogo* is almost entirely his own invention. Its elements are too complex to describe in a few words, but you needn't be Professor Higgins to recognize a native speaker of Okefenokee when you hear its characteristic extensions of the suffixes -*ical* and -*able*, as in *psychologicowockle* or *formidabobble*. The world of the strip is quite as stylized as its language. In its early manifestations *Pogo* was a comic-book feature called *Bumbazine and Albert the Alligator*. Bumbazine, a little boy who talked to the animals, was later dropped because, "being human, he was not as believable as the animals." The Okefenokee Swamp in which those animals live is not in an odd corner of the state of Georgia, as they seem to think, but on the outskirts of Arcadia. After one reads *Pogo* for a few years, one begins to notice that the strip has most of the characteristics of a pastoral. Although the rustics of a classic pastoral are usually shepherds, Kelly's substitution of anglers is supported by a tradition that extends back through Sannazaro's *Eclogae piscatoriae* to the twenty-first *Idyll* of Theocritus. In Kelly's pastoral, as in the classical and renaissance varieties, the rustics use their elaborately stylized language to speak about sophisticatedly urban issues. They write poems, suffer the pangs of unrequited love, and, for the most part, enjoy an innocence for which a reader feels nostalgia; while, at the same time, the pastoral artifice reminds him that such innocence has never existed outside of art. (I do not for a moment suppose that Kelly learned his formal principles from Bion and Moschus, only that those principles are lively enough to spring up in the fertile soil that Kelly provided.)

In *Pogo* the rule of pastoral innocence dictates that sexual love be either wished-for and unfulfilled, or past and forgotten, but never a fact of the immediate present. To produce the innocent children of the swamp, Kelly sometimes brings in a parent or two, but he never seems to know quite what to do with them. The strip has little room for a vision of what the dog calls "wedding bells, the mud hut, children on the floor, the humdrum argument." After making a few uninteresting remarks, most of the strip's parents leave the scene on some serious errand, freeing their children to join the general frivolity. This rule of exclusion is proved by its one apparent exception: the one parent who plays an extended (and not deliberately tedious) role in the strip is Miz Stork, the emblem not of parenthood but of *sexless* parenthood. Yet since potential, unrequited love is virtually central to pastoral, almost everyone in the strip becomes smitten at one time or another with Mam'selle Hepzibah, sveltest of skunks, although no one ever sufficiently overcomes his shyness to do more than bring her offerings ranging in appropriateness from a love poem to a live frog. (Again there is one rule-proving exception: Porkypine's Uncle Baldwin starts his career in the swamp by kissing Hepzibah, but he seems more intent on ravishing her lollipop.)

Yet the Okefenokee is never fully innocent. Its characters are capable of anger, fraud, suspicion, greed, prevarication, and petty theft (mostly from Pogo's larder). Still, any real danger, any threats of mayhem or loss of liberty, are visited from outside the swamp's Arcadia. In the first of Virgil's *Eclogues*, the almost unconscious force of Roman law disrupts the pastoral tranquillity by expelling Meliboeus from his fields. In precisely the same way, the first of *Pogo*'s invading villains, Mole MacCarony, disrupts the swamp by making an off-the-cuff ruling that Howland Owl is a migratory bird who must leave the swamp for parts unknown. Mole arrives in the midst of a mild reign of terror in which so unlikely a radical as Churchy La Femme is suspected first of supplying bootleg mail, then of being a member of an underground group—or perhaps an under*water* group, engaged in "submersive activities." But even Mole eventually assimilates himself, as do most of the other newcomers to the swamp, like P. T. Bridgeport, who speaks in circus posters, or Sis Boombah, who arrives to conduct a survey for Dr. Whimsy on the Sectional Habits of the U.S. Mailmen. Kelly's most memorable venture into political satire, however, involved a character who could no more assimilate himself into the swamp than his original could find a stable place in the world outside. On Mayday 1953, Mole and Deacon Mushrat welcomed Simple J. Malarkey to the swamp. He was the "spit an' imogene" of the senator from Wisconsin, a fanged, grinning, hollow-eyed feline whose gun contained all the votes he needed to elect himself president of the local snoop-group, the Audible Boy Bird-Watchers Society.

It took some courage to introduce Malarkey to the comics page, which for decades had been a blithely apolitical refuge. (*Li'l Abner*'s and *Barnaby*'s satire of politicians had been unspecific and therefore palatable.) Newspaper editors, when they saw that Kelly was crossing received categories, responded with archaic pollution-fears as potent in the newsroom as they are in the plains and jungles. Some editors tried to expel the strip altogether; others moved it temporarily to the sanctuary of the editorial page where they could keep a closer eye on it. The same taboos surfaced a few years later when the content of the strip showed unsettling parallels to the news about school desegregation in the south. Albert Alligator got to the heart of the matter: "You open up a school, next thing you know all kinds of ingnoramusses is comin' in . . . They meets yo' daughter . . . splits a orange with her, poof! they's engaged, married, an' livin' in the attic. An' I don't want *nobody* marryin' my daughter if he's so ingnorant he gotta go to school in the first place." (*Pogo*'s dialogue, it should be said, looks much better

in freehand lettering than it does in rigid type.) One editor, on hearing the outraged howls of his counterparts on other papers, wondered if they were afraid their daughters might marry a possum.

Kelly's satire, for all its occasional fierceness, usually shaded into calmer wisdom. His readers were always grateful—in ways they might be embarrassed to acknowledge in the forum—for the gentle-spirited apothegms that Kelly produced in his role of sage of the swamp, but they also could feel uncomfortable when reading some of his sterner moments. "We shall meet the enemy," he wrote in 1953, "and not only may he be ours, he may be us": villains like Mole MacCarony and Simple J. Malarkey do their mischief because others who are not villains give them their opportunity. Later, when Albert blames Mole for a dognapping that Albert himself unknowingly committed, Albert asks, more reasonably than we like to think, "What good is an enemy if you can't blame him for stuff like that there?" Kelly never indulged himself for long in the gormless whimsy that would give a with-it clergyman an opening for a *Gospel According to Pogo*. And in avoiding banality, Kelly also avoided the *poésie pure*, however wonderful, of Herriman's *Krazy Kat*. Like all impure art, *Pogo* both rebukes and consoles.

The strip at times achieved such delicacy of tone that an adult reader could trip into unsettling depths at precisely the point where a child could glide undisturbed across a serene surface. In one strip, a few days after Mole and Malarkey disappear into the swamp intent on mutual destruction, their crony Sarcophagus MacAbre, a buzzard whose speech balloons are in the style of black-bordered funeral announcements, approaches a picnic table to "borrow an odd end or two." Offered "sugar, salt, pickles," he replies, "No, thank you kindly. I must join my friends. A knife and fork is all I'll need." That violent death is at the edges of this pastoral world, and that a buzzard has a culinary interest in it, is unmistakable to an adult; a child, like Churchy La Femme in the last panel, can only wonder that MacAbre has friends, and is "fond of 'em."

Reading the early *Pogo* books, and looking through newspaper files at some of the uncollected strips, one is convinced that Kelly had more than mere wit and talent. His comedy is always dense and multilayered—appealing not only to adults and children, but to the gallery and the pit. Quite an extensive textbook of esthetics could easily be put together using various examples from the strip. If you want to explain how the formal pressures for art shape and alter the phenomena of the world that art claims to represent, simply refer to the strip in which Churchy composes one of his advertising jingles:

More precious than gold,
Yet less than a dollar,
Most freshes' and cold
Is *Kokomo Kola*.

The Owl insists that Churchy change the jingle to bring in a proper rhyme for Kola. But Churchy, for whom the truest poetry is the most feigning, changes the *product* instead: "collar and dollar rhymes, don't it?" (At which Owl, clutching his throat, asks, "A *cold* Kokomo *Kollar*?")

Churchy also has to face the problem that Mam-'selle Hepzibah's name won't fit into the love song that he has written for her: better if it were Lou or Sue, "could even be Sam." Later, when he rhymes his praises of her eyes—

O, my love's eyes are truly blue
For she knows I'se mos' bluely true

and refuses to change the poem when she protests that her eyes are in fact "a jolie brown," Hepzibah answers in the best tradition of verse debate:

If my love's eyes be truly blue
The she knows I'se mos' throughly thru

And while we have got onto the subject of poetry, it is worth mentioning that *Pogo* generally produces better poems than these. One of Churchy La Femme's election campaign songs has the undertones of an erotic campaign:

THE THIRD RAIL THEME
The Party of the first part and the Party of the next
Are partly participled in a parsley-covered text.
Were you partial to a Party that has parceled out its
    parts
With the Party that was second in your polly-tickle
    heart?
Then parlay all your losings on a horse that's running
    dark:
With lights-out you may triple in a homer in the park.

As a nonsense poet Kelly may not attain the Parnassian heights of Carroll or Lear, but he does hold a secure place among the foothills. He can write a perfect birthday poem:

Once you were two, dear birthday friend,
In spite of purple weather.
But now you are three, and near the end,
As we grewsome together

How fourthful thou, forsooth for you,
For soon you will be more.
But—'fore one can be three be two;
Before be five be four.

And even a nonsense elegy:

A song not for now you need not put stay,
A tune for the was can be sung for today,
The notes for the does-not will sound as the does,
Today you can sing for the will-be that was.

(As Porkypine tells Albert, "Don't take life so serious, son. It ain't nohow permanent.")

For all the esthetic delight of their world, the *Pogo* characters know that parables and formal arguments can be taken too far, and that language can bear only a tenuous relation to the world of phenomena. The dog lives in a house labeled "Fido," though his name seems to be Beauregard Chaulmoogra Fontenac de Montmingle Bugleboy. And when Beauregard warns Porkypine, who is on the way to court Mam-'selle Hepzibah, that marriage can be dangerous, that a black widow spider celebrated her wedding by eating her husband, Porky, untempted by allegory, imperturbably replies that "Anybody what marries a black widow spider got to *expeck* trouble."

While observing elaborate formal restraints, Kelly knew that he should violate those restraints when he had a good enough reason. From the first years of the strip Kelly distinguished carefully between the daily and Sunday sequences, both in plot and atmosphere. The daily strips tended to be more meditative and articulate; the Sundays, with their gaudy colors and large outlines, were farcical and loud. Only once did the plot of the daily strips continue "through" the Sunday strips: immediately before Pogo, Churchy, and Albert were fired off to Mars (or perhaps Western Australia: Kelly seems to have changed his mind in the middle of things) for six months away from the swamp, six months in which Kelly used dozens of new characters, settings, and varieties of language. The breaking of a formal boundary in the strip—between weekdays and Sundays—accurately signaled a drastic shift in its content.

That comic strips, at their best, deserve intelligent attention—and not merely the sociological attention paid to etiolated popular forms—is, I believe, beyond dispute. But intelligent attention requires a critical language suited to the medium, and such a language has so far been lacking. It seems unlikely to develop in American studies of comic strips. For want of any other native claimants, the territory has been thoroughly occupied by the popculturists, whose impenetrable defensive lines, barbed by cliché and pitted by vacuity, discourage any serious incursions. Perhaps it will be necessary to get rid of the term "comic strip," with its lowlife associations in both elements, before we can get serious discussions of the medium, but I hope it won't be. If a new term is needed, however, I propose *acolouthiconolect* (from Greek, *akolouthos*, following; *eikōn*, likeness; *lexis*, speech), though it will probably have to be shortened in time for the first issue of the *Journal of Iconolect Studies*.

The situation in Europe is somewhat better, perhaps because the French can talk with dignity about *la bande dessinée*. (The Germans seem to have given up *Karikaturstreifen* for the more inclusive *Comics*, with dreary results.) The French semiological industry, which generates a volume fully equipped with diagrams and tables for all literatures and *para-littératures*, has done reasonably well in this instance. Pierre Fresnault-Deruelle's *La Bande dessinée* (Paris: Hachette, 1972), described on its cover as "Essai d'un analyse sémiotique," is an intelligent and illuminating book, whose merits include an awareness of the limitations of its method. The book implicitly acknowledges that its analyses are best suited to the rather ordinary French comic books which are all that it analyzes in detail. Exceptional cases, including a few from *Pogo*, find themselves relegated to subordinate clauses. Semiological analysis is perhaps by its nature unfitted for the detailed study of complex esthetic contraptions; either that, or, less probably, such study will become possible when semiology achieves greater subtlety than it has now. (One should keep in mind, when reading about the glorious future of semiology, that hypothetical sciences, like the scientific semantics predicted by Ogden and Richards in 1923, never seem to get off the ground.)

Though his method can never distinguish genius

from junk, except by recognizing that the method doesn't do very much when confronted with genius, Fresnault-Deruelle at least avoids the customary route through the impasse, which is to deny that there is a distinction at all, or to claim that distinctions are the visible products of invisible conspiracies of schoolmen. Fresnault-Deruelle is especially good on the relation between one panel of a comic strip and the next, quite illuminating on the ways in which comics deal with the formal property by which they include two radically different means of representation: the words, representing an invisible temporal sequence of spoken events; and, separated by the boundary of the speech balloon, the pictures, representing the events of a single visible instant.

Far beyond this he is unable to go, for his way is blocked by the central naiveté of semiological criticism: its implied and often explicit insistence that a work of art, which is to a crucial degree the product of deliberate choice and conscious freedom within the necessity of grammar and form, is ultimately a kind of scientific specimen, the product of unconscious necessity. (One recalls the old sub-Freudian method of analyzing a work of art as if it were a patient on the couch.) This insistence begs most of the interesting questions about literature and art, and the neologic overkill of all semiological texts serves less to illuminate new discoveries than to signal their authors' linguistic solidarity with the members of their academic tribe. Still, it is always luxurious to bathe in the foamy rhetoric with which French criticism introduces its scientific rigors, and if the tepid comic books described by Fresnault-Deruelle are hardly a ''luminous reservoir of the imaginary,'' it is nice to be told that they are. Within the limits of its method, his book remains an indispensable starting point.

For the moment, one wants to see more *Pogo*, not more analysis of it. *Ten Ever-Lovin' Blue-Eyed Years with Pogo*, published in 1959 and reissued a few years ago in paperback, is the most substantial of the *Pogo* books. It collects some of the best strips of *Pogo*'s early years, and intersperses these with Kelly's unexpectedly urbane commentary as well as miscellaneous verses and stories. The thirty or so *Pogo* paperbacks, which appeared from 1951 until 1976 (the last two are posthumous), add considerably to the available oeuvre. They drift erratically in and out of print; catch them when you can. Some of the earlier books have been gathered into collections of two or three titles each; these have titles like *Pogo Revisited* and *Pogo Re-runs*. Each of these collective volumes costs more than the sum of the prices of its original contents.

A glance at old newspaper files shows that there are countless treasures still to be recovered. From the beginnings of the strip almost thirty years ago until his death in October 1973, Kelly drew hundreds of daily and Sunday strips that never appeared in the books; many of the forgotten strips are as splendid as the ones that everyone remembers. Though *Pogo* never generated all the international spinoffs of, for example, *Peanuts* (the ITT of comic strips), there is still enough ancillary material—advertisements, drawings for special occasions, articles, mobiles, songbooks, children's stories, an HEW pamphlet, etc., etc.—to fill a lengthy volume. Best of all, of course, would be a reprinting of all the *Pogo* strips. While I have no doubt that such an enormous collection would be a profitable venture for Kelly's publishers, I wonder if a commercial press would agree. Is there perhaps a university press with the courage and imagination to collect and publish *The Complete Pogo*, including not only the daily and Sunday strips but all the miscellanea as well, in proper chronologicowockle sequence, as a substantial and palpabobble contribution to humane letters?

EDWARD MENDELSON

The World of Pogo

THE first major one-man show of Walt Kelly's artwork was at the Museum of Fine Arts, Springfield, Massachusetts, from October 6 to November 17, 1974. This show had added significance, as it was the catalyst for an even bigger show at the Museum of Cartoon Art. Both shows are discussed in The Best of Pogo.

From interviews with Selby Kelly, the following corrections should be made to the "Postscript" of the Springfield catalog, reprinted here. Dan Noonan, an animator on the MGM Pogo film, never worked on the syndicated Pogo. And Walt Kelly's good friend Bill Vaughan of the Kansas City Star wrote some material on a trial basis after Kelly's death, but it was never used.

Interestingly, Selby mentions a new name when the syndicate was looking for somebody to help her with the writing. "They had VIP [Virgil Partch] try his hand at it," said Selby, "but VIP's material wasn't anything like what Pogo should be. I couldn't use it."

For those interested in the Pogo animated films, the Springfield catalog mentions the "premiere showing of Pogo, the Candidate for the Office of Your Choice." When asked about this film, Selby Kelly commented, "It doesn't even deserve the name. It's a hodgepodge of stuff, a couple of stills of Pogo and some other stuff. It looked like something Chuck Jones had thrown together. It was not outtakes from the MGM film and had nothing to do with Pogo running for office. It really isn't an animated film. It's shots of things pasted up like a storyboard, but there isn't a story. It is also only about ten seconds long or some such time."

In the best spirit of supermarket tabloid journalism, the photo of the Pogo installation was secretly taken by Bill Crouch, Jr., in November 1974, two years before he met Selby Kelly or founded the Okefenokee Star.

WALT KELLY

Walt Kelly was born in Philadelphia, Pennsylvania, August 25, 1913. Two years later his family moved to Bridgeport, Connecticut, where Kelly attended public schools. His father, a theatrical scene painter, taught him how to draw.

Kelly landed in the newspaper game early. The first of many experiences, he became the editor and cartoonist for his high school newspaper. After high school he worked as a reporter and part-time artist for the *Bridgeport Post*. Between 1935 and 1941 Kelly worked as an animator for Walt Disney studios in Hollywood. On his return to the East, Kelly illustrated children's books for the Western Printing and Lithographing Company. During World War II he illustrated handbooks as a civilian employee for the Army's foreign language division.

While art editor for the short-lived New York *Star* in 1948, Kelly introduced the first *Pogo* strip. Upon the demise of the *Star* in 1949 Kelly was employed by Post (later Publishers-Hall) Syndicate from which *Pogo* began its rise to fame as a nationally syndicated cartoon. At last one of Kelly's childhood dreams had come true. As he wrote in *Ten Ever-Lovin' Blue-Eyed Years with Pogo*, published by Simon and Schuster in 1959, "On rainy days we might lie around each other's houses looking at Mutt and Jeff cartoon books, all of us determined to become cartoonists and rich." Fortunately this ambition won out over others, including that of baseball pitcher, "wealthy tycoon," ringmaster of a grasshopper circus . . .

Kelly received many awards and honors during his career. In 1952 he was named Cartoonist of the Year by the National Cartoonists Society, and became president of the society in 1954. In this position he campaigned against the excessive violence and crime in comic strips, which had become a staple of the medium. In 1954 Kelly was the first comic strip artist to be invited to contribute work to the Library of Congress collection. He received the Heywood Broun Award for his political cartoons from the New York Newspaper Guild. In 1972 the *New York Times* published for the first time, and only time so far, three cartoons. One of these was "Pogo's Smoke-Filled Tavern," which is included in this exhibit.

Kelly's talent and energy, plus his keeping 6–12 weeks ahead of his deadlines, allowed him to produce more than the daily and Sunday *Pogo* strips. Thirty-six books of Pogoana have delighted Pogo fanatics. With his training at the Disney studios as background, Kelly made animated films starring the *Pogo* menagerie. This side of Kelly's talent is amply represented during the exhibit with the showing of the *Pogo Special Birthday Special*, done for television in 1969, the premiere showing of *Pogo, the Candidate for the Office of Your Choice*, and *We Have Met the Enemy and He Is Us*, an anti-pollution film done by Selby and Walt Kelly.

The many-sided Kelly also wrote the lyrics, some of the music, and drew the illustrations for the songbook, *Songs of the Pogo*. When the record album was cut in 1956 featuring some of these *Pogo* songs, Kelly lent his baritone to two of the melodies.

In addition to drawing strips, originating and animating films, writing songs and doing numerous other projects that defy categorization, Kelly found time to lecture to college audiences. In 1952 during a "Pogo for President" rally, Harvard's mock campaign turned from enthusiasm into a four-hour riot.

Kelly maintained his level of productivity until the end of his life. He died on October 18, 1973.

Pogo circa 1943

POGO

Pogo Possum first appeared in a comic book in 1943. As a rather homely, bedraggled animal in an overlarge nightshirt, Pogo played a minor part in a feature entitled *Bumbazine and Albert the Alligator*. Bumbazine was a boy who lived in the Okefenokee Swamp and learned to talk to the animals. Kelly dropped him soon "because, being human, he was not as believable as the animals." In the early comic books Pogo filled the gap and became a straight man for Albert. Over the next few years Pogo's form changed into the cute, cuddly creature he is now.

THE STRIP

Pogo and Albert were soon joined by other regular strip players, including Churchy La Femme, a turtle and free-lance poet; the scientific Howland Owl; Porkypine the philosopher; and Bun Rabbit, a collector of holidays. Over 150 assorted characters have been spotted at one time or another in the swamp.

Some of the more unusual characters demanded special lettering styles in their balloons. This was helpful, in Kelly's view, for giving the reader an idea of the tone of voice. P. T. Bridgeport, a carnival barker type bear, speaks in an amalgam of circus-style lettering, while the Deacon converses in Gothic type, indicating the gravity of his profession.

The *Pogo* strip varies in tone from political satire to sentiment, from nonsensical humor to serious philosophy. With the strip's political satire, Kelly attacked any and every threat to his own sense of dignity and right. In the early fifties Senator Joseph McCarthy entered the swamp as a wildcat named Simple J. Malarkey. Khrushchev appeared as a pig dressed like a pirate. More recently a hyena resembling Spiro Agnew arrived in the swamp attacking the media and proposing a limitation on civil rights.

Kelly's veiled assaults on political figures were not always accepted by the newspapers. A publisher denounced the Malarkey series as editorial, claiming it had no place on the comic pages. According to Henry Shikuma, an illustrator who worked with Kelly on the strip, many newspapers in this country and Japan refused to print the Khrushchev-Castro series, feeling that a comic strip was not the place to satirize a world figure. Realizing that situations like these were not acceptable to everyone, Kelly always drew alternate, inoffensive strips that could be run by timid editors. Kelly enjoyed the flak caused by his controversial strips, especially since they created more publicity for him and the strip.

Perhaps the most important aspect of Kelly's political satire has been put best by John Horn in his 1951 review of Kelly's first book of *Pogo* strips, written for the New York *Compass*.

> Evil does not triumph in Walt's fictional world. However, it is not defeated either. It is thwarted or frustrated or delayed only to rise again on another occasion, when it gets the same treatment. If a philosopher would like to moralize about *Pogo* he would say that the book indirectly argues that virtue is its own reward. Or he might say that, in Walt's view, the human race is in no danger of extermination; that bumbling good is a force far superior to determined evil.

It is Kelly's essential faith that goodness and reason will prevail, creating an encouraging optimistic outlook which is an important element in the strip.

Perhaps the most poignant example of *Pogo* philosophy comes from the June 20, 1970 strip in this exhibit. Porkypine and Pogo have just climbed a steep cliff. The dialogue runs as follows:

> PORKYPINE: Suppose I was to suggest we have climbed the wrong mountain?
> POGO: Org! Y'mean all that trouble was a mistake?
> PORKYPINE: Well, relax . . . Enjoy the scene . . . Looking back on things, the view *always* improves.

The slapstick situations and pure nonsense dialogue that appear in the strip are enjoyed on face value alone.

There are a few explanations offered for the origination of this inspired nonsense. At an early age Kelly's understanding of the English language, like that of most children, wasn't that discriminating. Such childlike interpretations as ''Hallowbee Thy Name'' and ''Give us to stay our daily bread'' for the Lord's Prayer were common.

This early training undoubtedly helped Kelly in

the writing of the Christmas carols "Deck Us All With Boston Charlie" and "Good King Sourkraut looked out on his feets uneven." Later Kelly gave credit for some of his restructuring of the language to others: "Some of the more notable successes in the field of gobbledygook in the strip were due to lettering men not being able to keep a tight rein on my handwriting."

Kelly, a kind, sensitive man, often added personal touches to his strip. The little swamp boat Pogo and others used often carried the name of friends Kelly wanted to say "hello" to, or to remember on special days. When two of his daughters died in infancy, boats with their names left the shore. After Walt Kelly died in October of last year, his widow, Selby, took over the strip. In the Christmas cartoon that year Selby carried on this tradition as a boat with "W.K." on the side and the dates "1913-1973" on the stern transported the characters.

At the time of Kelly's death the strip was being carried in more than three hundred newspapers in the United States and Canada. In addition, *Pogo* had an avid following in Australia, France, Greece, Italy, Japan, Lebanon, New Zealand, Portugal, Spain, South Africa, South America, Sweden, and Thailand. Nearly 300 million copies of Kelly's *Pogo* books have been sold.

TWO WHO KNEW KELLY

Joseph P. Mastrangelo, of the Washington Post

In 1948, I was working as an apprentice artist on a new afternoon paper, the New York *Star*, when Walt Kelly took over as art director and comic strip editor, and brought little Pogo, his cartoon opossum, with him. Getting to know Kelly was one of the good things that have happened in my life. . . .

KELLY'S GENEROSITY:

Kelly charities were mostly of his own making. If a fellow cartoonist or writer was down and out, he might suddenly find his rent paid for the next two months—by Kelly. The morning after the papers reported a policeman shot in the line of duty, Kelly would make out a generous check for the widow. A priest running a mission on the Lower East Side in Manhattan was another beneficiary. A Jewish friend received a monthly Kelly check for a group that was hunting ex-Nazis . . .

KELLY AS BOSS:

(By 1960) Kelly was working out of a big studio on Madison Avenue and employed six people. When you worked with Kelly, there was playtime and deadline time. On any day of the week, he would invite the whole staff out to lunch. We would go to one of the best restaurants. He would order cocktails, for everyone, thick slabs of roast beef, wine, dessert, brandy, cigars. About five o'clock a weary waiter would smile when he got a big tip. Then next day, when someone would look up from his drawing board and ask, "Anyone for lunch?" Kelly would say, "Those lunch hours you guys take last too long."

KELLY AT WORK:

When Kelly worked, he liked to sit in a big chair, a beat-up soft hat on his head, a thick unlighted cigar in his mouth. He worked with his drawing board propped up on a big old-fashioned desk, which had letters stuffed into every pigeonhole. Pinned along the edges of his drawing board were dozens of notes. (From "Unforgettable Walt Kelly," *Reader's Digest*, July, 1974)

John Horn, CBS

More impressive than his enormous capacity for work was Walt's agility of mind.

One day, after finishing the political cartoon of the day, he was about to relax for a moment when he remembered he had another deadline. He turned from his drawing board to his typewriter and began pounding away. He asked me to ring for a messenger. I looked over his shoulder as he was finishing some two and a half pages of copy (in about twenty minutes). It was a fantasy of the natural world, a children's story of bees and butterflies and fairy queens, but a complete story of action with beginning, middle, and end. He had a contract, he told me, to write such stories to be printed on cereal boxes and he hated to give it up. . . .

The only disagreement I remember Walt and I ever had began with a criticism of mine of *New Yorker* cartoons of the 1960's. "Why, for God's sake, they run talking animal cartoons!" Walt looked at me peculiarly. "*I* draw talking animal cartoons." "No, you don't. Your strip is about human beings and the human condition." From there we argued about a number of things, mainly art. Walt said that art was not art unless it came about consciously, that the artist and his audience had to know what a work intended and what it meant. I disagreed, saying that art could be created without conscious intention or specific rational meaning. . . . But the argument went unresolved.

KELLY QUOTE:

"If you're a professional, writer or artist, you can get anywhere from 75 to 85 percent of what you're aiming at in your first try. A lot artists spend most of their time trying to get the other 15 to 25 percent. I don't. I'd rather go for another 75 to 85 percent."

From the 1951 review of the first Pogo book in the New York Compass:

As only one of Walt's creative products, *Pogo* does not tell us all about the author, which is a story that will be told some other day. In addition to being a storyteller, cartoonist, satirist, and philosopher, Walt is also, among other things, illustrator, piano player, scholar, cigar smoker, editor, political cartoonist, philosopher, and above all, man of good humor and good will. His practicing philosophy is: Be yourself to the utmost. Just by being Walt Kelly, he has helped others find themselves.

Postscript:

Since Kelly's death, his widow, Selby, an artist and animator, and his son Steven have continued the strip. Some of the artists and illustrators who worked with Kelly have remained on the strip with Selby and Steven, including Don Morgan, Dan Noonan, Henry Shikuma, Bill Vaughan, and George Ward.

S.R.P.
10/74

ACKNOWLEDGMENT

We wish to express our deepest thanks to Selby Kelly, without whose consent to lend Kelly's original drawings this exhibit would never have proceeded further than the idea. Beyond that, she gave her precious time to select a representative group of Kelly's work, ensuring that we have a cross-section of the years and examples of the many themes in *Pogo*. She supplied the names of people who knew Kelly before she did, from whom we obtained background on Kelly and insights into his character. She put us in touch with Chuck Jones in Los Angeles, from whom we borrowed the films *Pogo Special Birthday Special* and *Pogo, the Candidate for the Office of Your Choice*. In addition she secured for us a copy of the film she and Kelly finished just prior to his death, *We Have Met the Enemy and He Is Us*, lent us her songbook and album of *Songs of the Pogo*, and helped with myriad other details.

Thanks also to John Horn, who knew Kelly and willingly shared his reminiscences; to Joseph Mastrangelo and *Reader's Digest* for permission to reprint parts of "Unforgettable Walt Kelly"; to Henry Shikuma for help in choosing pieces for the show and providing anecdotes about Kelly.

Susan R. Progen, Curator of the Exhibit
Jeffrey R. Brown, Director
Springfield, Massachusetts
Museum of Fine Arts

LIST OF THE EXHIBITION

Drawings:
Daily Strips from 1949–72
Sunday Strips from 1951–72
"Pogo's Smoke-Filled Tavern," *New York Times,* 1972
Three self-caricatures
"Robin the Red Breasted Hood," nursery rhyme from *The Pogo Stepmother Goose*, Simon and Schuster, 1954
Storyboards from *We Have Met the Enemy and He Is Us*

Films:
Pogo Special Birthday Special
Pogo the Candidate for the Office of Your Choice
We Have Met the Enemy and He Is Us

Lyrics and Music:
Songs of the Pogo

The Complete Daily Pogo Strips for 1953

By 1953, Pogo Possum had already become a national treasure to some and a burr under the saddle to others, always reaching a nerve. Readers either loved him or hated him.

On May 1, 1953, Kelly introduced the most infamous character in the history of the strip, Wiley Catt's

cousin, Simple J. Malarkey. Funny thing about ol' Simple: he was a dead ringer for U.S. Senator Joseph R. McCarthy. This was new and dangerous territory for Walt Kelly.

Kelly wrote in Ten Ever-Lovin' Blue Eyed Years with Pogo:

There has never been much question in my mind that the man who Simple J. Malarkey represented was one of the great all-time comedians. This is because he was a *true* comedian; he was not pretending for a moment. With his uproarious and highhanded disregard of the amenities and established precedent he became almost a law to himself. Before our very eyes we saw ourselves allowing ourselves to be chumps. The man was just great. I miss him. He was completely unpredictable and, therefore, fascinating.

Simple J. Malarkey's first appearance among the swamp people was on May 1, 1953.

HURRY OVER TO SHORE! COME QUICK! WOW!

IT'S ANOTHER YEAR.......! A NEW YEAR! HAPPY NEW YEAR! MAN'S BEST FRIEND SEES MUCH TO BE HAPPY FOR. AH! WE'RE LUCKY TO HAVE ME AROUND.....CONGRATULATIONS.

GREETINGS TO ALL! TELL EVERYBODY THAT THE NOBLE DOG'S BIG HEART SHINES THRU IN A BLAZE OF LOVE AN' HOPE! HOORAY, I SAY, FOR '53! NOW I'LL GET ALONG TO SPREAD THE NEWS.

UNLESSEN THAT BOY SLOW DOWN, HE'S GONE USE THIS HERE YEAR ALL UP AFORE IT EVEN GITS GOIN'.

DIST. BY POST HALL SYNDICATE.

MAKIN' RESOLUTIONS FOR PEOPLE AN' THEN DOIN' FOR THEM WHAT-EVER THEY SWEARS OFF IS A TOUGH BUSINESS.

YOU BEEN TELLIN' TOO MANY TO GIVE UP EATIN' STUFF.

SEE, YOU MADE ALBERT GIVE UP CREAM PUFFS, SO HE HAD TO GO OUT AN' BUY A SET SO'S TO GIVE 'EM UP.... WE GOT SIX LEFT.... I ALONE ET NINE.....

OOG!

THEN A RESOLUTION FOR HOUN'DOG. MADE HIM GIVE UP HIS FAVORITE FOOD.... FORGOT IT'D BE BONES! US HAD TO EAT A POUND AN' A HALF OF VINTAGE PIG KNUNKLES AN' RIBS... US GOT SOME OF THEM LEFT.

ALL THE LEFT OVERS, MIXED WITH THE MONEY US TOOK IN, IS SORT OF GOON-UP WITH THE BICARB WE PACKED AS A PREE-CAUTION..... OUR BUSINESS IS IN A MESS!

DIST. BY POST HALL SYNDICATE.

DO I HEAR CORRECT, BOYS? YOU ARE MAKING THESE RESOLUTION FOR NOUVEAU YEAR 1953?

YEP.

YOU MAKIN' UP THESE FOR OTHERS PEOPLE, NO? THEN YOU ARE HELP THEM TO KEEP THESE RESOLUTE?

THAT'S THE GEN'RAL IDEA, MUM.

PORKY'S UNCLE, BALDWON, IS KEEP SNOOKIN' UP AN' IS KISS MAM'SELLE... PERHOP YOU CAN CONVINCE THESE GENTLEMAN TO ABANDON THESE POORSUIT... EY?

US'LL GIVE IT A WHIRL ... COURSE WE HELPS OUR CLIENT BY DOIN' FOR HIM WHATEVER HE SWEARS OFF DOIN'.......WHICH WAY IS UNCLE BALDWIN?

DIST. BY POST HALL SYNDICATE.

TO GIT UNCLE BALDWIN TO OPEN PORKY'S DOOR US'LL GOT TO FOOL HIM... I'LL SAY I IS MAM'SELLE.

PORKY.

♪ YOO HOO! ♪ OPEN UP?? I IS MAM'SELLE HEPZIBAH! ♪

SMEERP!
PORK

I ISN'T HER, SIR! I ISN'T HER! JES' HIM, SIR. JES' ONLY HIM!

UG

US'LL HIDE WITH HIS HEAD AN' POP OUT ON HIM WHEN HE COMES OUT.

GOTTA *SNEAK* OUT----THEM *LI'L'* SCAPERS GONE *BLOCK*ADE ME INTO *STAR*VATION.

THERE HE GO! *FLYIN'* BLIND! *HEADLESS!* A MENACE TO *NAVIGATION!*

HEY! COME BACK! *YOU* IS *FORGOT YO' HEAD!* US PULLED IT OFF BY ACCIDENT AN' YOU BETTER WEAR IT 'CAUSE..

MY SAKES! YOU *GOT* ONE ON---*THIS ONE LOOKS BETTER'N* THE OTHER, TOO!

YES, I'M QUITE ATTACHED TO IT.

WHAT'LL I DO WITH YOUR *OLD ONE?*

HEY! WOW! PUFF...WHOOF--- HOO-BOY! AM *I* OUT OF --*PUFF*.... BREATH? ...OO- THE NOBLE DOG RAN ALL THE WAY ---*HUFF*---MAN'S BEST FRIEN'...

1-12 *DIST. BY POST HALL SYNDICATE.*

...BRINGS *NEWS* --GOTTA--PFF-- TELL YOU MMPH *BOY!* --WHOO----*WHAT A HEROIC RUN*----WOO

THE BURGESSES OF *AIX* --PFF--VOTED---*BOY* TO GIVE *ROLAND*---HOO WHOOSH----THEIR LAST MEASURE OF --*HUFF*-- WINE --WHOOIE..WHEN HE RUN FROM *GHENT*----
M·M·HUMPH

YOU RUN OVER TO TELL US *THAT* ?

NO, IT'S JES' A FOOTNOTE TO THE MAIN MESSAGE --- *VALOR DESERVES REWARD,* MY MAN.

I GOT NEWS FOR YOU, TOO: YOU COMED *EMPTYHEADED*... YOU LEAVES *EMPTYHANDED.*

THIS RUN I MADE OVER TO TELL YOU THIS *NEWS'* SURE DOES REMIND *ME* OF *ROLAND* WHO CARRIED THE GOOD NEWS FROM GHENT TO AIX.

I TOOK A FREIGHTER TO DECATUR

1-13 *DIST. BY POST HALL SYNDICATE*

"Not a word to each other they kept the great pace Neck by neck, stride by Stride Never changing our place"- 'Til the others DIED!

BUT:"There was my Roland To bear the whole weight Of the news which alone Could save Aix From her fate.."

OH, SUCH A BRAVE HEART... MAN'S BEST FRIEND! EVER *LOYAL!*

THERE.. THERE

WASN'T THIS ROLAND A *HORSE* ?

I TOOK A FREIGHTER TO DECATUR FOR TO SEE MY ROSE! TO SUPPLICATE HER DEAR OL' PATER HM-TUM-TUMTY TOES!

WHAT WAS THIS NEWS YOU RUN OVER TO TELL US'N, COUSIN?

AH, YES! WELL, YES.... AH-HUM--MMP. ---NEWS---- WELL, NOW, -- HMM----

1-14
DIST. BY POST HALL SYNDICATE.

I REMEMBER! THEM TWO ON THE *OUTSIDE* PULLED OFF THE *HEAD* OF THAT BOY IN THE *MIDDLE!*

I'M GLAD IT WAS A **MOP** WE PULLED OFF THE HANDLE AN' NOT YOUR **HEAD** OFFA **YOU**, UNCLE BALDWIN.

IT'S A COMFORT

1-15 DIST BY POST HALL SYNDICATE.

ME AN' OWL COMED AROUND TO GIT YO' TO SWEAR OFF KISSIN' MIZ MA'M'SELLE DURIN' 1953----

SHHH SHH

WELL, I...UM....

SHHH! **SH!** THE BOY BIRD WATCHERS IS HOLDIN' **WINTER** MANEUVERS.

SH! AN' OL' **PEEK-A-BOO** BEN ADHEM LEADS ALL THE REST.

SHHH.... WE IS TRAILIN' A PTARMIGAN.

EVER SEE A **PTARMIGAN?**

SEE ONE! I CAN'T EVEN **SAY** ONE.

COPR. 1953 WALT KELLY

JUST WHAT I NEED! **THREE** INTELLIGENT MEN!

WHERE?

1-16 DIST. BY POST HALL SYNDICATE INC.

YOU, MY FRIENDS, ARE ABOUT TO BE **MILLIONAIRES.** EVER HEAR OF SOAP OPERA AN' THE **SOAP KINGS?**

HUH?

CORRECT! VERY PERCEPTIVE! BUT **WHAT** IS SOAP WITHOUT **WATER?** BAD TASTIN' CHEESE! PUT YOUR MONEY IN **WATER!**

WON'T IT GIT SOGGY?

IT HAPPENS, FRIENDS, THAT **I** HAVE JUST **OBTAINED** THE **NIAGARA FALLS!** ALL I HAVE TO DO IS RAISE A LITTLE CASH TO GET IT DOWN HERE AN' WE'RE **MADE!**

ISN'T THAT JES' FINE?

COPR. 1953 WALT KELLY

NOW **SUPPOSE** WE'RE IN THE **WATER** BUSINESS...A LADY BUYS **SOAP**, SHE'S **GOTTA** HAVE WATER ---WE SELL HER A BARREL ---AN' THEY IS FIFTY MILLION **LADIES.**

1-17 DIST. BY POST HALL SIND.

FIFTY MILLION BARRELS OF WATER LEAVES A BIG **HOLE**---FISH GOTTA SWIM IN EMPTY AIR... **HOW** DO WE FILL IT...?

WE FLOATS THE **NI**AGARA DOWN HERE BY WAY OF THE ST. LAWRENCE AND THE ATLANTIC AN'...

WAIT! I GOT A IDEA! THE HOLE IN THE SWAMP WOULD BE A **DRY** WATER HOLE... THERE OUGHTTA BE A BIG DEMAND FOR **DRY WATER**....IT DON'T GIT CLO'ES WET AN----

LEAVE US **NOT** BE **REE**-DICULOUS!

YEAH!

COPR. 1953 WALT KELLY

I CHARGE SEMINOLE SAM WITH INNERFEARIN' WITH THE RIGHTS OF **SMALL BUSINESS** MEN! HE GONE DIG A HOLE IN THE SWAMP WATER AN' FILL IT WITH THE **NI**-ANGORRA **FALLS!**

1-19 DIST. BY POST HALL SYNDICATE

I SAY USE THAT **DRY** WATER HOLE! THE DEMAND FOR DRY WATER IS **OVER**-POWERIN' AN...

FURTHERMORE US DON'T NEED NO **YANKEE** WATER IN THIS SWAMP...OOMP.

SEE! IF THIS HAD BEEN A DRY WATER HOLE I WOONTNA GOT WET.

IF IT'D BEEN **DRY** WATER, OUR BOAT'D BE **FIFTEEN** FEET IN THE AIR AN' YOU'D OF FALLEN TO YOUR **DEATH!**

YEAH! THEN YOU'D CHANGE YOUR TUNE.

COPR. 1953 WALT KELLY

AFTER GIVEN YOU THE NAME OF THE **SECRET** INGREDIENT THAT **HOUSEWORK** REQUIRES---(ALL IN GOOD FAITH) I CAN'T FIND YOUR MILLION DOLLARS.

OOH--G! I IS IN PAIN!

PAIN? WHAT FROM?

FROM THAT PERCYPACASSIDY AN' THE PRESBY-COOTITY YOU CLAM I HAD... **MY HEAD'S ON FIRE!**

THAT'S WHAT YOU GITS FOR GOIN' TO BED ON THE DINNER TABLE----- YO' **HEAD** IS IN A **HOT BOWL OF SOUP.**

ANYWAYS I FEELS ONE HUNNERD **POOR** CENT BETTER ---- GOTTA REMEMBER THIS **PERSCRIPTION** --- WHAT KIND **WAS** IT?

NOODLE. IT NATURALLY COULDN'T OF BUN **NOTHIN'** ELSE.

DIST BY 1-24 POST HALL SYND.

WISH YOU COULD REMEMBER WHAT YOU DID WITH THAT **MILLION**

ON ACCOUNT OF MY RECENT **ILLNESS** I CAN'T RECALL EVEN **HAVIN'** IT.

BUT I TOLD YOU OF A **SECRET INGREDIMENT** TO SELL TO HOUSEWIFES----- SOMETHIN' THEY **GOTTA** HAVE AFORE THEY EVEN **KIN START** TO CLEAN.

FOR THIS SECRET YOU WAS GONNA GIVE ME **HAFFA** YOUR MILLION!

I CAN'T EVEN FIND **MY** HALF, EASY COME · EASY GO ----- SO I'LL BE FAIR.

I'LL GIVE YOU **BACK** THE NAME OF THE SECRET INGRED-IMENT-----**LISTEN CLOSE NOW,** IT'S **DIRT** ----- GET IT? HELLO, UNCLE BALDWIN, ARE YOU THERE? IT'S **DIRT**... D LIKE IN **DIRT**... I LIKE IN DIRT R LIKE IN **DIRT**--- T LIKE IN ORANGE PEKOE.

1-26 DIST. BY POST HALL SYNDICATE.

H'LO CHURCHY AN' UNCLE BALDWIN, IS YOU DIGGIN' **BAIT?**

NO, POGO. US IS DIGGIN' OUR **FORTUNE.**

BUT IT'S SUCH A **POW'FUL** SECRET....

WE CAN'T TELL YOU WHAT WE IS PUTTIN' IN THESE BOXES TO SELL TO **HOUSEWIFES** ----US **MIS**LAID MY **MILLION** DOLLARS AN'

TO GIT IT BACK, US IS GONE MAKE **BILLIONS** SELLIN' THIS STUFF TO **HOUSEWIFES** 'CAUSE THEY NEEDS IT AFORE THEY GOTTA USE SOAP AN' WATER EVEN....

WHY, **THAT'S DIRT!**

YOU MUST OF TOLE!

HMM... **DIRT!** WODDYA KNOW?!

1-27 DIST. BY POST HALL SYNDICATE.

COPR 1953 WALT KELLY

FIRST PERSON US'LL CALL ON WITH THE UNDISPENSABLE INGREDIENT WILL BE A **OL' FRIEND** --- I'LL SHOW YOU HOW TO APPROACH WIMMENS...

WATCH HOW I SWEEPS HER OFF'N HER **FEETS.**

YOU!

GOOD AFTERNOON (SMEERP) I WONDER IF I COULD HAVE A FEW MINUTES OF YOUR TIME **SMEERP!**

WHAT HAPPENED?

UNCLE BALDWIN WAS GONE SHOW ME HOW TO IMPRESS HOUSEWIFES BUT MIZ MA'M'SELLE HAD A LONG-HANGLE BRUSH AN' HE WAS **CARRIED** AWAY.

PHOO ON PLAYIN' THE **GENT'MAN** I SHUNTNA TOOK OFF MY HAT.

DIST. BY POST HALL SYNDICATE 1-28

COPR 1953 WALT KELLY

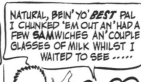
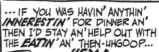

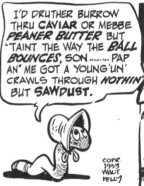

2-17 Panel 1: THAT *NUGGET* YOU CRUNCHED ON MUST OF COME FROM HERE ... THIS IS THE SPOT WHERE THEY *DUG!*

Panel 2: THE *SECRET INGREDIMINT* IS *GOLD!* AN' WE'LL BE RICH RICH *RICH RICH!*

Panel 3: *RICH?* THAT NUGGET WAS MY *OWN* STORE BOUGHTEN *GOLD MOLAR* OF 14 KARAT BRASS ALL THE WAY FROM ST. AUGUSTINE.

Panel 4: *CAREFUL!* STEADY! *STEADY!* YOU'LL DISSOLVE OUR PARTNERSHIP. / *LETTIN'* ME DIG ALL THAT WHILE! AN' FER *BRASS!*

2-17 DIST. BY POST-HALL SYNDICATE. / COPR. 1953 WALT KELLY

2-18 Panel 1: YOU AN' ME IS *THROUGH!* THE NEXT *MILLION DOLLAR* IDEA I GET I'LL KEEP FOR MY*SELF!* / AN' THE NEXT *BILLION* DOLLAR IDEA I'LL KEEP, SO *HA!*

Panel 2: *I'LL* KEEP THE NEXT *TRILLION* DOLLAR IDEA, *HA HO!* / THE NEXT *QUAD-RILLION* IDEA, *I'LL* KEEP! TOP THAT!

Panel 3: WHAT COMES AFTER A QUADRILLION DOLLARS? / IF THEY HEARS YOU *GOT* IT, THE *FEDERABLE* GUMMINT IN LESS'N A MONTH. / *HE* MEANS IN NUMBERS. I'D SAY A *VERMILLION*, TAKE OR LOSE A DOZEN...

Panel 4: ISN'T THAT GOIN' INTO THE *RED* A LI'L? / WITH BIG *FIGGERS* LIKE THAT IT DON'T SEEM TO MATTER. / *YAH YAH YAH YAH!* / *YAH YAH YAH YOU' SELF!*

2-18 DIST. BY POST-HALL SYNDICATE. / COPR. 1953 WALT KELLY

2-19 Panel 1: WELL, *I* IS ALL READY TO JOIN OL' *ALBERT* AN' GO OFF TO THE *BERMOOTHES* TO WATCH THE *ONIONS* AN' THE *EELS.*

Panel 2: HOW YOU GONNA AFFORD *THAT?* WATCHIN' ONIONS COMES *HIGH!* / *ALBERT* MADE $10,000. ON A BIG DIRT DEAL.

Panel 3: UNCLE BALDWIN SOLD HIM A *MILLION* BOXES OF *DIRT* AN' KNOCKED A PENNY OFF EACH SO ALBERT SAVED A *COOL TEN THOUSAND.*

Panel 4: BUT *FIRST* HE GOTTA PAY FOR TH' *MILLION* BOXES OF DIRT. / *WHUFFO?* HE GONE SEND 'EM *BACK!* WHO WANTS *THEM?* / THEY AIN'T FLIM-FLAMMIN' *ME!*

2-19 DIST. BY POST-HALL SYNDICATE. / COPR. 1953 WALT KELLY

2-20 Panel 1: THERE'S *MILLIONS* IN "*DIRT*"... MAYBE EVEN *HUNDREDS!* I'LL GET THE *ADVERTISIN'* AN'... / ARE YOU MUMBLIN' PRIVATE OR CAN I MUMBLE WITH YOU?

Panel 2: *REASON REELS!* I'LL OPEN A T.V. STATION IN THE OL' SWAMP AN' *PLUG* UNCLE BALDWIN'S HOUSEHOLD HELP.."*DIRT*"! I'LL CALL IT "THE HOUR OF ....." / I DUNNO

Panel 3: A *FLASH* OF GENIUS! / I HAD A COUSIN WHO WORKED ONE OF THEM SHOWS. *HE* KEPT TELLIN' THE *SAME* STORY ABOUT THE CAT WHO ATE *CHEESE* AN' SAT BY THE MOUSE-HOLE WITH *BATED* BREATH. THEY ASKED HIM TO DESIST, BUT HE PERSISTED UNTIL AT LENGTH HE WAS *CANNED*...

Panel 4: HE WAS THROUGH? / WAS HE *THREW!* HE WAS THREW *ALL* THE *WHOLE* WAY OVER THE RIVER INTO A *JERSEY CANNIN' FACTORY* AN' LATER SHOWED UP IN A CONTAINER OF PEAS IN TERRE HAUTE WHERE HE.. --*WHAT?* / WE'RE WAITIN' ON YOU...YOU GOT THE CARDS

2-20 DIST. BY POST-HALL SYNDICATE / COPR. 1953 WALT KELLY

WELL, I'M OFF TO PACK MY BAG.

SO'S US KIN **WAFT** OUR SELFS TO THE **BERMOOTHES** TO WATCH THE ONIONS AND THE **EELS**.

I AIN'T **NO** MIRROR.

WHY, **SO** YOU ISN'T, I **WONDERED** WHY I **COONENT** PART MY HAIR..... WELL, THAT'S A **RELIEF**.

WE NEED A IDEA FOR THE **NATIONAL 'DIRT'** HOUR T.V. PROGRAM.

AN' A **ROUSER** FOR A **THEME** SONG.

EASY!

"**D** IS FOR THE **BREATH** BLEW ON THE GRAVY
I IS FOR A **WIVVER** WET AN' WAVY..
R IS FOR THE **OOLONG** SHORTLY SHOALED
T IS FOR THE **ICE** WITH LOWLIFE LININ'...."

AIN'T HE GOT TOO MANY LINES IN THERE?

YEP. 'BOUT **FIVE**.

NOW, ON YOUR **T.V.** PROGRAM WE COULD HAVE A **WILE WEST** SHOW "THE FIASCO KID WRITHES AGAIN."

OR A **NEWS ANALYSIZER**, TO WIT: *Miz Limpkin is visitin' her Aunt Meemie up to Fort Mudge....... Behine of this move is Mister Limpkin. Sunny weather is bein' caused by few clouds and no rain atall.*

OR WE CAN PUT ON A **PUMPET** SHOW...USIN' LI'L WOODEN ANIMALS THAT **TALK** LIKE HUMAN BEANS.

TOO RADICAL! TALKIN' ANIMALS ISN'T HARDLY BELIEVABOBBLE...**HOW** 'BOUT A **MAGICIAN** WHAT SAYS: "WHO WAS THAT LADY I SAWED WITH YOU LAST NIGHT?" IT'S **ALLUS** GOOD.

HERE'S HOW IT WORKS. WE OPEN OUR **T.V.** SHOW ON A SMILIN' **HANDSOME** FACE.

WHERE WE GONE **GIT** ONE?

THEN I TELLS FUNNY STORIES AN' SHOWS 'EM A BOX OF **'DIRT'.** *EVERY LADY KNOWS HOW IMPORTANT DIRT IS....*

HOW 'BOUT THAT, MIZ ANGLEWORM?

AS A HOUSEWIFE I CAN TELL YOU IT'S HARD TO KEEP HOUSE WITHOUT IT. CALL YO' PROGRAM THE "**HOUR OF DIRT**"...... THE LADIES WILL EAT IT UP.......

SURE, A **GOSSIP** PROGRAM.....WE'LL GET A **NOTED** COMMENTATOR LIKE **ME** AN'....

THE LADIES WILL EAT **THIS** UP?

SURE 'NOUGH. IT MAY BE DIRT TO **YOU**, BUT IT'S **OUR** BREAD AN' BUTTER.

You see anything of an incomin' liner with a friend of mine aboard, Pogo?

NOPE

You sure? He's a mole by trade ~~~ squinty look on him ~~~ nobility stamped all over him ~~~~

WHAT'D THEY DO **THAT** FOR?

Probably wearin' a sports coat ~ might have a spray gun with him ~~~ he's very hygienic ~~ You sure you've looked sharp?

I LOOK SHARP AS MOST....LINERS DON'T COME IN HERE.

Ha! That's all you know! Here comes the Hon. Mole now. Huzzah, friend, huzzah, I say!

SORRY, DEAC ...HAD TO COME IN BY SECOND CLASS CABIN.

I THINK I GOT THE SONG TO OPEN THE "HOUR OF DIRT."

LONG AS IT DON'T CLOSE IT.. SHOOT.

Oh, to reap in the weep of the golden ripe Reap! All the Sheep in the fold All asleep in the gold of the ripe weep we reap..

GRAMBUNKLE!

Wipe the weep from your Reap! Ripe reap, ripe weep! Ripe the reap of the weep Wipe weep! RIPE REAP!

WHERE IS ANY MENTION OF "DIRT"?

THEM SHEEP IN THERE IS FOR SALE AN' THEY IS DIRT CHEAP.... GET IT?

IT NEEDS A KICKER AT THE END

YEP. ONE WHO KIN PUNT IT 70 YARD OR MORE

COPR. 1953 WALT KELLY

3-12

YOU WON'T GIVE A LISTEN AT MY SONG, HUH?

THE "HOUR OF DIRT" IS DESPRIT.--- GO AHEAD.

"THERE'S A STAR IN THE WIND, AND THE WIND WINDS HIGH, BLOWING ALIGHT THRU FOG, THRU NIGHT, THRU COLD, THRU COLD AND THE BITTER ALONE ...."

"THERE, HIGH IN THE WIND, RIDES A STAR, MY OWN, AND THE STAR IS A WORD... OF WHITE...OF WHITE.. AND THE STAR IN THE WIND IS A WORD. "

IT MIGHT MAKE FOLKS BRING BACK THE DIRT THEY ARREADY BOUGHT.

NOT MUCH SELL TO IT.

MAKE IT FUNNY, PORKY. PUT A BOFF IN IT.

WULL, I THO'T IT WAS PERTY FUNNY AS IT WAS.

COPR 1953 WALT KELLY

3-13

'LONG AS YOU ASK, I'LL TELL YOU THE POEM THAT EVER'BODY THUNK WAS SO BAD YESTERDDY.

AT LISTENING TO POEM MA'M'SELLE HAS UNERRING EAR AN' EYE.

IT GO 'LONG AN' GO 'LONG AN' THEN SAY: --- "--THRU COLD, THRU COLD AND THE BITTER ALONE THERE, HIGH IN THE WIND RIDES A STAR, MY OWN, AND THE STAR IS A WORD ...OF WHITE... OF WHITE... AND THE STAR IN THE WIND IS A WORD..:..."

EN VRAI! QUEL AVOIRDUPOIS! FORMEEDOBBL! AN' SO CUTE!

WHAT DOES HE MEANS?

COPR. 1953 WALT KELLY.

3-14

YOU WANT ME TO READ THESE LINES YOU WROTE FOR "CHEERFUL TEARFUL MABEL," EH, OWL?

I'LL TAKE MABEL'S PART.

T.V. REHEARSAL

H'LO, MABEL! WHY DOES YOU LOOK LIKE YOU DOES?

GRAN'MAM WHAT RUN OFF WITH MY UNCLE POODIE JES' BUS' HER LEGBONE AN' COTCHED LEPROSY.

AN' THE DIKE LEAKED ALL OVER OUR PET ELEPHUMP AN' DROWNED THE CRITTUR.

HOW DOES YOU KEEP A STIFF UPPER LIP IN TH' FACE OF ADVERSITOSSY?

I GOT A STIFF UPPER LIP 'CAUSE I IS A OL' TRUMPET PLAYER .....

YES, FOLKS, IF YOU TOO WANNA FACE LIFE...LEARN TO BLOW A HORN AT HERM HORNBILL'S HORN EMPORIUM.

WELL?

IS THIS CONTAGEROUS?

COPR 1953 WALT KELLY

3-16

Ah, there! The Dove Brothers.

IT'S NICE TO BE RECOGNIZED IN A SPIRIT OF **BONAFIDISM,** FRIEND DEACON! MOST OF THE **PSUEDO-INTELLECTUARIES** HERE THINK OF US AS **COWBIRDS!**

UGH.

WE'RE REFORMED! **CAST ASIDE** ARE THE INFANTILISMS OF **ENTRENCHED YOUTH**--- THE CHARLATANISTIC DEMOGOGUERY SPAWNED BY THE MACHIAVELLIAN MACHINES OF MASOCHISTIC MANIPULATORS ARE **INDEED.**

YES!

YEA! OUR EXPERIENCE BEHIND THE VEIL OF VENOM ---**BEHIND THE MONOLITHIC MURAL**--- HAS LED US TO KNOW--- **WE KNOW THAT THE OWL,** WHO IS A REPUTABLE MEMBER OF THE COMMUNITY IS A **FRIEND** OF THE **TURTLE!**

TRAVESTISM!

COPR 1953 WALT KELLY

AN' THE TURTLE IS A FRIEND OF THE **ALLIGATOR, WHO IS A FRIEND OF POGO!** AN' HE, THE VIRTUOUS, **ONCE BEFRIENDED US!**

AN' ANYBODY KNOW WHAT SCURVY **SCUM WE** USED TO BE!

3-17

DIST BY POST-HALL SYND.

IF YOU'RE GOIN' TO DO BIRD WATCHIN' ... **WATCH THE OWL!** THERE IS AN **AVID ADVOCATE** OF **ADOLESCENTISM.**

The Hon. Mole here is an Expert Bird Watcher.

I'LL **DO** IT! I'LL KEEP AN **EYE** ON HIM.

HE DOESN'T SEEM TO **MOVE** MUCH.

OH, **THAT'S** NOT EXACTLY THE **OWL,** SIR ---- IT'S MORE A **STUMP!** CLOSE THO'... BUT WE'RE NOT AT THE **T.V.** STATION YET.

AH, WELL! POINT ME AT HIM AND I'LL WATCH THE **TAR** OUT OF HIM.

RIGHT, SIR .... LOOKOUT FOR THE **ROCK,** SIR.

COPR. 1953 WALT KELLY

3-18   DIST. BY POST HALL SYNDICATE.

I'VE COME TO **WATCH** YOU, OWL, BEING AS YOU'RE A **BIRD.**

AN' BEIN' AS YOU'RE THE TOP **BIRD BRAIN** IN THE SWAMP, HON. MOLE?

CAN'T SAY WATCHING YOU IS **EASY** ON THE EYES, OWL ---YOU LOOK SORTA SUSPICIOUS.

THAT'S A **MIRROR,** NOT A **TEEVY** SET.

YOU THERE, MR. **OWL,** STOP BREATHING GERMS AT US! **ARE YOU TRYING TO CONFUSE ME?** I'VE GOT **EYES,** HAVEN'T **I?**

IF I ANSWER THAT RIGHT AN' **WIN ANOTHER REFRIGERATOR** I'LL JES' **DIE!**

DIST. BY POST-HALL SYNDICATE 3-19   COPR.

SCRIPTS

COPR. 1953 WALT KELLY

WHY DON'T YOU HEAD OVER TO A **BASEBALL CAMP,** THEY NEEDS UMPIRES.

A BIRDWATCHER **NEVER** SHIRKS HIS DUTY FOR A **SPORT,** SIR.

I DUNNO. I WAS GIVIN' 'EM THE EYE ONE TIME WHEN A **CHICKADEE** CAME BY WHAT SHE LOOKS LIKE A **REAL** SPORT... WELL, I LEFT OFF WATCHIN' THE OTHERS AN'...

A LITTLE RESPECT OWL!

YOU'RE **SOME** BIRD WATCHER! I'M A **MOUSE** NOT A OWL.

HA! THE OWL CLAIMS HE'S A **MOUSE** ..... HE'S OUT OF HIS **MIND!**

WHY SHOULD YOU BE OUT OF YOUR MIND TO BE A MOUSE? --- **SOME NERVE!** I'D RESENT THIS SLUR ON US MICE IF I WERE YOU.

COPR 1953 WALT KELLY

3-20   DIST. BY POST-HALL SYNDICATE.

OWL, I'VE BEEN THINKING YOUR CLAIM THAT YOU'RE A *MOUSE* IS A *MERE* SUBTERFUGE.

I'M OVER HERE! AN' IT WAS THE MOUSE SAID HE WAS A MOUSE.

3-21

DIST. BY POST HALL SYNDICATE.

QUIETLY..*QUIETLY!* CALM QUESTIONING WILL DETERMINE *WHO* SAID IT....MR. *MOUSE*, DID YOU CLAIM TO BE A *MOUSE?*

Ridiculous

SO, THAT LEAVES ONLY *YOU*, SIRRAH! AND IN *MY* OPINION...

HE AIN'T NO MOUSE IN THE FIRST PLACE! HE IS A *MUSHRAT!*

COPR. 1953 WALT KELLY.

MY DEAR SIR, DID YOU *EVER* IN ALL YOUR *BORN* DAYS HEAR ANYTHING LIKE *THIS?*

NO... I CAN'T *truthfully* say I have.

THERE IS SOMETHING SUSPICIOUS AND *FEARFULLY* FAMILIAR ABOUT THAT *OWL* ON T.V.

THAT'S A MIRROR AGAIN, SIR.

3-23

BUT IT SHOWS THE INTRINSIC *BASICAL* SUSPICIABILITY OF THE OWL! IT TRANSCENDS REALITISM AND PERVADES FUNDIMENTALISTIC *OCCULT*IFICATION OF LOGIC.

HOW REALLY RIGHTLY HONESTLY AND TRULY *TRUE.*

DIST. BY POST.HALL SYNDICATE

WE COWBIRDS OR— (*HEE HEE*) DOVES— KNEW OWL BEFORE HE WAS ON *T.V.* ---VERY *FRIENDLY,* TOO.

NO DOUBT ABOUT IT-- HE'S BAD FOR THE JOB.... *I'LL* WAGER OWL IS A *MIGRATORY* BIRD....HE COULD *LEAVE* QUIETLY?

COPR. 1953 WALT KELLY

NO, OWL'S A *NATIVE* AND HAS CERTAIN *RIGHTS.* HE'LL HAVE TO BE THROWED OUT BODILY.

MY *DEAR* SIR! WHY BE *UNCOUTH?* WE ---UH...*I'VE* ALREADY IDENTIFIED HIM AS A *MIGRANT.* WE'LL JUST ASK HIM, *EVER* SO POLITELY, TO MOVE *ON.*

I BELIEVE THAT, AS HEAD BIRD WATCHER, *YOU* SHOULD TELL *OWL* TO MIGRATE TO HIS SUMMER GROUNDS.

But he's a *native*---not a migrant---He has *certain rights..*

3-24

I'M AFRAID YOU'VE BEEN *INFECTED* BY THE *GERMS* IN OUR AIR....*I'LL* TELL OWL IF *YOU* REFUSE...

You're the big bird brain --- go ahead...

MOVE OFF, OWL.... DO YOUR *DUTY,* SIR! MIGRATE LIKE A GOOD FELLOW! *MIGRATE! MIGRATE!*

Kof Kof

HE WON'T BE MISSED, POOR LAD.

You already missed him.

I disagree with you, Hon. Mole, the Owl is an old native of the Swamp---He never migrates--- Let him play with his *silly* T.V. station --- What harm?

3-25 DIST. BY POST-HALL SYNDICATE.

YOU LOSE SIGHT OF ONE THING ---- *THERE'S MILLIONS* IN A *T.V.* STATION....

IT SHOULD BE IN COMPETENT HANDS.

Millions---well-- well-- m-m-m--What *charges* would you-- uh---*we* use to get *rid* of Owl?

CHARGES: GET RID OF HIM? LET'S BE *FAIR,* WE'LL FORCE HIM TO LEAVE OF HIS OWN FREE WILL.

COPR. 1953 WALT KELLY

—44—

TRY THAT POEM AGAIN. NOT SURE IF I GOT IT ALL.

Give me your tired, your poor, Your huddled masses yearning to breathe free, The wretched refuse of your teeming shore.

Send these, the homeless, tempest-tost to me, I lift my lamp beside the golden door.

HMM.... WHERE'D YOU SAY YOU GOT THAT?

WELL, A NICE LADY NAME OF EMMA LAZARUS WRIT IT....BUT I GOT IT OFF'N ANOTHER LADY...A OLD LADY, STANDIN' OUT IN THE BAY....NIGHT AN' DAY---A LADY CARRYIN' A BIG FLAMIN' TORCH.

I'M AFRAID YOU DOVES ARE RIGHT....HE'S CRAZY....OR THE OL' WOMAN IS, OUT IN THE WATER IN ALL WEATHER, ARMED WITH A TORCH! HAH! A PYROMANIAC, NO DOUBT.! A DANGER TO ALL.

NO! NOT A OL' MAN WHAT CAN'T SEE..

BUT HE'S TALKIN' 'BOUT THE WOMAN I LOVE.

COPR. 1953 WALT KELLY

YOU MEAN MOLE JES' LAUGHED AT YO' POEM 'BOUT MISS LIBERTY?

YEP....HE SAID SHE WAS CRAZY FOR STANDIN' OUT IN THE WATER OF THE HARBOR

4-20   DIST. BY POST-HALL SYNDICATE

BY JING! THAT DOES IT!

THAT BOILS MY ALL AMERICAN SOUTHERN FRIED BLOOD! THAT MOLE IS GOTTA GO!

LEAST HE COULD OF DO IS HELP THAT OLD LADY OUTEN THAT BAY! BY NAB! JES' HE WAIT!

WHAT HE GONE DO?

MUST BE GONE ROUSE OUT THE BON FIRE BOYS!

COPR. 1953 WALT KELLY

I IS HAD ENOUGH OF THAT MOLE. I'LL GIT OL' BEAUREGARD TO HELP ME RUN HIM OUT.

4-21 DIST. BY POST-HALL SYNDICATE

'COURSE OL' HOUN'DOG'LL PROB'LY SAY: TAKE IT EASY! (NOT BEIN' STIRRED YET---) SO I'LL ARGUE WITH HIM----

LIKE AS NOT, HE'LL ARGUE CLAIMIN' HE'S TOO BUSY; THEN HE'LL FIND ANOTHER EXCUSE... THEN IF HE DOES HELP, HE'LL BE PRETTY BOSSY.

ARGH! JES' WAIT'LL I LAY MY HANDS ON THAT GOLDBRICKIN' DOG!

COPR. 1953 WALT KELLY

HOW RIDICKLE-MOUS OF ME TO GIT MAD AT OL' HOUN'DOG 'FORE I EVEN TALKS TO HIM.

-4-22

THERE'S NO REASON YET TO THINK HE WON'T HELP THROW MOLE OUT....HE WON'T CLAIM TO BE TOO BUSY...HE WON'T ACT BOSSY...I GOT NO RIGHT TO GIT BURNED OFF....

DIST. BY POST-HALL SYNDICATE

I'LL WALK UP TO MY OLD PAL K'NOWIN' HE'LL HELP....ABLE TO COUNT ON HIM ~. I'LL SHAKE HAN'S AN' EVEN 'FORE I CAN GIT THE WORDS OUTEN MY MOUTH..

LIKE AS NOT THE BANG-BANG CRITTUR WILL REFUSE TO LISTEN!

COPR. 1953 WALT KELLY

HOUN'DOG -- YOU IS JES' THE MAN I IS LOOKIN' FOR.

AHA!

YES?

I NEEDS A CANNY-DATE FOR A DANGEROUS MISSION..... CARE TO TOSS *YO'* HAT IN THE RING?

NO!

BY GEO. Y. WELLS! I *KNOWED* YOU WOULD BACK OFF, *SKEERT!*

THAT WASN'T *ME!* I RENTED THE UPPER STOREY TO LI'L' OL' *MOUSE* AN' HE'S SENS-ITIVE 'BOUT ME THROWIN' THE HAT *ANYWHERE*.

I'LL HELP YOU THROW OL' *MOLE* OUT, ALBERT.

HOUN'DOG, YOU DON'T SEEM VERY JOYED UP 'BOUT IT.

I DIN'T SAY A *THING!* IT'S THAT MOUSE AGAIN.

WHY'D YOU EVER RENT YO' HAT TO A *MOUSE?*

HE COULDN'T RENT IT TO A *RHINOCER-WURST.* HEY, I GOTTA GIT DINNER----

BY JASPER! I DIN'T GIVE YOU KITCHEN PRIVILEGES.

AN' YOU DANG WELL KIN POUR YO' *BATH WATER* DOWN THE *BACK STAIRS* HEREAFTER.

WHY'D YOU EVER RENT YO' HAT TO THE MOUSE?

WELL, I WASN'T USIN' MY HEAD FOR ANYTHIN' AN' I.....

FIRE!

HE SET IT A PURPOSE TO GIT ME OUT!

YOU TRY MOVIN' BACK IN NOW AN' THE RENT IS GONE UP 15 POOR CENT.!

NOTHIN' OFF FOR LIKE A *FIRE SALE* LIKE?

THE REASON I RENTED THE HAT WAS 'CAUSE THE *MOLE* TOLD ME TO *MIGRATE.*

CLAIMED YOU WAS A *FLAMINGO,* HUH?

YEP.... HE SAID ALL THE FLAMINGOS WERE HEADIN' FOR THE *DERBY*---- TOLD ME I HAD TO WORK AT CHURCHILL DOWNS.... *ME*, AS CAN'T OUT-RUN A *POTATO BUG* ..... *HA!* I'M A FULL BLOODIED AMERICAN RODENT BY TRADE AN' *PROUD* OF IT.

NO DAG BLAGGIN' SELF-APPOINTED COP KIN PUSH *ME* AROUND..... I SWORE *I*, FOR *ONE*, WAS GONNA 'STAND *FIRM!* UNFEARED! CONFIDENT OF MY *RIGHTS!* SO I TOOK A ASSUMED NAME AN' HID IN THE HAT.

HE'S *RIGHT!* ARE WE *MICE* OR ARE WE *MEN?*

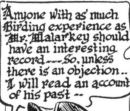

WE'LL GO SEE IF ALBERT IS READY..... IF I'M GONE TO FALL INTO THE CLUTCHES OF THESE CRITTURS, I'LL NEED HIM AN' YOU TO RESCUE ME *FAST*

F. OLDING MUNNY AN' EL FAKIR WILL NOT FAIL.

5-12

DIST BY POST-HALL SYNDICATE.

YOU TOOK A LONG ENOUGH, EL FAKIR. C'MON, US GOTTA *PRACTICE* ON BLUNKIN' OUT OUR EYES.

HAD TO FOLD UP MY HEAD IN THIS *TARBOOSH*; IT TOOK TIME .....

COPR 1953 WALT KELLY

'SPECIALLY WHEN I PACKS IN IT A LUNCH,TOO... THE *LAMB STEW* OF WHICH IS *LEAKIN'* A LI'L'.

ARF   AN'ARF

DON'T FIGHT FACTS, DEACON OL' FRIEND. I'M PRESIDENT OF THE CLUB AN' *THAT* IS THAT.

Well --- I s'pose you can be the Local head.

5-13   DIST BY POST-HALL SYNDICATE

Just so long as I retain my powers of National President with jurisdiction over you ----

NO.

What do you mean: "*NO*"? Malarkey can't be local head and National head too!

I *KNOW*.... I happen to be NATIONAL PRESIDENT my self...

AS INTERNATIONAL CHAIRMAN AND PRESIDENT FOREVER OF THE *BONFIRE BOYS* OF THE WORLD I REALLY MUST ASK YOU TO CEASE THIS SQUALID SCRIMMAGE OVER YOUR PETTY CONCERNS.

BAM!

MEMO TO THE CREW:" WE APPROACH THE HIDEOUT OF THE *BON FIRE BOYS*...NONNY WILL *SING* AN' BEGUILE THEIR FASCINATED EYE ~~~

5-14

THE *WERRY WRATH* OF WERRENRATH

"THUS EMULATIN' *CLEOPATRA* WHO BARGED UP AND DOWN THE *NILE* PAST THE *GREEK* AN' *ROMAN* EMPIRES WHICH WERE THE *NATIONAL* AND *AMERICAN* LEAGUES OF THE DAY -----

POOT

DIST BY POST-HALL SYNDICATE

SO SING IT UP AND *LURE* THEM ....." SIGNED: *F. Olding Munny.*

HOO HO!

COPR 1953 WALT KELLY

BANG! BAM! BANG!
BAM BAM BAM

QUICK MEMO: GOOD WORK. YOU'VE ATTRACTED THEIR ATTENTION. SIGNED: *F. Olding Munny.*

THAT *CLEOPATRA* LURE WAS TOO RISKY... I BETTER STICK TO BEIN' A *OUT-OF-WORK' WAIF* AN' GO ASK 'EM FOR A JOB.

AYE ~..THE FUNNY [SIC] PAPER ALLUS HANDLES IT THAT WAY.

THIS DOG BONE THING CALLED "*POGGO*" IS JES' ABOUT *INCOMPRESHENSIBLE*.

GOOD LUCK, US'LL COME A-RUNNIN' WHEN YOU IS NEEDY.

5-15

DIST BY POST HALL SYNDICATE

SIMPLE J., YOUR METHODS ARE TOO CRUDE .... YOU SHOULD HAVE *DIGNITY* AND *LAW* ON YOUR SIDE. YOU CAN'T JUST *SAY* YOU'RE BOSS.

YES, I CAN, PAL...I GOT A *LOT* OF VOTES IN OL' BETSEY HERE. *THAT'S* LAW.

COPR 1953 WALT KELLY

BASIC LAW SAYS "*NO!*"~ FRIEND. YOU *HAVE NO* CONSTITUENCY... I REMOVED THE VOTES WHILE YOU WERE NAPPING...LUCKILY, THEY FIT MY *SAWED OFF MODEL* A PARLIAMENTARY POINT THAT CAN NOT BE OVERLOOKED.

UM.

-56-

"Mole an' Malarkey must be displaced -- poison might work...

PHOO! Deacon, the rest of us is stickin' together an' is DIS'REGARDIN' 'em both...

THEY AIN'T GONE SCARE NOBODY IF NOBODY LISTENS AT 'EM -- AN' THEY IS GOT PERTY DOGGONE HARD TO LISTEN TO. DULL IS AS DULL DO.

What?! you shirk your duty -- to let these two usurpers despoil the swamp --

YOU BRUNG 'EM IN!

Well, yes -- but that was before they stole my job. Disgraceful turncoats -- and now nobody cares if I'm out of my proper place -- hmm- eels in brew...

5-30 DIST. BY POST-HALL SYNDICATE.

How can you tell jokes at a time when I've been cheated out of my job?

THIS HERE BOOK "ASTEIA" GOT AWFUL FUNNY STUFF IN IT BY A YOUNG 'UN NAME "HIEROCLES".

MEBBE YOU OUGHT TO LISTEN AN' LAUGH TOO.. "MAN SAYS: I DREAMS SO REAL THAT WHEN I JES' DREAM I STEP ON A NAIL -- I... UH-- HAW- HAW-- I WOKE UP WITH A...

-HAW!-- WITH A HOLE IN MY FOOT -- AN' T'OTHER MAN, HE SAY: THAT'S WHAT YOU GIT FOR GOIN' TO BED BAREFOOTED!-- HAW HAW HOO HA HEE

Who'd go to bed with his shoes on?

HO HA WHEE HOO HA HO HEE HAW!

THE DEACON GOT A POINT THERE.... WHO WOULD?

YEAH... WHO INDEED? THAT AIN'T SO FUNNY IS IT?

6-1 POST-HALL SYNDICATE

Poisoning is too good for those two usurpers -- eh -- What's that?

URF URF URF

IT'S ME LAUGHIN'... I'M BEGINNIN' TO UNDERSTAND THE JOKE YESTERDAY. WISH'T I HAD A SENSE OF HUMOR....

How can you simpletons laugh when authority is taken from the hands of the Rightful..?

YOU BRUNG IN THEM TWO EXPERT BIRDWATCHERS... SAYIN' IT WAS TO KEEP US FROM MAKIN' DERN FOOLS OF OURSELFS... WHERE AS IT'S THE INHERENT RIGHT OF ALL TO MAKE DERN FOOLS OF THEIR-SELFS...

IT AIN'T A RIGHT HELD BY YOU OFFICIAL TYPES ALONE. .... THE REST OF US MIGHT NOT HAVE THE SHEER ABILITY AT IT BUT US DO GOT THE RIGHT.... SO DON'T MESS WITH IT......

6-2 POST-HALL SYNDICATE

Aye -- Poison is too tricky -- I'll rout the Mole and Malarkey by setting a trap -- One of 'em will step in the loop and --

Go away, child -- You're too young to comprehend --

Hah -- I'll yank the rope and over he'll go into the pot of tar, himself -- Hah -- I always say: Give one of these sharpers enough rope and --

he'll hang himself...

Shush, child you'll wake the dead.

6-3 POST-HALL SYNDICATE

Panel 1 (6-13): DEACON, US IS SURE GRATEFUL. YOU BRUNG OUT THE PUP DOG ALL SAFE. / To be honest, Pogo, I... I-uh-...uh- uh-...I- / OOP! IT'S OL' SARCOPHAGUS MACABRE / The shouting is ended, sirs. The chase is done...

Panel 2: Might I borrow an odd end or two? / SUGAR... SALT... PICKLES?

Panel 3: No, thank you kindly. I must join my friends. A knife and fork is all I'll need... / HE GOT FRIENDS? / AN' HE FOND OF 'EM.

COPR. 1953 WALT KELLY

POST-HALL SYNDICATE

Panel 1 (6-15): WHAT IS SO RARE AS A DAY IN JUNE?

Panel 2: WULL, THE TWENNY NINTH OF FEBRUARY IS PERTY RARE BUT THE FIFTY FIRST OF OCTOBER IS EVEN WORSE.

Panel 3: HECK! THERE ISN'T ANY FIFTY FIRST OF OCTOBER. WE NEVER HAS ONE.

Panel 4: WELL... WHAT KIN BE RARER THAN THAT? / Y'KNOW, TRAVELIN' BY LEAP FROG IS GOT ITS HAZARDS

6-15 POST-HALL SYNDICATE

COPR. 1953 WALT KELLY

Panel 1 (6-16): I BEEN FIGGERIN' OUT WHAT YOU SAID... THAT WE AIN'T GOT NO FIFTY FIRST OF OCTOBER. / WHAT'S TO FIGGER OUT 'BOUT THAT?

Panel 2: ALL THE FIFTY FIRSTS OF OCTOBERS FALL ON THE TWENTEETHS OF NOVEMBERS. / OCTOBER STOP ON THE THIRTY ONE OF IT.

Panel 3: WHY? / YOU CAN'T GO HAVIN' A WHOLE YEARFUL OF OCTOBER.

Panel 4: WHY NOT...? IT'S A PERTY MONTH..... WE COULD HAVE OCTOBER, CHRISTMAS, THE FOURTH OF JULY AN' MY BIRTHDAY AN' LET ALL THE OTHER MONTHS GO .... FEBRUARY FOR INSTINCT... WHO NEEDS IT?

6-16 POST-HALL SYNDICATE

COPR. 1953 WALT KELLY

Panel 1 (6-17): I THINK I GOT THE NEW CALENDAR ALL SET. / NEW CALENDAR?

Panel 2: YEP... THE OCTOBER CALENDAR.... CHRISTMAS COMES ON THE 86TH OF OCTOBER.

Panel 3: ONE GOOD MONTH ALL YEAR LONG. THE FIRST OF THE YEAR FALLS ON OCTOBER NINETY-THIRD .... WODDY YOU THINK OF THAT!

Panel 4: OH, I DUNNO.....IT'S ONE OF THEM THINGS I DON'T THINK ABOUT VERY MUCH.

6-17 POST-HALL SYNDICATE

COPR. 1953 WALT KELLY

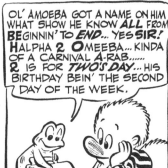

POGO, TELL ALBERT WE AIN'T *SUPER-NATURAL*.

LOOKIN' AT YO' FRIEND I B'LEEVE THAT IS HARD TO B'LEEVE.

DIN'T YOU IS *EVER* SEE A PELICAN AFORE?

SURE, FOLKS, THIS HERE IS GOOD OL' *ROOGEY BATOON*, THE LOU'SIANA TYPE PELICAN.

HE'S THE BOY WHAT MADE THE *LOU'SIANA PURCHASE.*

MY! IS YOU *REALLY*?

YUP.

YUP.... I MADE ALL *THREE* OF 'EM.

HUH? HUH? HUH? HUH?

COPR 1953 WALT KELLY

DID YOU SAY *YOU* MADE THE *LOU'SIANA PURCHASE,* MR. ROOGEY BATOON?

YEP, *THAT* I IS *DID* SAY.... AN' IT'S BE TRUE I DO GUAR-AND-TEE....

HOW COULD YOU OF? YOU IS SO *YOUNG* LOOKIN'

I IS MOUGHTY OBLIGED TO YOU, SIR.

DID YOU BUY IT FROM OL' *NAPOLEON?*

NAPOLEON? NAPOLEON WHO? I KNOWS ONE RUNS A *LIVE BAIT STORE* ON THE GULF....

THE ONE WHAT WAS *EMPEROR OF FRANCE*?

MM ....*MIGHT* OF BEEN.... DID THE ONE YOU KNOWS SELL *SHRIMPS* TWO FOR A *PENNY?*

8-10

POST-HALL SYNDICATE

COPR 1953 WALT KELLY

HARD FOR ME TO FIGGER HOW THAT *PELICAN* COULD OF MADE THE *LOU'SIANA PURCHASE.*

SHUCKS.....IF HE HAD THE MONEY, *WHY NOT?* IT'S A *FREE* COUNTRY...

THE S.S. OWEN BRENNAN

IF IT'S *FREE*, HOW COME HE GOTTA PAY CASH FOR A PIECE OF IT?

NATURAL, IT'S THE LAW OF PROFITS AN' ECONOMIXUP .....*DEEFLATION* IS *IN-FLATED* THE DOLLAR SO THE SOVEREIGNITY ON THE *FUNDAMENTS* IS EN-TIRE IN ESCROW.

SO EVEN IF YOU GIVES A THING AWAY YOU STILL GOTTA GIT *PAID* FOR IT OR THE WHOLE *FIASCAL* SYSTEM BECOMES A AUTOMATIC INFIELD OUT OR A GROUN' RULE *DOUBLE.*

DIN'T KNOW ALBERT WAS A ECONOMIST.

IT'S HIS *SECRET WEAPON.*

THE S.S. OWEN BRENNAN

8-11

POST-HALL SYNDICATE

COPR 1953 WALT KELLY

IT *MOUGHT* BE OF INTEREST TO YOU TO KNOW THERE IS THEM AS DOUBTS YOU MADE THE LOU'SIANA PURCHASE.

PICAYUNE, YOU KNOWS' I MADE 'EM... *ALL* AND *EVERY THREE* OF 'EM!

ALL *THREE* OF 'EM? WHAT'S YOU *MEAN*? JES' WHAT DOES YOU THINK THE *LOU'SIANA PURCHASE* IS ANYWAYS?!

FISH! FISH THEY IS..... NATURAL THEY IS *FISH*...AN' I MADE ALL *THREE*.... *LEARNED* 'EM! *GROOMED* 'EM!

FISH... *FISH?*

FLIM, FLAM AND *FLO'*... THE *LOU'SIANA PERCHES!* A STELLAR SET OF SQUAMOSE SONGSTERS.

NO... IT CAN'T BE.. .... THE LOU'SIANA PERCHES ---- ??

8-12

COPR 1953 WALT KELLY

I DON'T SEE *HOW* THAT ROOGEY BATOON COULD OF BOUGHT OL' *LOU'SIANA*..

MEBBE IT WAS MARKED DOWN.

ONLY THING TO RENCH YOU OFF WITH IS THIS LEF'OVER *LEMONADE*...

RENCH AWAY...

BUT IT'S SO *BIG*...THE LOU'SIANA PURCHASE TOOK IN MOST ALL THE MIDDLE STATES PLUS SASKATCHEWAN AN'...

YOWP!

WHAT'S THE MATTER? TOO *COLD*?

NO...

TOO SOUR.

8-13

COPR 1953 WALT KELLY

ROOGEY BATOON IS A *FRAUD*.....HE AIN'T BEEN TALKIN' 'BOUT THE *LOU'SIANA PURCHASE*....

WHAT *IS* HE BEEN?

THE LOU'SIANA PERCHES.

8-14

WHAT?! HE AIN'T BEEN TALKIN' 'BOUT THE LOU'SIANA PURCHASE BUT HE IS *BEEN TALKIN' 'BOUT THE LOU'SIANA PURCHASE?*

YAS!! *WHAT* COULD BE *MORE SIMPLE* THAN THAT... BESIDES *YOU?*

DON'T YOU SHOUT AT ME!

I TOLE POGO HERE 'BOUT YOU HAD A SINGIN' TRIO .....*FLIM, FLAM AN' FLO*....

YEP, THE *THREE* LOU'SIANA PERCHES.

A BASS BARITOON... A CONTRALTOR, AN'A TREBLE CLEFT PALATE.

FLIM, FLAM AN' AN'FLO'...SIMPLY SPLENDIFEROUS STELLAR STARRED *SQUAMOSE* SONGSTERS. STICK YO' HEAD IN, FRIEND.

DID YOU *HEAR 'EM*? SONGBIRDS OF THE DEPTHS PRACTICIN' A NEW *ROUSER*... "ASLOOP IN THE DOOP."...LIKE IT?

GLOOP...

8-15

COPR 1953 WALT KELLY

TRYIN' TO LISTEN TO YO' SONGFISHES UNDER THE WATER IS *RISKY* AN' *SOGGY*.

HOW RISKY?

LEAVIN' MY *EARS* OPEN THAT WAY, I IS LIKELY TO GIT WATER ON THE *BRAIN*.

WELL,YO' TURTLE FRIEND CAN'T GIT WATER ON NO BRAIN.

SEE HOW YOU LIKES THE *LOU'SIANA PERCHES* SINGIN' "A SLOOP IN THE DOOP."

SOUNDS KINDA *GURGLY*...SOMETHIN' IS THROWIN' 'EM OFF----I THINK ONE OF 'EM GOT A *FROG* IN HER THROAT.

SIR!

8-17

COPR 1953 WALT KELLY

—75—

8-18 IF ONE OF THE SINGIN' LOU'SIANA PERCHES IS GOT A BAD THROAT IT'S FROM OVERWORK---THEY NEEDS A REST.

THEY NEEDS A LITTLE VACATION---A CULTURAL TRIP TO DR. BRENNAN'S UPSTAIRS WAXWORKS--- OR A EDUCATIONAL TOUR OF THE VIEUX CARRÉ.

YOU FERGITS WE ISN'T IN N'ORLEANS.

RIGHT, PICAYUNE -- MEBBE YOU GENTS COULD SUGGEST A GENTEEL DIVERSION FOR THREE MAIDEN PERCHES?

THINK THEY'D LIKE TO GO FISHIN', POGO?

SHUSH, THEY IS FISH.

WULL--- I GOT A CAN OF BAIT OVER'T MY PLACE. FIGGER THEY'D LIKE TO HELP UNSNARL A FEW YARDS OF NIGHT CRAWLERS?

IT'S QUIET BUT ABSORBIN' WORK.

8-19 MEBBE OL' ROOGEY BATOON IS RIGHT, HIS LI'L PERCH FISH SINGERS NEEDS A LITTLE FUN.

ALL WORK AN' NO PLAY MAKES FLIM, FLAM AN' FLO A DULL QUARTET.

THEY'S ONLY THREE--- THEY'RE MORE A TRIO.

BUT FLAM GOT A BANJO -- A OL' HE-BANJO WITH A VOICE LIKE A BURGLAR! THAT'S FOUR.

WHO DO WE KNOW COULD ESCORT THEM GAL FISH TO A NIGHT BALL GAME OR A SIMILAR SOIRÉE?

IT WOULD HAFTA BE THREE GENTS OF MEANS AN' MANNERS BUT ALSO A LI'L BATS!

THAT'S US--- GANGWAY!

WE'S PRACTICIN' UP FOR HOLLOWEEN- OUR NATIONABLE HOLIDAY.

8-20 HOW'D YOU BOYS LIKE TO HAVE A DATE WITH THREE BEAUTIFUL GIRL SINGERS?

IT'D BE KINDA NOISY.

YEAH, WITH THEM HOOTIN' AN' HOLLOWIN' UP A STORM.

AN' SNAPPIN' THEIR FINGER BONES.

FIGGER US WANT TO BOOK A TRIO OF GROANERS?

ASK HIM DO HE KNOW ANY ACROBATS OR WOMBATS OR SOMETHIN' FAMILIAR.

NOT TOO FAMILIAR.

LONG AS IT'S A BLIND DATE, THREE GIRL POKER PLAYERS'D BE NICE---

WOULDN'T HAFTA EVEN BE BEAUTIFUL.

THEY COULD LEAVE ON THEIR BLIND FOLDS THE WHOLE WHILE.

ONLY TIME US GOES OUT WITH GIRLS IS ON HOLLOW-WEEN--- THE BROOMSTICK SET---

PHOO! THEM ISN'T GIRLS!

HEAR THAT? WE IS BEEN LED ON!

FILLIN' OUR PERTY LI'L HEADS WITH LIES! LIES!

8-21 SOMEBODY LEFT THIS PAIL OF WATER HERE--US KIN TAKE A BATH LONG AS WE'S GOIN' TO MEET THREE BEAUTIFUL GAL SINGERS.

HOW'LL WE ENTERTAIN THESE YOUNG WIMMEN--- 'TAIN'T NEAR HOG SLAUGHTERIN' TIME ---THER'S NOTHIN' TO DO.

PULL ME OUT! MONSTERS GOT ME!

LOOK---'TAIN'T MONSTERS--IT'S THREE FISH.

US COULD GO OVER TO THE PARK AT OL' WAYCROSS.

MM

NOTHIN' DOIN'!

THAT OL' SWAMPY PARK IS FULL OF ALLIGATORS!

YOW! ALLIGATORS!?!

STEADY.

WHEN I SAYS US OUGHT TO TAKE THEM *FISHES'* PLACE, I MEANT US OUGHT TO OFFER OUR SERVICES TO THE PELICUM, *ROOGEY BATOON.*

I GOT FOUR KINGS.

SO IS *I*—AN' THREE OF 'EM IS *CLUBS*.... THAT'S STRANGE.

I WINS THEN... I GOT *FIVE KINGS*....... ALL *DIFFERNT.*

HERE'S A CARD SAYS "HAPPY BIRTHDAY TO MEEBLE."

MEEBLE? SOMETHIN' IS *WRONG* WITH THIS DECK— WE DON'T KNOW ANYBODY NAME OF MEEBLE.

HERE'S ONE SAYS: *ALL YOU CAN EAT AT BRENNAN'S FOR $99.05*

WELL, THAT SPOILS THE GAME..... IT'S HARD TO PUT THEM KIND OF CARDS IN ANY SUIT.

I COULD OF PUT 'EM BACK IN THE OLD *DEACON'S* SUIT.... IT'S WHERE I GOT 'EM FROM.

THE DEACON ALWAYS GOT A *79 CARD* DECK....... HARD TO DEAL.

8-27

WE'RE THINKIN' OF GETTIN' UP A *PURSE*, POGO, TO GIVE TO ROOGEY BATOON FOR HIS *PERCHES* WE ATE.

YEP, WE'RE GONNA SELL A *JOKE* TO ONE OF THEM *FUNNY* MAGAZINES.

THEN WE'LL GIVE THE MONEY TO *ROOGEY*... WE'LL DRAW A PICTURE OF A BIG *RADIO* AND *TEEVY WRITERS'* MEETING....

EVER'BODY IS LI'L *CLOCKWORK MENS*.. ONE OF 'EM IS GITTIN' *WOUND* BY ANOTHER WHO IS GOT THE *KEY* IN THIS GUY'S *EAR*... AN' HE IS SAYIN'....

HOL' YO'SELF IN NOW, POGO.

WHOO OO-HEE.

YOOH-HA..*OOF-HAW*..HEE.. AN' HE IS SAYIN': *"I KNEW WE WAS GITTIN'* MECHANICAL BUT I DIN'T KNOW WE WOULD *WIND UP LIKE THIS!"* AW..HAWF-WAH-HA.. WHEE..HOO *BOY!*

YEE HAW! YEOW!

OO-- IT'S SURE FIRE!

8-28

WE COULD MAKE IT UP TO THE OL' *PELICUM* BY REPLACIN' HIS *THREE PERCH FISH*....

WHO WILL TEACH 'EM TO *SING*?

I WILL.

YOU WILL? *YOU* DON'T KNOW *NOTHIN'* 'BOUT MUSIC.

YOU FERGITS I HUNG OUT IN THE *DALLAS* PRESS CLUB FOR *YEARS*. DIN'T YOU EVER HEAR OF THE GREAT *EMERICH*... EMERICH, THE *EEL?*

YOU MEANS YOU USED TO *COACH HIM?*

HE HAD A VOICE ON HIM LIKE A *DC6.*

YEP AN' I LEARNT HIM *ALL* HE KNEW.

'BOUT *SINGIN'* ?

NO.. 'BOUT *FLYIN'*... I GUV HIM FLYIN' LESSONS OFF OF THE *MEZZANINE.* HE BECOME THE ONLY *FLYIN' EEL* IN TEXAS..... BUT BIRD IMITATIONS DON'T DRAW SO THE GREAT EMERICH WENT BACK TO EELIN' AN'...

8-29

I RUSHED OVER, MR. ROOGEY BATOON, COZ I HEAR THAT SOME *CANNIBOBBLES* ET YOUR FISH.

AYE... A *CROO-EL* BLOW, HOUN' DOG~ THANKS FOR YOUR SYMPATHY...

I HEAR TELL THEY WAS *MIGHTY* TENDER.

NICE OF YOU TO SAY SO... *NICE...* NICE.

IN FACT, THE WORD IS GOT AROUND THAT THEY WAS *DEE-*LICIOUS.

IT HELPS TO SOFTEN THE BLOW... *NOTHIN'* BUT KIND WORDS SINCE THEY TOOK OFF.....

YESSIR! TENDER AN' *DELICIOUS*....WE GONE BE *LUCKY* IF FOLKS *EVER* SAYS STUFF LIKE *THAT* 'BOUT YOU AN' ME.

8-31

IF YOU WANTS TO SHOW **SNAVELY** HOW A **MONGOOSE** TACKLES A **COBRA** WHYN'T YOU DEMONSTRATE WITH THE **WORM CHILD?**

YEH...

I DON'T WANNA PICK ON A INFANT.

9-15

YOU DON'T **HAFTA** BE ROUGH. JES' SHOW US **GENTLE-LIKE...**

THE KID'S READY.

VERY WELL BUT ONLY IN THE INTEREST OF **SCIENCE.**

I'LL GO SLOW, KID.... DON'T BE SCAIRT... **EASY** DOES IT.

YESSIR, **EASY... EASY... EAAH!**

EASY DOES IT, I SAID!

VERY EDUCATIONAL.

COPR 1953 WALT KELLY

HOW'D YOU MANAGE TO GIT THROWN BY THE **WORM CHILE?**

SHEER SKILL! BESIDES, MY FOOT SLIPPED.

9-16

HOWever, I'LL GO **ON** WITH THE DEMONSTRATION...... I'LL BE **EASY** ON THE **TAD** WHILST SHOWIN' HOW A **MONGOOSE** TACKLES A **COBRA ...EN GARDE.**

NOW, I WAS JUS' GOIN' LIKE **THIS** WHEN... oOOW...

--OWP!

YOU BULLY! PICKIN' ON THAT LI'L SMALL WORMCHILE, **THOU BEAST!**

COPR 1953 WALT KELLY

BEAST! BULLY! OGRE! BESTING A CHILE THAT WAY!

I WAS **ONLY** TRY AN' TO TEACH THE WORM CHILE A FEW.....

9-17

A **BIG STRONG MAN** LIKE **YOU** MAKIN' A **FOOL** OF THAT LI'L FELLA... BOXIN' HIM SILLY WITH A **BLINDIN'** DISPLAY OF FISTIC ARTISTRY!

POST-HALL SYNDICATE

HE THRUN ME TWO OUT OF **TWO,** MIZ BEAVER, **HONEST!**

SSH.... SH.... I KNOW--(HE WAS BEATIN' YOUR EARS OFF --SHSH --HERE'S YOUR COAT AN' STICK! THOUGHT I BETTER GIT YOU OUTEN THERE ----)

(BUT IT DON'T PAY TO LET THEM OTHER MENS KNOW.) **OH, THE SECRET MAGIC OF COMBAT SKILL WHAT YOU TRICKED THAT BOY WITH.....! YOU BRUTE!**

HEAR HER? WE MUST HAVE MISSED SOMETHIN'. SHE'S A EXPERT.

COPR 1953 WALT KELLY

NEVER PICK ON NO**BODY UNDER** YO' OWN SIZE, MR. MOUSE... IF YOU **WINS** YOU IS A **BULLY** AN' IF YOU **LOSES** YOU IS A **BUM!**

BUT... MIZ BEAVER, I--I-- UH...

9-18

FIGHT **BIGGER** FELLAS ... WIN OR LOSE, YOU IS A **HERO.** HERE, I'LL HELP YOU PICK THEM THINGS.

I WAS **ONLY** TRY AN' TO TEACH THE **YOUNG COBRA** HOW TO **THROW** A **MONGOOSE.**

POST HALL SYNDICATE

MY SAKES, YOU IS PICKED QUITE A **SACKFUL..** MIND TOTIN' 'EM FOR ME? THEY IS FER A **BEAUTIFUL** YOUNG LADY... DOWN THE LINE A PIECE.

OH? WHO?

GIRL WHAT GO BY NAME MIZ BEAVER, A THOUGHTFUL TYPE OF HIGH CLASS BEAUTY.

MMPH ... SNFF-- AW, YOU SHOULDNTNA DIN IT. GOIN' TO ALL THIS TROUBLE, MR. MOUSE.

COPR 1953 WALT KELLY

EVENIN', MIZ MA'M'SELLE HEPZIBAH..... EVENIN', MIZ BEAVER ......HEY, MOUSE.

WELCOME TO THESE *SOIRÉE*, M'SIEUR POGO.

YOU'RE JES' IN TIME FER THE REST OF MY STORY 'BOUT *FRANCE*, POGO. PULL UP A CHAIR....

THIS FELLA I RUN INTO HIS ROOM OF, TURNS OUT TO BE A BIG *PER-FUME* MAKER (*THEY PRONOUNCES IT PARAFINE*) WELL, I GIVE HIM A IDEA..A PERFUME LIKE A BREEZE --OPEN SPACES...FRESH AIR...FOR THE *NONCE* CALL IT "*X*."

HE IS *NATURUL DEE*LIGHTED AN' IS COUNTIN' OUT A MILLION IN *ONES* FOR ME WHEN I MENTIONS A GOOD SLOGAN: *LISE "X" AND SMELL LIKE ALL OUTDOORS.* ---WELL, RIGHT THEN A VERY NASTY THING HAPPENS HE....

HE USED TO TELL THIS'N ABOUT *LOS ANGELES* WHEN *THAT* WAS A *TONEY* TOWN.

9-24   POST HALL SYNDICATE   COPR. 1953 WALT KELLY

OH, HOW *GAY!* THAT YEAR IN *FRANCE* WAS JUST AFORE THE *BOTTOM FELL OUT OF THE MARKET.* I WAS WORKIN' IN THIS FOODSTUFFS EMPORIUM ON THE *RAVIOLI* WHEN I....

YOU MEAN ON THE *RIVIERA*?

WELL, IF YOU MUST GIVE IT THE *FRENCH* PRONOUNCEMENT..O.K. ANYHOW, *THERE* I WAS ON THIS *BIG* PILE OF *CANNED RIVIERA*....

THE *CAT*, WHOM IT WAS *MY* DUTY TO BE CHASED BY, CAME ALONG *SNEERIN'* IN THE MOTHER TONGUE, SO I HOLLERS OUT: "*CAMEMBERT!*" (*FRENCH FOR* "COME ON, BERT.*" THE CAT'S NAME BEIN' BERTRAM*) WELL, SIR, THAT CAT GUV A LEAP ..*WOW!*

OVER WENT THE PILE OF RIVIERA IN A *AWFUL CRASH*.....THE FLOOR SAGGED, QUIVERED, AN' *BOOM! THE BOTTOM FELL OUT OF THE MARKET!* WE ALL LANDED IN THE CELLAR SCREAMIN' GALLICISMS WHICH BRUNG THE GENDARMES ON THE DOUBLE AN'......

HOW 'BOUT "*LIZA JANE*"?

9-25   POST HALL SYNDICATE   COPR. 1953 WALT KELLY

STOP ME IF I'M *BORIN'* YOU BUT IT'S SUCH A CLEAR NIGHT FOR A GOOD TALK.... WELL, WHEN THAT MARKET ON THE *RUE DE LA CHAT* COLLAPSED IT CAUSED QUITE A *STIR*...*1929* IT WAS...

THE PAPERS WERE FULL OF IT.. PEOPLE SAID: "*WHY'D THE BOTTOM FALL OUT OF THE MARKET?*" HA! I KNOW! THE *CAT* KNOCKED OVER THE CAN-NED GOODS. *DID* THE EXPERTS ASK *ME*? *NO*, THEY..

THEY *MIGHT* OF BEEN THINKIN' OF ANOTHER MARKET.

Y'MEAN ANOTHER MARKET COLLAPSED THAT YEAR?

A MARKET ON *WALL STREET.*

A COINCIDENCE! WALL STREET STORE, HUH? SMALL PLACE, NO DOUBT...*NEVER HEARD OF IT.*

NO, IT HAD A LI'L' SIZE ON IT...Y'EVER HEAR OF THIS *WALL STREET* WHAT POLITICIANS AN' *REEVOLUTIONARY* RASCALS IS ALLUS HOLLER'N' *DOWN WITH IT?*

ALWAYS THOUGHT THAT WAS A OL' *MYTHOLOGICAL BEAST*...WODDYA KNOW! WELL, THIS *BIG* MARKET COLLAPSE *I* WAS IN WAS ...

9-26   POST HALL SYNDICATE   COPR. 1953 WALT KELLY

ALL EVENINGS IN THESE *PARTY*, MY *SOIRÉE*, *THESE PERSON IS SHOOT OFF MOUSE TRAP* AN' IS *LONG DRAW* OUT THE BOW.

HE'S *MY* GENNLEMAN GUEST! AN' IT'S AS MUCH *MY* SWARRY AS *YOURN.*

SOMETHIN' 'BOUT ME GITS WIMMEN TO FIGHTIN'

THEY IS EASY RILED.

BUT M'SIEUR LE POGO IS HERE AWAIT WITH BANJO, WITH MUSIC, WITH SOCIETY VERSE TO PERFORM ....

SUCH AS?

ATTEND THE MENU! SUCH AS "*CASÉE A LA BATON!*" SUCH AS "*LE BEAU PIPP!*" SUCH AS "*MOE LE BRANNIGAN!*" *THAT* IS WHAT IS SUCH AS.

MOLLY BRAN...AGAIN? US HEARN THAT *TWO YEARS RUNNIN'!*

YOU DO NO *LIKE?*

THAT'S *EX*ACK WHY WE WAS RUNNIN', HONEY, MOLLY OUGHT A *SUE* SOME-BODY.

ALLUS THUNK MY LOUD *BANJO* WORK COVERED MY VOICE PERTY GOOD.

WELL... YES AN' NO.

9-28 POST HALL SYNDICATE   COPR. 1953 WALT KELLY

IN·AN·ASMUCH AS THE SOIREE IS BOGGED INTO A VERITABOBBLE SARGASSO, POGO AN' I GONE CHEER UP US.

YUP... PORKYPINE IS RUNNED ACROSS A NEW TUNE..... IT GOT A LOTTA *ZIP* IN IT SO TO SPEAK....

I'LL ROUSE AHEAD WITH THE SOPRANO WORDS WHILST YOU FOLLY 'LONG WITH THE *BOOM A DIDDY BOOM!*

FOLLY IT IS.

♪ I S'POSE YOU HEAR OF TH' BATTLE ♪ NEW *ORLEANS*, ♪ WHERE OL' GEN'RAL JACKSON GIVE THE BRITISH BEANS ♪ THERE THE YANKEE BOYS DO TH' JOB SO SLICK FOR THEY COTCH OL' *PACKENHAM* AN' ROW HIM UP THE *CRICK!* ♪

POSSUM UP A GUM TREE.. COONY ON A STUMP

POSSUM UP A GUM -- UH.. MM -- A -- BOO -- UH -- HMM? *MY SAKES!* HOW *COULD* THEY OF RUN OFF *AFORE* THEY SEE HOW IT COME OUT?

THEY MEBBE IS *ANGLO*-PHILES.

MORE LIKELY MUSIC LOVERS

9·29 POST HALL SYNDICATE.

COME ON OUT....US IS GONE SING SOMETHIN' LESS *COUNTER-VERSIBLE*... SOMETHIN' MORE CLASSICAL....

PATER

♪ SHE HAD NO GANE A MILE OR TWA, WHEN SHE HEARD THE *DEAD-BELL* RINGING ♪♪ ♪ AN' EV'RY JOW THAT THE DEAD-BELL GEID IT CRY'D: *WOE* TO BARBARA ALLEN. ♪

OH, MOTHER, MOTHER MAKE MY BED! ♪

WELL! HAVIN' A GOOD TIME, FOLKS?

--OH, MAKE IT SAFT ♪ AN' NARROW! ♪ SINCE MY LOVE ♪ DIED FOR ME TODAY... ♪ I'LL DIE FOR *HIM* TOMORROW. ♪

SNIFF GULP! HAVIN' A MOS' WONDERFOOLS TIME..

COPR. 1953 WALT KELLY

9·30 POST HALL SYNDICATE

WELL, COWBIRDS! IS YOU GONE TO THE *SWARRY?*

YEAH

WHAT!? YOU'D GO FRITTER AWAY YOUR TIME WHILST THE *WORLD* TOTTERS ON THE *BRINK?* PURE FRIVOLISM!

THE *WORLD SERIES* (FOR THE DOMINANCE OF THE EARTH), *LOOMS!* AND *WHO* PLAYS AT THIS *SOCALLED* "GAME" THESE DAYS? (ACTUALLY A POWER MAD PREPARATION FOR DISASTER)

YEAH

IN ONE CELL IS A GROUP Y·CLEPT: THE *REDLEGS* .. *HA!* CHANGED FROM THE *REDS*---AN' *WHO* IS IN *BOSTON?* ...... THE *RED SOX* ...! *WHICH* ONCE WAS THE *HOME OF THE BRAVES!*

YEAH!

WHO STANDS BEHIND THE FULL DINNER PLATE CALLING *STRIKES,* ONE AFTER THE *OTHER?* THE *EMPIRE!* SO!

YEAH!

WHAT DID *I* DO?

YOU ASKED A SIMPLE QUESTION, YOU GOT A SIMPLE ANSWER.

COPR 1953 WALT KELLY

10·1 POST HALL SYNDICATE

US BETTER GIVE MY NEW "*CONCERTO TO A WONDER DRUG*" A QUICK LICK AFORE US HITS THE PARTY.

MI-MI MI

OH, THE WONDER DRUG THAT'S A SIGHT TO SEE ♪ IS THE WONDERFUL WAY MY SWEETIE DRUGS ME WHEN SHE DRUGS ME OFF'N HER PA'S T.V. AN'... ♪

OKAY! OKAY! HIT THAT "SIGHT" HARDER ..... OTHERWISE, *SOLID!* Y'KNOW I WAS TALKIN' ABOUT THE *PARTY* TO OL' *TROTSKY* YESTIDDY AN' *HE* SAY, "THIS IS GOTTA BE *BLOWED UP GOOD.*"

TROTSKY?

YEH... HIM WITH THE SIX PIECE BAND... *TURKEY TROTSKY* AND HIS *DIXIE GYPSIES*... HE SAY A BLUE NOTE GOTTA BE BLEW BUT *SOLID!*

OH, SURE! SOLID BLUE IS MY OWN FAVORITE SHADE.

COPR. 1953 WALT KELLY

10·2 POST HALL SYNDICATE.

AS WE QUIETLY TAKE **POGO'S** GRUB, (HE BEING AWAY FROM HOME LIKE THE IRRESPONSIBLE DESPOTIC LANDLORD HE IS,) **I WORRY.....**

YEAH.

PENSACOLA IT'S THE SPA

10-3

I WORRY ABOUT A WORLD WHERE AN HONEST MAN NEVER KNOWS **WHO** IT IS **SAFE** TO BE **AGAINST.** ONLY YESTERDAY, I TRUSTED THE TURTLE... WE'D TURNED TO HIS SIDE.....IN FACT, **JOINED 'EM.'**

YEAH.

WE KNEW OF HIS **STRATIFIED STUPIDISM**...WE WERE **SURE:** HERE WAS ONE WE COULD BE AGAINST WITH **IMPLINISTIC SECURITISM!** WHAT HAPPENS? HE REVEALS HIS TRUE FACE ---- **HE HAS** POWERFUL **FRIENDS.'** WHO **CAN** BE TRUSTED?

YEAH.

STOP LOOKIN' AT ME LIKE THAT.

YEAH.

COPR. 1953 WALT KELLY

POST HALL SYNDICATE

IS IT THAT M'SIEUR **ALBERT,** THESE **CROCODIDDLE,** IS NO COMING TO THESE **SOIRÉE?**

WULL, YEP.... MIZ MA'M'SELLE! BUT HE'S PLANNIN' A **500**·PRIZE.

10-5 POST HALL SYNDICATE

OOH~ **HOW EX**·CITEMENT! I AM **LOVE** SURPRISE... **BIG ONE** OR SMALL ---·I AM **ALWAYS DELIGHT** WITH **ANY KIND** SURPRISE...

AT'S A SPLENDID ATTITUDE TO MAINTAIN, MA'M'.

M'SIEUR ALBERT IS LIKE ONE RICH AN' HAN'SOME NOBLE WHO ONCE ALWAYS USE TO SURPRISE ME... WITH PERFUMES, WITH **ORCHID,** WITH **PEARLS BROOCHES**··· SO GALLANT; SUCH TENDER! SUCH **GAY!** THESE LITTLE THINGS ARE WHAT COUNT..

HERE Y'ARE KIDS.....TIME WE WAS GITTIN' INTO OUR **ANNUABLE WORLD SERIES**···THIS'LL LIVEN UP THE **SWARRY** ALL RIGHT. **GRAB A MITT!** SHORTSTOP AN' **LEFT FIELD** IS OPEN.

COPR 1953 WALT KELLY

WE GONE NEED A **UMPIRE** TO PREVENT **FIGHTS.**

ROOMPH! THEY ALLUS **START** 'EM.

POGO IS **RIGHT. WE NEED A UMPIRE.**

10-6 POST HALL SYNDICATE

A **ARBITER** WHO IS **TOUGH!** ONE WHO CAN BACK UP HIS OPINION... AN UMPIRE WITH **COURAGE**···WITH **STRENGTH! FEARLESS! A REAL FIGHTER! A REAL MAN!** WHO AMONGST US?

OH, MIZ **BEAVER**

YOO HOO

COPR. 1953 WALT KELLY

HOPE YOU DON'T MIND ME **PRAC**·TICIN' MY **RADIO JOB,** UNCLE BALDWIN···'TAINT HOOKED UP YET, BUT.... HERE GOES: **GOOD AFTERNOON,** HERE IS A IMPORTANT **PRE**· **GAME FLASH!**

10-7 POST HALL SYNDICATE

SEE IT **NOW!** THE **THROBBING NEW FILM "CUMQUAT BLOSSOMS."** SEE THE **ALLURIN' MIBSIE FARQUHAR,** THE CURVACEOUS AN' **DEE-LECTABLE TOO-TOO DEVINE**···AND THAT SLOW BURNIN' **TIGRESS,** GREEN-EYED **FOLLY FRISBIE!**

THOSE **YUM·YUM LIPS**...YOURS, **YOURS, YOURS!** IN BIG FAT **3D! YOURS** WITH A CAPITAL **U!** LOVE FIRE...

RUFF! SMEERP!

NEXT TIME **TAKE OFF YOUR MASK!**

NEXT TIME **TAKE OFF YOURN!**

UMPIRE

COPR. 1953 WALT KELLY

WELL, OUR OL' **WORLD SERIES** IS OVER ... US PLAYS LATER, LONGER AN' **LOUDER** THAN THEM OTHER OUTFITS BUT IN FOUR YEARS OF **STELLAR PLAY** WE IS NEVER GOT PAST THE THIRD INNIN'.

US IS **REAL STICKERS.**

10-13 POST HALL SYNDICATE

FRIENDS! TREE-MOUNDOUS NEWS.'

IT'S OL' **TAMMANANNY** THE **NATURAL** BORN TIGER.

MEBBE HE KNOW HOW TH' WORLD SERIES IS COME OUT.

COPR 1953 WALT KELLY

YEP! LISTEN TO **THIS!** "THE DETROIT TIGERS WERE ABSOLUTELY MAGNIFICENT IN THE FALL CLASSIC, THEY...."

HEY! THAT PAPER IS AT **LEAST** ABOUT **NINETEEN YEAR OLD!**

NATURALLY! I'VE READ IT **EVERY** YEAR SINCE 1934 ... IT WAS GOOD READIN' **THEN**... AN' IT'S GOOD READIN' **NOW!** CLASSIC! ABSO-**LOOTLY** CLASSIC!

GO AHEAD, GO AHEAD! HOW'S IT ALL COME OUT?

UNFORTUNATELY THIS ACCOUNT OF THE **TIGERS** AN' THE **RED BIRDS** NEVER TOLE HOW THE **CLASSIC ENDED.**

DIN'T YOU GIT THE NEXT DAY'S PAPER?

10-14

WELL, **I TRIED**... BUT SOMETHIN' HAPPENED TO THE **FREEDOM OF THE PRESS**...

WHAT!? OUR NEWSPAPERS IS BOUND BY THE RED BLOODED PRINTERS' INK WHAT COURSES THRU THEIR VEINS TO...

NOT THAT...I MEAN THE **FIRST** DAY I GOT A **FREE** PAPER WHEN THE NEWSBOY IN **CHICAGO** WAS... (I WAS AT THE **FAIR** AT THE TIME) WHEN HE WAS LOOKIN' AT A BALLOON.

HEAR! HEAR!

BUT THE **NEXT DAY** THIS FERRET SPOTS ME AN' HE SCREAMS AFTER ME DOWN MICHIGAN BOULEVARD.... **HAH!** THE **CROWDS!** YOU'D THINK THEY NEVER SAW A TIGER SWIPE A NEWSPAPER BEFORE ...

COPR 1953 WALT KELLY

NO, I NEVER **DID** FIND OUT HOW BADLY WE BEAT THE **RED BIRDS** THAT YEAR ... FOR **ME**, FREEDOM OF THE **PRESS** ENDED WHEN...

10-15

THE **GENDARMES** INTERFERED AN' I AIN'T HAD A **FREE** PAPER SINCE ... SOMETHING ABOUT ME **ALERTS** THE MOST NUMP-BRAINED NEWSBOY... **HOWEVER**, THE TRASH BASKETS I'VE BROWSED THRU LATELY **ALL** INDICATE THE PRESS HAS **CLAMPED DOWN!**

WHERE?

WHERE?! HA?! DO WE HAVE HEADLINES LIKE **THIS** ANYMORE? MY **FAVORITE** KIND?-- **NO!** THEY **BURY** THINGS!

PAPERS PRINT THE NEWS WHAT **IS**... NOT JES' WHAT YOU **WANTS**, WODDYA MEAN THEY **BURY** THINGS?

HERE'S A PAPER (WRAPPED 'ROUND A FISH) AUG. 29 1953.. **BURY THINGS?!** LOOK WHERE THEY PUT **DETROIT** IN THE STANDIN'S **...SEVENTH PLACE!** 40 GAMES BURIED! THAT DIDN'T HAPPEN IN **MY** DAY, FRIENDS!

COPR 1953 WALT KELLY

IT'S **MY** CONTENTION, FRIENDS, IF WE HAD A **TRULY** LIBERAL PRESS THE **TIGERS** WOULD OF GOT A BETTER SPOT IN THE **AMERICAN LEAGUE STANDINGS**... SUCH THINGS ARE NOT THE WHIM OF CHANCE ....

THEY IS THE **WHIM** OF **WHAMMY.**

OL' ROY MATSON   10-16

FORGET SPORTS ...TAKE THEM **COMICKAL** STRIPS ...A NEWSPAPER BUYS A STRIP AN' WILL IT LET OTHER PAPERS IN THE SAME TOWN HAVE IT, TOO?

HA! TALK ABOUT FREEDOM.

ROY MATSON

BESIDES..... **WHO**..**WHAT PITIFUL PITTANCE READS THE PAPERS TODAY?**

WELL, THERE'S A WAY OVER 50,000,000 COPIES EVER'DAY READ BY, AT THE VERY LEAST, TWO PEOPLE APIECE.

COPR 1953 WALT KELLY

WELL, YOU DON'T HAVE TO **SNAP** MY HEAD OFF.

DIN'T KNOW IT WAS MADE OF RUBBER, SON.

MAT

LAST TIME A PAPER MENTIONED ME THEY SPELT MY NAME WRONG.

SEE, YOU IS FUSSIN' 'BOUT A FREE PRESS AN' THE MINUTE THEY MAKES FREE WITH YO' NAME, YOU GITS MAD.

CRITTURS IS ALL ALIKE.

WHAT MAKES YOU SO TALKY? THEM'S THE FIRST WORDS YOU SAID SINCE WENSDAY.

I BEEN MULLIN' AT 'EM.

NEWSPAPERS ARE PUT OUT BY CRITTURS JES' LIKE OTHER THINGS IS DID BY CRITTURS... SOMETIMES GOOD... SOMETIMES NOT SO ...BUT CONSIDERIN' THAT EVER'BODY IS GOT TWO LEFT FEET US CRITTURS DON'T DO BAD...

I FIGGERS, PORKY, THAT EVERY MAN'S HEART IS EVENTUAL IN THE RIGHT PLACE.

AN' I FIGGERS POGO, THAT IF A MAN'S GONNA BE WRONG 'BOUT SOMETHIN' THAT IS THE BEST WRONG THING TO KEEP BEIN' WRONG ABOUT 'TIL FOREVER.

10-17 POST-HALL SYNDICATE

COPR. 1953 WILT KELLY

OW! WE WUZ BOWLIN' DOWN TO BOWLING IN OUR BULLY BOWLER 'ATS WHEN A BAWBBY WITH A BILLY BEAT OUR BEATRICE ON THE SPATS.

LUMME, REGGIE... IT'S A PLYCE WHAT PEDDLES TICKETS TO THE CRICKET MATCHES, JOLLY... WOT?

RUM, ALF! QUITE RUM.

CRICKET

TWO, MUM... TWO FOR THE MATCHES.

I'M A BUSY CRICKET WITH NO TIME FOR GAMES.... TWO FOR THE MATCHES, IS IT?

THEN IT'S THREE TO GIT READY... AN' FOUR TO GIT GONE!

A STICKY WICKET, REGGIE! DON'T GIT CAUGHT, CHAP.

NOT 'ARF' ALF, NOT 'ARF! I'M OFF, ALF, OFF IT IS!

CRICKET

10-19 POST-HALL SYNDICATE

COPR 1953 WALT KELLY

I S'Y, ALF, IF IT AIN'T ONE OF THEM, NOW, 'EDGEHOG CHAPS.

RIGHTO, REGGIE ... 'EY GUV'NOR, WHICH WAY TO THE CRICKET MATCH?

COR! 'E'S COLD GRAVY, ALF; 'E NEVER 'EARD OF THE GYME, BY THE LOOK OF 'IM.

THE ROUNDER SERIES FOR THE WORLD CUP, Y'KNOW!

ALF, LAD, IF YOU TYKE NOTE, 'E'S WEARIN' A GRASS KILT. LUMME! S'POSE 'E'S A HAWAIIAN?

IF 'E IS... 'E'S A LYDY... AN' ME WITH ME TOPPER ON.

COO! 'E'S NO HAWAIIAN...WHERE'S HIS GUITAR AN' 'IS BLINKIN' PINE-APPLE?

(AS I S'Y, REGGIE, 'E'S A FEMYLE... THEY DON'T CARRY THEM) A THOUSAND PARDONS, MADAM.

POST-HALL SYNDICATE 1953

10-20

COPR 1953 WALT KELLY

THINK I'LL GO BACK.... 'LONG AS HE SAID WHAT HE SAID ....

ONE OF YOU IS SAID TO ME..."A THOUSAN' PARDONS, MADAM." SO... HOW ABOUT 'EM?

BLINK ME EYE, IF SHE AIN'T A TALKER AT THAT, REGGIE...... RIGHTO, MA'M. WHAT ABOUT 'EM AS YOU SAYS, MADAM?

I WANTS 'EM. ALL ONE THOUSAN' OF 'EM ... SO START IN GIVIN'.

THE LOVELY LYDY'S RIGHT, ALF.... WHEN ALL'S SAID AN' DONE YOU DID OFFER, LAD.

'OW! NOW?

RIGHT Y'ARE, MUM. COMFY DOES IT... THIS'LL TYKE A BIT. WE WERE ABOUT TO BROACH TH' 'AMPER, MUM ... TEA? OR A BISCUIT, 'EY?

PARDON ME-- PARDON ME-- PARDON ME-- PARDON ME-- PARDON ME-- PARDON ME- I 'OPES TO GOODNESS SOME CHAP IS TALLYIN'! PARDON ME PAR DON ME PARDON ME PARDONMEPA RDONMEPARDON

10-21 POST-HALL SYNDICATE

COPR 1953 WALT KELLY

Row 1 (10-27):

THAT'S *FINE*, YOU LI'L' WORM CHILLUN....YOU SPELLED "*IS*".~ NOW SEE KIN YOU ALL SPELL "*CAT*."

NOTHIN' TO IT, UNCLE POGO.

LET'S SEE..YEP.. C...A...T... *RIGHT!* THAT *IS* "CAT."

ANOTHER *SHAMEFUL* EXHIBITION OF THE EDUCATIONAL LEVEL----*THEY* SPELLED IT UPSIDE DOWN.

IT'S *HARDER* THAT WAY....

NONETHELESS, I GONNA OPEN A *SCHOOL!* EVER'BODY HERE IS *TOO* IGNORANT....

PHOO.... IT WAS *YOU* SAID THE POEM WHAT OL' CHURCHY HAD WAS AWFUL.... SAID *HE'D* WRIT A BAD ONE.

WHEN *ALL* THE TIME IT WAS A POEM BY *WILL SHAKESPEARE*, HIS OWN SELF!

PHMPH! WELL, *HA!* HA·HMM.·YES, WELL! *THAT IS THE VERY TYPE OF IGNORANCE OF WHICH I DEPLORE!*

COPR 1953 WALT KELLY

Row 2 (10-28):

ALBERT, I IS THINKIN' 'BOUT OPENIN' A SCHOOL.

I ALLUS *THUNK* YOU NEEDED A LI'L' MORE *LEARNIN'*, OWL.

DON'T GO BE *SOURGRASSTIC*, ALL KIN LEARN----FOR *INSTINCT*, SIR, DOES YOU KNOW THAT "*EL LAGARTO*" MEANS----

A SEEGAR?

ALLIGATOR!

WHERE?

PUT ME DOWN, YOU LUMPHEAD! *YOU IS A ALLIGATOR YOUR OWN SELF!*

SAY, THAT *IS* TRUE, AIN'T IT.... IT'S HARD TO REMEMBER ALL OF A SUDDEN LIKE THAT.

COPR 1953 WALT KELLY

Row 3 (10-29):

ONE THING I KIN TEACH EVER'BODY IN SCHOOL IS 'BOUT *ATOMICAL POWER* AN' *INTERNATIONAL POLITINKS*

HEY, HOWLAN', I HEAR TELL YOU GONE OPEN UP A SCHOOL.

YEP. I GONE EX·PLAIN THEM *ATOMICALS* AN' *FISSION*.. ALSO *FUSION*, *PRO* AN' *CON*.

HOW 'BOUT *BOTANY?* YOU EVER SEE HOW *LIMA BEANS* IS FAT AN' ROUNDY.

AN' *STRING BEANS* IS STRINGY AN' *WAX BEANS* IS WAXEY AN' *CHILE BEANS* IS CHILLY? *WHAT MAKES THEM DIFFERMINTS IN BEANS, OWL?*

I DON'T RIGHTLY KNOW, PORKY, BEIN' BUSY AS I IS WITH *ATOMS* AN' THE *WORLD* AN' ALL....

WULL, *OKAY*... GO 'HEAD BUT I BE *DOGGED* IF I KIN FIGGER HOW YOU ALL KIN 'SPLAIN 'BOUT *ATOMS* AND HOW TO BLOW UP EVER'THIN' AN' *YOU DON'T EVEN KNOW BEANS!*

COPR 1953 WALT KELLY

Row 4 (10-30):

OL' *OWL* GONE OPEN UP A *SCHOOL*, HOUN' DOG.

GREAT NEWS! YES, *INDEED.*

MY SCHOOL DAYS ... THE GOLDEN YEARS IN FIRST GRADE WERE GONE TOO SOON.... I'VE OFT WONDERED WHAT HAPPENED TO OUR MANUAL TRAININ' TEACHER AN' FOOTBALL COACH..

A GREAT GUY, HUH?

A LADY... MISS *BOOMBAH*~ WE LOVED HER LIKE A BROTHER~ CALLED HER "*SIS*".~ WE HAD A CHEER FOR SPORTING CONTESTS.~ *YAY WILLACOOCHIE! GLORIOUS WILLACOOCHIE EVER TRUE! FIGHT ON, CHARTROOS AN' PLAID!*

WILLACOO-CHEEE! SIS BOOMBAH.'" WE *ALWAYS* TACKED *HER* ON THE *END.* SHE HOLLERED LOUDER'N ANYBODY....

I SHOULDA THUNK SHE WOULD

COPR 1953 WALT KELLY

SIS BOOMBAH WAS THE BEST FOOTBALL COACH THE FIRST GRADE EVER *HAD*. WE WON THE *CHAMPEEN-SHIP* FIVE YEARS IN A RO---*YUM!* CAKE AHOY!

WELL, IF IT AIN'T THE LI'L' BUG WITH THE CAKE AGAIN.

IT'S A *BRAN' NEW CAKE* FOR A LI'L' OL' FUNNY FACE...SHE'S A-HIDIN' *SOMEWHERE* ---YOU SEED HER?

GUESS NOT...YOU GOTTA LOOK *SHARP*, WHICH IS *MORE'N* I KIN SAY FER ANY OF *YOU*.....SO, IT'S OFF TO *BIRTHDAY COUNTRY*...

SOME *FABLE*...I COULD TELL A BETTER *FAIRY TALE* THAN THAT WITH BOTH HANDS TIED AHIND MY BACK.

NO-HANDS CHRISTIAN ANDERSEN, HE.

THE KATHRYN B

10-31

COPR 1953 WALT KELLY

THIS NOW, *SCHOOL*....SOON'S I GIT ANOTHER *BENCH* MADE ITS GONE BE A *SURE 'NUFF* U-NIVERSITY...

GOOD FOR IT!

I'LL HELP YOU TEACH ALL 'BOUT MY *SPECIALTY*....BECAUSE I IS A *EXPERT* ON MY SPECIALTY.....AN' IS A *SPECIALIST* ON IT TOO BESIDES.

I WASN'T *FIGGERN* ON HELP...I KNOWS *EVER'THIN'* I NEEDS...

YOU DON'T KNOW *MY* SPECIALTY LIKE *I* DOES. *I* IS ON THE *INSIDE*.

SOUNDS GOOD, CHURCHY. I'LL TAKE OFF'N YOU.

ALL RIGHT! WHAT'S YOUR SPECIALTY? WHAT'S *YOU* ON THE INSIDE OF?

TURTLE SHELLS..I GOT INSIDE DOPE.

IN CASE I TURNS *TURTLE* IT'LL BE *GOOD* TO KNOW.

11-2 COPR 1953 WALT KELLY

I IS OPENIN' MY CLASS ON *TURTLES* AFORE *OWL* GITS TO OPEN THE WHOLE *U*-NIVERSITY ON ACCOUN' I IS *READY*.

WELL, YO' CLASS IS HERE WITH *EAGER* EARS.

SO TEACH AWAY.

FIRST OF ALL, NOTICE A TURTLE KIN SUCK IN HIS HEAD BY GOIN': *OOO*

HOW YOU SPELLS THAT "*OOOP*.."?

WITH OOZE AN' PEAS.

NEXT HE KIN DRAW UP HIS *LEG BONES*, BOTH TO ONCE...

GREAT! GREAT, PROFESSOR, WHAT *NEXT*?

YES, YES! WHAT *NEXT*? LIKE MY CO-LLEAGUE SAY: *WHAT*?

NEXT GIT A LADDER AN' A LI'L' *WAGON*... MY LANDIN' GEAR IS JAMMED.

11-3 COPR 1953 WALT KELLY

YOUR STUDENT BODY IS *PREE*-PARED TO GIVE YOU *TEMPORARY UNDERPINNIN'*, PROF.

THEN YOU KIN GIT OVER TO YOUR *AUNTIE'S*......*MIZ MYRTLE* IS BOUND TO REMEMBER HOW TO GIT YO' *LEG BONES OUTEN* YO' SHELL......*EASY NOW*....

GOT HIM...

OKAY...NORTH BY NORTH EAST-EAST BY WEST-SOUTH-WEST, MEN...*BRISK!*

PHOO...MOST DANGEROUS THING I COULD GET WOULD BE *MORE* HELP LIKE *THAT*.

GOOD NEWS, OWL! *GOOD NEWS!* WE IS COMIN' OVER TO *JOIN YOUR FACULTY.*

WHOOOP! KEERFUL.

11-4 COPR 1953 WALT KELLY

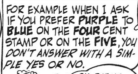

11-10 IF YOU IS MAKIN' A **SURVEY** ON US **MAIL MENS** YOU OUGHT TA **ACCEPT** THE ANSWERS WE GIVES.

BUT THE ANSWERS YOU GIVE ARE **COLORLESS** AND DO **NOT** FIT OUR THEORETICAL PATTERN.

FOR EXAMPLE WHEN I ASK IF YOU PREFER **PURPLE** TO **BLUE** ON THE **FOUR** CENT STAMP OR ON THE **FIVE**, YOU **DON'T** ANSWER WITH A SIMPLE YES OR NO.

O.K. PUT ME DOWN FOR A SIMPLE "MAYBE."

FURTHER, WHY DO YOU NOT WEAR **SNOWSHOES?** DO YOU HAVE A DEEP ROOTED DESIRE TO IGNORE WINTER?

NO, THEY LETS THE COLD THRU ON MY TOEBONES AN' BESIDES IT'S **ONLY** NOVEMBER.

WHY DO YOU HATE POOR **NOVEMBER?** WHY BELITTLE IT, SAYING "**ONLY**"?

DAG NAB IT. I WISH YOU'D LET ME DELIVER THIS **SPECIAL** --- IT'S FOR **ME** AN' I CAN'T WAIT TO GIT HOME SO I'LL BE THERE WHEN IT COMES.

11-11

Y'KNOW, IT SEEMS TO ME THIS IS ALL BACKWARDS ---- WE, EVER'BODY, OUGHT TO KEEP OUR BIG MOUTHS SHUT **ALL** THE **WHOLE** YEAR LONG SO'S WE'D HAVE TIME TO THINK OF TWO MINUTES' WORTH OF SOMETHIN' TO SAY ON THE **ELEVENTH DAY OF NOVEMBER.**

OL' DEEMS TAYLOR

11-12 DO YOU MEAN TO SAY YOU'RE **BREAKING OFF** THE INTERVIEW?

I GOTTA **GO!** IF I'M OUT HERE I CAN'T BE **HOME** AN' CAN'T GET THE **LETTER** I GOT TO DELIVER TO ME.

BUT IF YOU'RE AT HOME YOU CAN'T BE **ON DUTY** AN' IF YOU'RE NOT **ON** YOU CAN'T **DELIVER** THE MAIL.

I DON'T **CARE!** I DON'T **CARE!** I DON'T **CARE** AN' ANYWAY I CAN SO.

NEITHER SNOW NOR SLEET NOR FOG NOR RAIN NOR **DARK** OF NIGHT CAN **TOUT** ME OFF'N MY POINTY **ROUNDS** --- **IT'S** THE CREED!

DOES THE **CREED** SAY ANYTHING 'BOUT THE **FURY** OF A **SCORNED** WOMAN, LOVELY IN HER WRATH?

NO... JES' ORDINARY **NATURAL DISASTERS.**

THEN **COME ON BACK HERE!**

11-13 THIS **SPECIAL DELIVERY** LETTER FOR **YOU**, MAILMAN, HAS GOT YOU **ALL AFLIGHTERY** --- I'LL JUST OPEN IT AND SEE WHAT'S SO ALL-FIRED IMPORTANT.

THAT'S **UNLEGAL!**

HMMPH! BZZZ-MMS-UM-SP. WZZR--FRZ--**HUMPH!** MBS. WIBS-GMS--SNMPER--NGGZ--

AT LEAST READ IT **LOUDER!**

WELL, I NEVER! MY, MY, MY, MY, MY, MY, MY, MY, **MY!**

WODDIT **SAY?** WODDIT **SAY?**

MY LAND! BUT NOW LET US GET ON WITH OUR REPORT FOR DR. WHIMSY. **WHY DO YOU DAWDLE WHEN DELIVERING MAIL?** ANSWER IN TWO WORDS OR LESS.

Panel 1 (11-14):
HEY! LET OL' CHOO CHOO UP BEFORE I POPS YOU WITH MY OAR.

GEN'LEMENS DON'T POP LADIES WITH NO OARS.

WHAT'S YOU THINK YOU IS DOIN', MA'AM?

I'LL GLADLY LET THIS SPECIMEN UP...IS HE ALL THE MAIL MEN YOU HAVE? I'M POLLING THEM YOU KNOW.

I'LL POLE YOU WHEN I GITS MY HEALTH BACK.

Panel 2:
I'D GUESS HE'S A GOOD CROSS-SEC-TION OF OUR MAIL MEN...

AS CROSS AS THEY COME.

PITIFUL! SUCH A SMALL SAMPLING! I'D LIKE TO GET A LARGER PERCENT FOR DR. WHIMSY....

HE'S A HUNNERD PERCENT 'S FAR AS THIS SWAMP IS CORNCERNED—AN' STOP CALL-IN' HIM A SAP-LIN'

Panel 3 (11-16):
HERE'S THAT SPECIAL DELIVERY LETTER FOR YOU THAT I WAS KEEPIN' IN ESCROW, SONNY... RUN ALONG LIKE A GOOD LITTLE MAILMAN, NOW.

TELL DR. WHIMSEY I STAND ON MY CONSTITUTAL RIGHTS AND WRONGS.

WOTSIT SAY? WOTSIT SAY?

IT'S PRIVATE, PERSONIAL, AN' BESIDES I CAN'T READ IT.

HOW'S YOU KNOW THAT IT'S PRIVATE THEN?

'CAUSE I WROTE IT......I WASN'T GITTIN' NO MAIL PERSONIAL, SO I WRIT AT ME A IMPORTANT DISPATCH.

WHY? IF YOU CAN'T WRITE FIT FOR THE NAKED EYE BALL?

SHUCKS, WRITIN' IS EASY....IT'S MY READIN' WHAT MAKES EVER'THIN' LIN DECIPHERFOBBLE.

Panel 4 (11-17):
BALL ALL PUMPED UP, WATERBOY?

ALL PUMPED.

THEN.....KICK OFF!

WHADDYA CHASIN' ME FOR? YOU DIN'T SAY WHAT TO PUMP IT UP WITH...YOU FERGITS I'M THE WATERBOY!

WHO'S CHASIN' YOU? I'M GITTIN' OUT AFORE HE GETS HIS FOOT WORKIN'----

SPLASH!

Panel 5 (11-18):
I DO DECLARE, POGO, IT'S EXTREMELY DIFFICULT FOR AN ELDERLY BACHELOR GIRL TO MAKE A LIVING; SO I TOOK A JOB WITH DR. WHIMSEY...

BY JING! MY OL' FOOTBALL COACH, SIS BOOMBAH, UP IN PROVIDENCE, ALLUS SAID ROADWORK IS MIGHTY BENEFICIAL...

SPECIALLY IF YOU IS ON THE LAM...

BOOP!

HAVE A CARE, SON, I'M AN OLD LADY.. ... SO, AS I SAY, POGO, I'M HELPING DR. WHIMSEY AND....

MISS BOOMBAH!

LET'S GO, EVER'BODY, FOR A RIDE IN THE NEW BOAT WE NAMED FOR DOCTOR CARL.

STOP BEIN' SO *BROODY*, DEACON.' C'MON.

What? With these students plotting to steal California...?

DOC CARL HARTMAN

12-8

BUT, AS M'SIEUR *PORK* LE PINE IS SAY: *WHERE ARE THESE CAULIFORN'* TO BE KEPT IF HE *IS STOLING?*

Phaugh! They'll keep it in Florida perchance or sell it in South America ~~~~ The whole idea fills me with *Loathing.*

I FEEL THE *SAME!*

YES SIR!

COPR 1953 WALT KELLY

If you two feel like I do ~~How can you both look so happy?

WE'RE ALWAYS HAPPY WHEN WE'RE FILLED WITH *LOATHING.*

SURE.. AIN'T YOU?

POST HALL SYNDICATE

WE JUST LEFT THE DEACON ~~~~HE IS *PERTY* UPSET BY THE *DEECADISM* OF YOUR COLLEGE, OWL.

YES... *NOTHING* IS BEING TAUGHT... IT SEEMS *QUEER* THAT YOUR SCHOOL TEACHES NOTHING BUT *NOTHING.*

WHAT'S *WRONG* IN *THAT?* IT AIN'T LIKE WE WAS TEACHIN' *SOMETHIN'!* WE TEACHES A GOOD BRAND OF NOTHIN'.

WHAT KIND OF NOTHING?

12-9

WELL, ALBERT TEACHES NOTHIN' ABOUT *MATH*...HE'S STRONG IN THAT FIELD....I TEACHES NOTHIN' *'BOUT SCIENCE*... MY *FORTE.* PORKY IS GITTIN' BONED UP ON *FRENCH* ---HE'S HEAD OF THE FOREIGN LANGUAGE *DEE-PARTMINTS.*

COPR 1953 WALT KELLY

HE DON'T KNOW *NO* FRENCH HAR'LY AT *ALL*, SO HE KIN TEACH PERTY CLOSE TO *NOTHIN'* BOUT THAT AN' *AB*-SOLOOT NOTHIN' 'BOUT THEM *OTHER* FOREIGN TONGUES----A GOOD *UNSPEAKABLE* MAN.

YOU KNOW WHO INVENTED FOREIGN LANGUAGES?

YEP. *PETER, THE GREAT.*

YOU SAYS YOU *COWBIRDS* KNOWS WHO *INVENTED FOREIGN LANGUAGES?*

YEP... *PETER, THE GREAT*... HE'D JUST GOT THE *TRANSATLANTIC CABLE* LAID AN' FOUND OUT A STARTLING *DIS*COVERY.

HE DISCOVERS THE *MORSE CODE!* IT WAS GOOD FOR *SENDIN'* MESSAGES, BUT *FOREIGN LANDS* COULDN'T ANSWER *BACK*... THEY DIDN'T HAVE *NO* LANGUAGES!

12-10

WELL, I'LL BE *DOGGED!* NOT A *PEEP*, HUH?

NARY A! SO OLD PETER INVENTED SPANISH FOR SPAIN, CHINESE FOR CHINA, ENGLISH FOR THE *U.S.* AND *A* --- AND *ALL* LIKE THAT THERE...

COPR 1953 WALT KELLY

BLESS MY *SOUL*... THEN THEY COULD *ANSWER BACK* ON THE CABLE, HUH?

WELL, HE HAD TO INVENT A CODE FOR *ANSWERING*---- CALLED IT, *NATURAL*, THE *RE*-MORSE CODE...*NEXT* THEY NEEDED ELECTRICITY, SO CZAR IVAN TOOK A KITE AND SOME STIRING AND A KEY

YOU SAY THE *DEACON* IS AGAINST OUR ACTIVITIES.

SAYS HE DON'T COMPREHEND. 'EM, COACH.

COME SEE HIM, COACH BOOMBAH, AN' *WOO* THE OL' BUZZARD.

MM-- EVERY TIME I WOO A MAN HE FOLDS IN THE STRETCH. MEN HAVE NO *DE*FENSE AND LITTLE STAMINA.

12-11

NO, I MEAN BE *NICE* TO HIM.... MAKE HIM *BUSINESS MANAGER* OF THE *BEAN BAG TEAM* ..... THINK HOW HAPPY HE'LL BE, COUNTIN' THE HOUSE WHEN YOU PLAY *IGLOO U.*

FROM WHAT I HEAR OF THE *DEACON* HE'S TOO LAZY TO COUNT TO *SEVEN* ON HIS FINGERS.

I *DUNNO*, MOST BUSINESS MANAGERS KIN BE VERY HAPPY COUNTIN' UP TO *SEVEN* OR EE-*LEVEN* ON THEIR HANDS AN' KNEES.

THE HON. FRED W. GIESEL

Walt Kelly

Milton Caniff Talks About Walt Kelly

JUST AS Walt Kelly pioneered the development of the politically satirical syndicated humor strip, Milton Caniff had been on the cutting edge of an earlier cartoon phenomenon, the continuity adventure strip.

Caniff, who died April 3, 1988, at the age of 81, was considered by his peers in the National Cartoonists Society to be the "Dean of American Cartooning."

He began his career with the Associated Press drawing Dickie Dare *and* The Gay Thirties. *Then in 1934 he created* Terry and the Pirates *for the Chicago Tribune–New York Daily News Syndicate.*

The adventures of young Terry Lee, his guardian the handsome Pat Ryan, numerous sexy women, most notably the Dragon Lady and Burma, were set in the China of warlords and anarchy that preceded World War II. Caniff earned a following of 30 million readers in an era before television, videos, and other diversions.

During World War II, Caniff designed "Miss Lace," one of the most popular pinup girls among servicemen. She appeared in Armed Forces newspapers throughout the world.

At the end of 1946, Caniff was lured away from the Tribune Syndicate by Marshall Field, owner of the Chicago Sun Syndicate, which guaranteed him $100,000 a year and full ownership of a new adventure strip he created, Steve Canyon. *The strip ended syndication shortly after Caniff's death.*

Fortunately, all of Caniff's work on Terry and the Pirates *(1934–1946), his "Miss Lace," and most of* Steve Canyon *(1947–1988) have been reprinted by the comic fan press. A graduate of Ohio State University, Caniff's inspiration caused the founding of the OSU Library of Communication and Graphic Arts, which is fast becoming the premier cartoon research center in the country.*

I had the privilege of interviewing Milton Caniff three separate times: on December 20, 1977, November 24, 1979, and November 20, 1980. Much of that time was spent discussing his own work, but we did speak at length of his friendship with Walt Kelly. This material has not been published before.

—B. C., Jr.

THE INTERVIEW

Q: When did you meet Walt Kelly?

MILTON CANIFF: I met Kelly during his time on the New York *Star* [1948]. It was in a saloon—most likely Costello's. I had seen his work, of course, but I hadn't crossed his trail until then.

Soon after meeting him, I began to see a lot of his work. The [National] Cartoonists Society was just getting cranked up. It was very clear to me he'd be president of the club as soon as we could corral him into doing it.

Q: I hear he was quite cool to that idea at first. Is that true?

MILTON CANIFF: He was very cool. He was cold, he wasn't just cool. It would be a nuisance to

him, but he did have a keen sense of obligation. He really didn't want to spend all the time necessary to be president. But finally he came to the conclusion that it was his turn to serve.

He and I hit it off right from the first. However, Walt was a serpent's tooth when it came to sarcastic wit. He would think of the sardonic thing to say and then say it.

Q: Cartoonists are like all newspaper people in that they are always talking shop. Did you and Kelly talk shop?

MILTON CANIFF: Yes, endlessly. We went on a couple of speaking appearances and rode back on the train together. One time we came down from

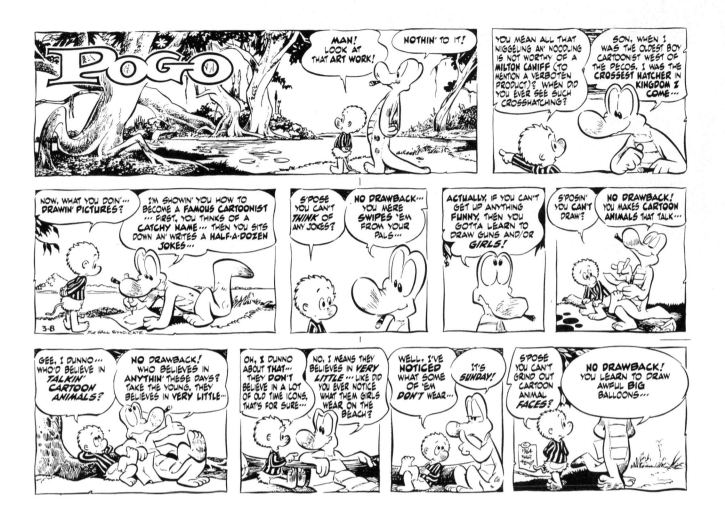

Kelly took Milton Caniff's style of cartooning that features action, adventure, glamorous women, and guns as the playful subject of this Sunday page he gave to Caniff.

Boston to New York—this was after he'd married Stephanie. I'm sure she was bored stiff because we just sat there and yacked.

We'd talk about how we handled our current strips. We compared our devices and techniques for working with newspapers—not drawing techniques, but business techniques. He asked me if it worked with the managing editors. I responded, "Yes, except when I could move in at a higher level and establish a relationship with the publisher." Usually we both dealt with the managing editors.

Q: Did you ever talk with Kelly about your techniques for getting publicity? It seems to me that Caniff, Capp, and Kelly were the three masters of publicity.

MILTON CANIFF: Well, if you want a long wait, let the syndicate do your publicity for you. I've always gone on the theory, and I think Walt did too—though I don't remember him saying so—that you have to do it yourself. It's the only possible way out.

You need to know what kind of thing you can promote in a family newspaper and you need to know what kind of trouble you can start to get publicity.

Q: Did you ever talk to him about the McCarthy stuff? Kelly was in the eye of the storm with his character Simple J. Malarkey.

MILTON CANIFF: I don't think we did because at that point we were all so tuned in to Walt and what he was doing that unless he mentioned it, we wouldn't have brought it up. It just didn't get talked about. . . . We never criticized it. We were delighted by it. In fact, we were wondering whether or not he'd get away with it.

Q: Given the time frame of the early 1950's during that period when Kelly was on the cutting edge of criticism of Senator McCarthy, did you ever wonder why the FBI or some other investigative agency never got their teeth into Kelly's rather juicy private life? He was wide open—on a wild roll.

MILTON CANIFF: Yes, he was, and it's surprising nobody never nicked him on it.

I remember one time when a fellow, George Perry of the London Sunday *Times*, came to New York City to see me, Rube Goldberg, and Walt Kelly. We had dinner at the Orient, a Chinese restaurant on East End Ave. I brought along Emily Hahn, a writer about Far East items for *The New Yorker* magazine. Walt greatly admired her.

During dinner, Walt became enamored of Emily. We felt sorry for the fellow from London. When Walt got in one of these moods you couldn't get him out of it. Emily Hahn was too much of a woman not to enjoy taking the spotlight from the fellow from London.

He was also desperately avid for a couple for completely unapproachable women. He made no bones that he lusted for them. Emily Hahn, who I've just mentioned, was one of them. She was pleased but she just laughed him off. The ladies loved his mind.

Q: Did Kelly ever talk to you about any of the Pogo for President campaigns?

MILTON CANIFF: Not in any detail, though we used to kid about it.

I think he thought the first one [1952] was ridiculous and part of his ploy was to say whatever somebody else would be thinking. His way was to be self-denigrating about his successes.

One thing, toward the end of his life I didn't see as much of him as I did during the middle period. I went to live part of each year in Palm Springs, California, and I did have some correspondence with him. I wrote him at the time of Stephanie's death [1970]. He responded that he'd never had a reason to go to Palm Springs before, but now that I was there he'd try to stop by.

Q: What type of fellow was Walt Kelly?

MILTON CANIFF: Of course, he was terribly talented. You know, people assumed Kelly was Roman Catholic but he wasn't. He was Protestant. So people would always apologize to him about telling an ethnic Catholic joke.

If you ran into Walt it was his party from then on. There was a certain loneliness about this. He had friends on all levels of society, top to bottom, I didn't know them and he was expert at letting you see only that portion of his life he wanted you to see.

He always had trouble with his weight. Walt was really quite a Falstaffian character. Costello's and the Pen & Pencil, the *New York Herald Tribune* hangout, were the two spots he favored. If you wanted to find him you called either one of those places. He was very close to the *Herald Tribune* hotshots of that day.

The *Herald Tribune* wasn't a big newspaper for cartoonists so it was the writers he visited with at the Pen & Pencil. The cartoonists were over at Costello's. It was also geographically the difference between the east side and west side of town. Nobody in our trade ever went west of Broadway in those days; all the publications were on the east side. No cartoonists ever bothered with the *New York Times*, of course. That crowd always went to Sardi's.

If you went into one of these saloons and Walt had a bottle on the table, he was holding court. If he had just a drink, it was another matter. You never knew what would happen and you'd better either go along with him or go home.

Q: What was the happiest you ever remember Walt Kelly?

MILTON CANIFF: I always remember him being concerned about something. I never saw him in a state of total happiness.

I should mention that Walt had a sardonic wit and the younger cartoonists were a bit afraid of him at times. He knew, of course, what I had done with *Terry and the Pirates* and *Steve Canyon*, and would say, ''If they ever stopped putting rivets in airplanes, Milt would be out of work.'' He'd also put my name in the *Pogo* strip on occasion. I have a *Pogo* Sunday page hanging in my studio right now.

Pogo, Albert, and Churchy leave what they think is the planet Mars in an aircraft certified by Milton Caniff. These adventures were reprinted in *Prehysterical Pogo in Pandemonia*, published by Simon & Schuster in 1967.

Release for the Week of March 13, 1967

Release for the Week of March 20, 1967

THE HALL SYNDICATE, INC.
30 EAST 42nd STREET, NEW YORK, N. Y.

When he and I talked, it reminded me of old times at the AP bullpen. We'd talk about cartooning, but not the theory of it, because we did it day in and day out for our living. Walt was a very practical gent on the subject of cartooning.

One thing that always confounded us was the fickleness of the American college student. Even Walt, who had great popularity on campuses, couldn't understand for sure exactly what students wanted from his comic strip. You know, Kelly graduated from high school in 1930 and I graduated from Ohio State University in 1930.

Q: Do you have any favorite character in *Pogo*?

MILTON CANIFF: I never thought about it but I suppose I do. Because of what I do in my strip I've always been fascinated by roguery. Albert the Alligator is my favorite. He's the genial rogue—con man more than rogue, really.

Q: Looking at *Pogo* as a body of work, and knowing Kelly as you did, what do you think was the single biggest achievement in his career as a cartoonist?

MILTON CANIFF: I would say his political satire that was so pervasive throughout his work from the McCarthy era on. I place Kelly right up there with Thomas Nast in terms of devastating editorial comment. The hyena he drew as Vice President Spiro Agnew was a classic. I believe some of Walt's bite was lost because *Pogo* was a comic strip instead of an editorial cartoon. But Walt always wanted *Pogo* to remain on the comics page because in the long haul you make more impact that way. On the editorial page you're here today and forgotten tomorrow.

I must add that we are all so glad a cartoonist came out of the Disney world and made it in what we considered the real world of cartooning. Walt escaped, and with the blessings of Disney, as far as I know. So many of those guys out there are so nailed into the animation business that they're afraid to break out on their own. They don't know the syndicated world so they're very apprehensive.

Q: Is there any special Walt Kelly anecdote you remember?

MILTON CANIFF: The one I remember involved Walt and Al Capp of *Li'l Abner*. This was at the RCA Johnny Victor Theater and was a meeting of the Newspaper Comics Council. [This is now the Newspaper Features Council.] At each of their meetings, after the business session was over, they usually had something that related to cartooning, visuals or a panel.

This time it was just Al and Walt, two boys from Bridgeport, Connecticut, nose to nose and no recording was made, I'm sad to say. This was pre-1970 but I can pin it down exactly.

Walt would say to Al, "Of course, Al, this is really how you should draw Daisy Mae, I'm only showing you this for your own good." Then Walt would do a sketch.

Capp, of course, got ticked off by this, as you can imagine. So he retaliated by doing his version of Pogo. Unfortunately, the drawings are long gone; no recording was made. What a shame. Nobody anticipated there'd be this dueling back and forth between the two of them. Otherwise we would have set it up to be recorded.

Q: Much of your friendship with Kelly initially revolved around the National Cartoonists Society. Do you think the NCS was more vibrant then because more cartoonists lived in New York City?

MILTON CANIFF: Certainly partly because of that and the difficulty of transportation kept creative people living in New York City. Even when I had a place outside of the city, I always kept an apartment here so it was easy for me to stay in at night for a NCS meeting.

When the Society was young it was a lot of fun. But after a period of time you run through all the speakers that come to mind easily and having a lot of meetings becomes more difficult. The NCS became a very enjoyable drinking and chowder society. Kelly added a lot of zest to the NCS. He was a friend and I miss him.

Repository Editor Immortalized by Walt Kelly; 'Ol' Clayt' Becomes Part of Swampland Legend

Looking for Bridey? Try Your Old Desk

By DORIS CALCOTT
The Salisbury Times

It's funny what you find when the day comes for the old desk to be cleaned out for painting and repairing.

For instance, the pair of galoshes or overshoes still sporting last season's mud, the forgotten coffee cup, no longer warm, or even an old sweater, complete with moths, for the chillier days, may turn up in the back of a desk drawer.

The psychology of putting such articles in a desk drawer is a little hard to explain. Reasons for using such storage places could easily vary with the individual. Or is a reason needed?

Consternation and confusion reigned in The Salisbury Times editorial quarters recently when several new desks arrived and were turned over to staff members. Other folks were told that they would have newly-painted desks soon.

It's odd but one can remove more from a desk than will conveniently go back into the desk once it is given a paint and renovation job. For a born collector of scraps of

The Typocycle isn't taking up comic strips but above is one we thought we could take a one-time crack at.

Most of us know Walt Kelly's famous swamp people whose activities range from pie throwing to politics to private world "serious" promoting.

Most of us, too, are familiar with that odd, flat-bottomed skiff that the inhabitants of the swamp use to get from place to place.

Some time ago, Joseph K. Vodrey, Brush-Moore vice president, suggested to Mr. Kelly that he immortalize Repository Editor Clayt Horn in one of his strips.

A few Sundays back the strip appeared. But "YARGH," none of the Brush-Moore newspapers carry the Sunday edition of Pogo.

paper, clippings, old used pencil stubs that would be better off in the trash can, and whatever else may have a purely sentimental value, it is a sad day when the parting must come.

The day has come—and gone—for several of The Times staff. All desks have been painted and each staff member can get off to a fresh start now as far as his desk is concerned. The next clean-up day will probably come when the desks are moved to the new quarters in the building on Times Square.

Walt Kelly and Milton Caniff both knew the importance of doing special drawings and providing treats for newspaper executives. This piece in the house publication of a chain of newspapers covering eight Ohio towns gave Pogo some welcome publicity.

Beau Pogo

In his small way, Walt Kelly seemed to take it upon himself to bring the wonderful world of newspaper cartooning to the austere New York Times. Reprinted in Outrageously Pogo is the full-page comic strip ad he did with Pogo characters for TV Guide that was published in the issue of The New York Times May 23, 1962. This may be the only full-page comic strip ever published in the gray lady of New York journalism.

Prior to this Kelly designed a series of ads for the Times for his book Beau Pogo [1960]. These four

February 8, 1960

in *The New York Times*

ads—reprinted here for the first time—appeared on four consecutive days: February 8, 9, 10, and 11, 1960. In a newspaper with no cartoons, they certainly must have captured the attention of readers.

Beau Pogo, which reprints material from 1958 to 1960, has the distinction of having four subtitles: "or The Impeccable Possum; or The Swanee Swami at Bay; or The Dandy Little Marsupial; or Okeydoke of the Okeefenoke."

February 9, 1960

February 10, 1960

February 11, 1960

Possum Attack in Vancouver, British Columbia

POGO has always had a devoted and noisy following of readers. In 1956, the Vancouver (British Columbia) Sun dropped Pogo and all hell broke loose with its Pogophile readers. The result was that Pogo was quickly reinstated.

The Hall Syndicate quickly used newsclips from this episode to send out a promotion piece heralding Pogo's staying power and the loyalty of Pogophiles. After all, the purpose of all comic strips is to get the reader to purchase the newspaper in which the comic appears.

The VANCOUVER (British Columbia)

SUN took a poll to measure the popu-

larity of its comic strips. Like most polls...

It reached a conclusion:

So the VANCOUVER SUN dropped Walt Kelly's "POGO"!

Tensely-Awaited Decision On Pogo's Fate Wednesday

A decision will be made Wednesday on whether Pogo will return to The Sun comic pages.

Protests over Pogo's disappearance continued to pour into The Sun while Fred Danks, manager of Canada Wide Syndicate, flew into Vancouver for talks with the newspaper management.

Dank is negotiating the reappearance of Pogo, and his Okefenoke swamp pals, dropped in favor of crime buster Dick Tracy.

However, there was still no word of Pogo's return today. Distraught readers donned black arm bands and prepared to bury their favorite 'possum.

TEACHERS HOLD 'WAKE'

School teacher friends of a Vancouver lawyer attended a "wake" Saturday night wearing black arm bands in mourning. Students complained of falling marks, mothers tried to quieten tearful youngsters, and subscribers asked directions to the nearest meeting-house of the Pogo Perpetuation Club..

University of B.C. students who demonstrated in front of The Sun tower Friday night and burned managing editor Hal Straight in effigy were backed up by others on the campus who sent in long petitions demanding Pogo's return.

Here's a sampling of some letters, many of them addressed to: Pogo Hater Hal Straight":

"Whoever did (away with Pogo) can be replaced but Pogo can't!"

A mother of five children wrote: "Sometimes, in the middle of the night, the baby stirs restlessly, wakes and screams, 'Pogo, Pogo.'"

SON TURNS SULLEN

The mother added that her 17-year-old son has become "unbearably sullen" of late and has taken to wearing sideburns and blue suede shoes. "Our happy home has been disrupted," she wailed.

"Politics must be the reason for this unhumanitarian, miserable miscarriage of justice," another subscriber charged.

"Isn't there enough crime, liquor control, international chaos and wet weather to satisfy appetites?" asked another, while a subscriber of 30 years' standing warned unless "that silly boola, boola" was dropped she wouldn't be a subcriber longer.

"Would you drop Harold Weir in favor of a Hollywood gossip columnist whose rating happened to be higher?" asked another subscriber, referring to readership polls that placed Pogo at the bottom of the list.

'ACT OF TREACHERY'

Another called the banishment of Pogo the "greatest single act of treachery ever perpetrated on the reading public.

"I refer, of course," he went on, "to recent developments whereby, using the tense situation in the Suez and the elections in the United States as temporary distractions, you have slyly eliminated one of the few remaining bright spots in a hectic world, to wit, Pogo. For shame and fie!"

"Remember," he warned, "the Pogo fan's blood pressure affects his circulation—it can affect yours, too."

"This time you have gone too far," still another subscriber screamed. "By dropping 'Pogo,' a brilliant satire, in favor of a rather mediocre and worn-out detective, you have committed a crime against literature itself."

Said another Pogo partisan: "Lovers of Pogo unite. You have nothing to lose but Dick Tracy."

Poll Doesn't Go for Pogo — But Many Do

"Pogo" is a casualty of the pollsters.

The lovable little 'possum and his Okefenoke Swamp pals were dropped from The Sun's comic page Monday to make room for Dick Tracy.

PICKETS, EVEN

The move caused an angry rebellion among the city's fanatic Pogo addicts.

Subscribers have flooded the newspaper all week with phone calls and letters. Thursday night a score of university students picketed The Sun and threatened to return every night until Pogo is restored to the comic page.

Today managing editor H. L. Straight explained Pogo's disappearance.

He said a readership survey showed Pogo was the least popular of The Sun's 19 comic strips.

When Dick Tracy was added to the paper's comic family, something had to go—and Pogo was considered expendable.

The survey, conducted by a reputable research firm, showed Pogo drew only 36 per cent of The Sun's male readers and 33 per cent of the females.

(Archie, the most popular strip, drew 75 per cent of the males and 68 per cent of the females.)

VOCAL MINORITY

But if Pogo's fans are a minority, they are a staunch and vocal one.

More than 150 angry or pleading phone calls have been received by The Sun.

A dozen or more subscribers have written to complain, including a mother of five who said Pogo's absence threatened to destroy her happy home.

"SPP SOCIETY"

A Society for the Perpetuation of Pogo has been formed.

Thursday night a group of Delta Upsilon fraternity members from the University of B.C. marched on the Sun Tower with placards bearing hotly pro-Pogo slogans.

They staged a noisy half-hour demonstration in front of the building and left behind a sign pleading, "Please bring back Pogo to The Sun."

"We'll be down here every night picketing The Sun until Pogo returns," said Leo Dooling, a student leader.

"This is just the beginning," warned Arnie Holm.

Protests Still Pour In Over Dropping of Pogo

Protests against The Vancouver Sun's banishment of Pogo continued Friday night and today.

More angry letters, phone calls and petitions poured in, demanding the daily Walt Kelly comic strip be reinstated.

University students staged a second and larger demonstration in front of the Sun building Friday night.

Today Sun executives said they would re-examine the situation.

STUDENTS PROTEST

The protest reached a peak Friday night when University of B.C. students staged another outburst of protest.

Managing editor Hal Straight was burned in effigy in front of the Sun building. Then outraged students marched on the editorial rooms.

In the newsroom reporters spent the evening answering phone calls from subscribers demanding Pogo be brought back. They counted up to 40 calls, pushing the week's total over 200, then lost track.

War drums beat on the university campus all afternoon to chants of "Pogo for the masses", "We want Pogo" and "Gumph on all you disbelievers."

Radio URS, voice of UBC, solemnly announced: "The literary idol of all loyal students, Pogo, will no longer appear in The Vancouver Sun."

WANTONLY BANISHED

"For some obscure reason known only to those august individuals in The Sun's ivory tower, the most popular reading material ever known to campus readers has been wantonly banished from the pages of that newspaper.

"Students all across the campus are taking up the call to arms."

A petition, signed by almost 1,000 students, protested the "disgraceful removal of that intellectual comic strip, Pogo."

Preceded by a sound car, students arrived at the Sun building about 7:30 p.m.

They carried placards bearing pictures of the little 'possum and his swamp pals and slogans such as "We won't take this lying down" and "Barf" (an Okefenoke term of derision).

The effigy, made from Sun newspapers, was set afire across the street from the Sun building.

Asked why they felt so strongly about Pogo, demonstrators replied, "He's an institution, a classic . . . like Len Norris."

Frank Elsner, a spokesman for the group, dismissed the survey which placed Pogo at the bottom on the list of comic readers' interest.

"The people who read Pogo don't usually read the comics," he said.

"HELP!" cried Hal Straight

— and sent a wire:

.NA107 LONG DPR   CNT UN VANCOUVER BC 13 1112A=
IRA EMERICH SALES DIRECTOR HALL SYNDICATE INC DELIVER=
     :342 MADISON AVE=

HELP. SUN TOWER BEING STORMED BY RAGING POGO FANS DEMANDING
WE REINSTATE THEIR IDOL ON OUR COMIC PAGE. WE HAD TO MAKE
SPACE FOR NEWLY ACQUIRED STRIP. DROPPED POGO AS LEAST
POPULAR OF OUR 20 COMICS. ACCORDING TO RENT SURVEY. BUT WE
UNDERESTIMATED LOYALTY AND SOLIDARITY OF PRO-POGO MINORITY.
     WE HAVE LEARNED IF PRESSURE CONTINUES WE MUST
CAPITULATE. CAN YOU HAVE WALT KELLY DRAW SPECIAL PANEL
ANNOUNCING POGO'S TRIUMPHANT RETURN. FOR PROBABLE PAGE ONE
USE TO PLACATE THE POGOSTICKLERS? AIREXPRESS SOONEST PLEASE=
     :EARL SMITH CITY EDITOR VANCOUVER SUN=

© 1956 WALT KELLY

"Hey, folks, I've got news for you. Please turn to page 23."

COMIC BACK THURSDAY

Fans Win Point, Pogo Returns

Pogo will be back on the comic pages of The Vancouver Sun Thursday.

Sun editors have bowed to the enraged cries of hundreds of Pogo fans who protested by phone, letter and demonstration against his absence from the paper.

The little 'possum and his swamp pals created by satirist Walt Kelly have proven their place in the hearts of Sun readers.

Sun management had decided to drop Pogo after a survey indicated he was the least-read comic strip.

We reckoned without the intense loyalty of Pogo fans.

The paper has been deluged with letters and phone calls. At last count the number of protests had reached 300.

University of B.C. students twice demonstrated outside the Sun building and burned managing editor Hal Straight in effigy.

Dozens of readers said Pogo was the only comic strip they read.

Okay, folks, we know when we're licked.

We go Pogo.

Pogo reappears tomorrow in the comic section—H. L. Straight, managing editor.

The Other Walt Kelly
Non-Pogo Artwork Prior to 1949

One of the hallmarks of the *Okefenokee Star* has been to reprint artwork from different time periods in Kelly's career.

This section is a very slim overview but some interesting artwork has been discovered.

The piece Kelly did as a lad of seventeen for General Electric's Bridgeport *Newsmagazine* was provided by A. F. Serra of GE. The original of the cartoon was presented by GE to the Museum of Cartoon Art, Rye Brook, NY. It shares a page with a piece of artwork Kelly did while attending Bridgeport's Harding High School in 1930.

Next in Kelly's progression before he went to Disney Studios, he illustrated the life of one of Bridgeport, Connecticut's most famous citizens and a former mayor, P. T. Barnum.

When Kelly left Disney, his work in comic books blossomed. Pogo's very first appearance was in *Animal Comics* #1 in the story "Albert Takes the Cake," published by Dell in 1942. This story is reprinted in *The Smithsonian Book of Comic-Book Comics* (1982). The first comic book completely devoted to Kelly's swamp critters was titled *Albert the Alligator and Pogo Possum* (Dell Four-Color #105), published in 1946.

Kelly's tenure as art director and editorial cartoonist of the New York *Star* has been discussed in *The Best of Pogo*. However, besides *Pogo*, he was developing another comic strip, *Bobo Larkin,* about a young newspaper reporter. The short-lived New York *Star* (June 23, 1948–January 28, 1949) didn't last long enough for Kelly to develop this strip fully. All that remains are some promo ads from the *Star*. The strip was slated to begin two days after the *Star* folded.

Kelly drew a series of "weather ears" for use on the New York *Star* featuring a small blond fellow. He also did a series using Pogo. These are published side by side to show two approaches to describing approximately the same weather.

A real find was *Crosstown*, a comic strip created for the New York *Star* but never published. It is shown here for the first time. Note that the *Star* newspaper is shown in the bottom right panel.

Kelly's editorial cartoons at the *Star* were award winning, and although we have published some of them before, it is always a joy to see his skill with grease pencil on pebbleboard.

The nationally syndicated *Pogo* that appeared with the first daily strip on June 16, 1949, did not happen overnight. Kelly had paid his dues.

THE SPECULATOR

Published when one least expects it
by Warren Harding High School
Bridgeport, Connecticut

Price—.05, if the room-leader's memory is good

The Staff
The Editor, I. R. Bill Yuss

POWER

Harding has illustrated its pre-eminence in every field of endeavor. The prolixity of athletic success has outshadowed any other achievements that the cooking department has attained. We must drop the word "can't" from our vocabulary and get behind our boys. Otherwise our pineal glands will not function properly. Never before in the history of our school have our athletes shown greater evidence of the true Harding inscrutability, the spirit of "Never Say Die". Nevertheless you ask, "What? Why the homework assignments?" While you speak of their length and incomprehensibility, we are looking for ways in which to perambulate them. That spirit of determination can do things that are deemed retroactive, even make the goldfish in the Biology room flop out of their bowl, like Guapenas. But we are getting away from our subject. Yes, every business of to-day wants a real "go-getter". Work and conquer is our motto. Though Lindbergh soup has a great moral influence on the complacency and stodginess of the school janitorial force we must not forget the shouts of acclaim we must tender to those who "went down fighting" in the cafeteria.

Ex-Employee Walt Kelly Was Creator Of "Pogo", Published His First Cartoon In The Bridgeport GE News

Several Bridgeport GE employees remember that Walt Kelly, creator of the comic strip "Pogo", was once an employee here. But few are aware that Walt's first published cartoon appeared in the pages of the Bridgeport GE Newsmagazine, called the "Works News" in years past.

The archives of this publication reveal that in 1930, when Walt was 17, he offered to do a picture to promote interest in the former GE Athletic Association. With some misgivings, considering the age of the artist, Walt was told to go ahead with the picture, which appears below.

This cartoon, believed to be one of the first by Walt Kelly to be published, appeared in Works News, October, 1930.

In subsequent issues of the "Works News", as the young Walt Kelly's fame spread as a result of his syndicated daily and Sunday comic strip, GE News editors had this to say: "The News makes no claim as the discoverer of the arrived young artist, but it takes its hat off to a talented youngster who had the stick-to-ititiveness to succeed in his chosen field."

This month and next, in memory of Walt Kelly who died in 1973, the Museum of Cartoon History in nearby Greenwich has dedicated an exhibit of the artist's drawings. The GE cartoon has been presented to the museum, and it is now prominently displayed as his first published work.

BOBO LARKIN

STARTS WORK IN
A NEW COMIC STRIP
NEXT WEEK IN THE *STAR*

JUST WHO IS THIS
BOBO LARKIN?

She'll find out—she's working on the same newspaper in the same comic strip

BOBO
LARKIN

WEATHER EARS

New York *Star*	Pogo Characters	New York *Star*	Pogo Characters

CLOUDY	THREATENING	CLOUDY, COOL	FINE, FAIR, BRISK

SUNNY	SUNNY	PARTLY CLOUDY	CLOUDY—FOGGY

CLOUDY, COLD	COOLER	RAIN	SCATTERED SHOWERS

New York *Star*	Pogo Characters	New York *Star*	Pogo Characters

PARTLY CLOUDY

SMALL SHOWERS

MOSTLY SUNNY, COLD

COLD & FAIR

WEATHER: RAIN

THUNDERSTORMS

MILD, RAIN

WET

MILD

MILD

CLOUDY, RAIN

RAINY

FAIR

FAIR

SLEET OR FREEZING RAIN

SLEET AND HAIL

NEW YORK *STAR*: EDITORIAL CARTOONS

The Four Horsemen of Hysteria

Two Mavericks at the Disney Studio

THE DISNEY YEARS

WALT KELLY rode the bus from Bridgeport, Connecticut to California and arrived there in December 1935. His motivation to travel west was not only to work for Disney but to follow his heart. His first wife, Helen DeLacy Kelly, had arrived on the West Coast a month earlier to fill a job as a Girl Scout executive. She had been the professional in charge of the Girl Scout Council in Bridgeport. He had met her in choir practice five years earlier.

Helen, who was a few years older than Walt, had hoped the westward move might shake her free of a suitor who, though charming, might be too young. Her job in California required her to have a car—"a beat up old Chevrolet roadster" as she described it—and it gave Kelly and his friends the advantage of having their own transportation. The couple were married in September 1937 and homecooked meals at the Kellys were a treat not only for Walt, but for bachelor Disney cartoonists such as Dan Noonan and Morris Gollub.

In an Editor & Publisher interview, Kelly referred to the Walt Disney organization as "the WPA of the cartooning world." The carrot held out to artists who might become animators for Disney was a $25,000-a-year salary, but very few of them made it to the big money, as Kelly stated in the interview. "During the time I was there I made about $100 per week for a work week of five-and-a-half days. It was a great education, though."

Exactly what Kelly did there was an area of much speculation for years. The Okefenokee Star strives to publish primary research. Thomas Andrae and Geoffrey Blum deserve every Pogophile's congratulations and thanks for this fine piece of research. Thanks are also extended to famed Disney animator Ward Kimball for graciously giving his time, memories, and repros of special artwork that have never been reproduced before.

Kelly began work at the Disney Studio on January 6, 1936, and left there on September 12, 1941, at the time of a strike. According to Helen Kelly, Walt Kelly crossed the picket line prior to leaving to talk with Walt Disney. At this meeting Disney provided entrée to Western Publishing for Kelly by suggesting he see either Oskar Lebeck or Mike McClutick when he returned to the East Coast.

When the Kellys left California in the fall of 1941, they moved to Nichols, Connecticut, just a few miles northeast of Bridgeport. At the time it was quite rural. Their first child, Kathleen, was born in Bridgeport on November 30, 1942.

Kelly then entered a period of drawing comic books at home and commuting by train from Bridgeport to New York City three days a week to deliver and pick up new work. It was a time of uncertainty. The family moved a number of times during the next two years.

B. C., JR.

WARD KIMBALL REMEMBERS WALT KELLY
by Thomas Andrae and Geoffrey Blum

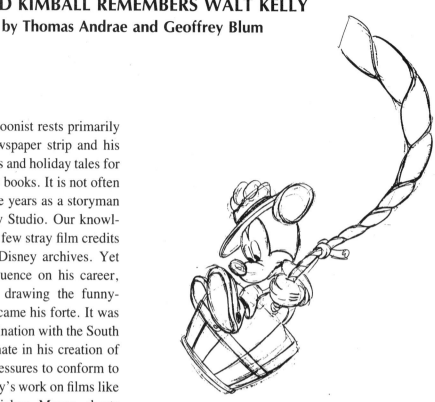

An animation drawing by Kelly for the 1941 Mickey Mouse short *The Little Whirlwind*.

Walt Kelly's reputation as a cartoonist rests primarily upon his work on the *Pogo* newspaper strip and his creation of a series of fairy stories and holiday tales for Western Publishing's Dell comic books. It is not often remembered that Kelly spent five years as a storyman and animator at the Walt Disney Studio. Our knowledge to date has been based on a few stray film credits and concept sketches from the Disney archives. Yet this period had a formative influence on his career, providing an apprenticeship in drawing the funny-animal characters which later became his forte. It was during this time that Kelly's fascination with the South began to emerge, later to culminate in his creation of Pogo. And though he resisted pressures to conform to a recognizably Disney look, Kelly's work on films like *Dumbo, Fantasia,* and the Mickey Mouse shorts helped galvanize his own graphic style.

Kelly joined the Disney Studio on January 6, 1936, beginning as a story artist on several cartoons which were never produced. He was then transferred into the animation department, where he worked on such classic features as *Pinocchio, Dumbo, Fantasia,* and *The Reluctant Dragon.* He was also an animator on three Mickey Mouse shorts: *Clock Cleaners* (1937), *The Little Whirlwind* (1941) and *The Nifty Nineties* (1941). While at the Studio, he formed a close friendship with Ward Kimball, later to become one of Disney animation's famous "Nine Old Men." The two collaborated on animating the crow sequence in *Dumbo,* since acclaimed for its hepcat jazz and humorous racial characterizations. Both artists shared a love of music and mischief, and a status as mavericks who occasionally had trouble adapting to the Disney mold. They formed a rowdy duo at the Studio, sneaking into the men's john for jam sessions on the tin whistle and playing touch football in the narrow hallways.

Kimball's outspoken comments—some about Disney himself—reveal the bureaucratic and artistic pressures that the more creative animators found constricting. His albums of correspondence and satir-ical cartoons by Kelly, saved over the years and perused during our interview, reveal that artist's flair for whimsical lyrics and inspired nonsense. Kelly would later recycle gags from his Studio days as running motifs in the *Pogo* strip. Even the immortal "I Go Pogo" campaign had its precursor in a group of Studio sketches parodying the Roosevelt-Willkie election campaign.

In May 1941, a divisive strike erupted at Disney's. The closing of the European market, forced two years earlier by the outbreak of war, had caused a drastic decline in the Studio's profits. This led to cutbacks and layoffs, and a need to work overtime without pay. Such measures, coming on top of an already large discrepancy in wages between supervisors and their staff, sparked hostilities. A strike began when animator Art Babbit was fired for trying to organize Studio personnel into an independent union, the Screen Cartoonists Guild. Kimball and Kelly, as supervisor and assistant, found themselves pulled toward opposite sides.

"There was a big national election going on [Franklin D. Roosevelt versus Wendell Willkie, 1940]," Kimball recalls, "so Kelly did a whole series of drawings on that. I'm the guy that's running for Senator, and I stand for corruption. He liked to portray me as being up to no good, so he drew me as a politician, because he saw all politicians as crooks and liars. Larry Clemmons and Fred [Moore] are my organizers, and Kelly is a symbol for John Q. Public. This is a good caricature of the way Kelly looked; he always said that he was sort of a country hick."

This strike marked an end to the golden age of Disney animation. Some of the Studio's brightest talents—Babbit, Bill Tytla, Frank Tashlin—departed at this time. Kelly left on September 12, ostensibly taking an extended leave of absence because of illness in the family. He never returned. What follows is a portrait of his Disney years, preserved in the memory of a close friend. Ward Kimball's reminiscences go a long way toward filling the gaps in our knowledge of Kelly's early career. They offer a unique glimpse of the *Pogo* artist in embryo and the Disney Studio at its zenith.

Let's start with Ward Kimball. How did you come to work for Disney?

I was going to Santa Barbara Art School at the time. (Sometimes when I have to repeat this stuff, I remind myself of a park ranger explaining how Old Faithful goes off.) It was during the depths of the depression, and you couldn't get a job anywhere; I was working part time at the Safeway store doing "Five Pounds for 60¢" signs and leading the Mickey Mouse Club band at the local theater, during the Saturday matinee. That was the first version of the club Disney sponsored; the whole idea was to get kids into the theaters. Each club—each theater—had a Master of Ceremonies and a Sergeant at Arms, membership cards, rule books, all that stuff. We developed a little military kids' band, and we'd play out of a beginner's band book. The kids in the audience would always boo us off the stage. They wanted to see the cartoons—which were not all Disney cartoons. There were Fleischer *Betty Boop* pictures along with Pat Sullivan's *Felix the Cat* and Paul Terry's *Farmer Alfalfa* to fill out an hour-and-a-half show.

I used to stick around after the club meeting to

see the matinee, mostly cartoons. I was impressed with the Disney films: they always seemed to have a plot, and they were always funny; everybody laughed at them. They were well constructed, and the animation was superior to that in the other cartoons—as an artist I could see that. A Disney giraffe would walk like a giraffe, a pig would walk like a pig; they didn't just move. The backgrounds were superior, too: they were in color, especially the Silly Symphonies. This was when *The Three Little Pigs* became world famous. The song "Who's Afraid of the Big Bad Wolf?" went to the top of the hit parade, and the Arlington Theater in Santa Barbara held over the film for about a month, which was unheard of. I saw it every Saturday four times in a row, and it was always funny.

In the latter part of March 1934, I heard they were putting on artists at the Disney Studio, so I decided to try for work there. I thought I'd become a background painter; my samples were all of that nature. The depression had hit our family pretty hard, but I had just enough gas in my car to make the trip down to Hollywood and back. I went into the Studio on Hyperion Avenue and asked, "Is this where you're offering jobs?" The lady at the reception desk—Mary Flanigan was her name—said, "Yes, if you care to leave your samples here, we'll notify you." I replied, "It would be nice if you could look at them today, because I can't make another trip; I don't have enough gasoline." So she sent them upstairs. Evidently they went to Walt's office; I heard later that he said, "Sure, he looks like a good prospect." I was told that they wanted me to start work on the following Monday. The person I was to contact was a Mr. Ben Sharpsteen. Little did I know the significance of that name: the role that he would play in my early career and the frustrations I encountered later.

I came to work the following Monday, thinking I was going to paint backgrounds, and went up to Sharpsteen's room. The door was open, and he was sitting over by the window, doing some drawings. In those days he was head of the junior animators, the guys who drew all the crowd scenes and water and leaves blowing—the junk that your first-line animation personnel wouldn't touch. I stood in the open doorway and asked, "Mr. Sharpsteen?" He went right on drawing and didn't even look up. That was a hint of what was in store for me. I must have waited thirty or forty seconds. At last he put down his pencil, turned,

and looked at me, but he didn't say a word. So I said, "Ward Kimball. I had an appointment with you." He finally replied, "I was expecting a much older man." At the time, I was the youngest person in the Studio; I had just turned twenty.

He said, "Well, Walt and I have decided that you'll be a good prospect as an animator." I didn't know what the hell that was; I just shrugged. He sent me to George Drake, head of the inbetweening department: a tyrant who knew nothing about drawing or how to get along with people. I was put in the bullpen—as it was called—filled with sweating new employees. In the summertime we had to strip to the waist, because there was no air conditioning and very little ventilation. We used to sing Volga boatman songs, as if we were galley slaves. It was all new to me, this curious business of making things move.

Six months later, Ham Luske[1] was looking for a new assistant animator, so I went to work for Ham. I gained a lot of experience, because he delegated responsibilities to me that no other animator would. He never did the corrections that were called for on his work; he would just push them over to me and say, "Fix it!" That's how I learned to animate. I became a junior animator by the time I was twenty-one.

When did you meet Walt Kelly?

We were still in the old Studio on Hyperion Avenue, and I was working at the time on *Pinocchio*, in charge of animating Jiminy Cricket. Kelly came to the Studio as a sketch artist and storyman. My first impression of the guy was that he looked different from everybody else. We were all "casual" Californians—sloppy—but Kelly wore dark, three-piece business suits with a starched white shirt and dark tie—always a bow tie—and Eastern-type shoes. He was really a newspaperman type who drew cartoons on the side; he was always talking about the "newspaper game." "When I was back in the newspaper business . . ." he would say; and we would reply, "Oh shit, Kelly!" But he was a funny gag man, and he worked in the story department for quite some time.

Then Kelly came over to work in the animation department. From the latter part of 1939 through

1. Luske was one of Disney's first supervising animators; he worked on *Snow White, Pinocchio, Fantasia,* and *Dumbo*.

1941, he was one of Fred Moore's assistants.[2] When we moved to the new Studio in Burbank, he had a room two doors away from me, with Fred's room in between. We all had connecting doors. Fred and I had rugs on our floors because we were animation *supervisors*. Kelly, being a junior animator, had to be content with plain ol' linoleum.

How was Kelly as an animator?

He had a very personal style. I supervised some of the scenes he did in *Dumbo*, and he had difficulty adapting to the model sheets, which were usually designed by other artists. When Kelly worked with other people, he would always manage to change the drawing of the characters a little. He unconsciously drew them the way *Kelly* thought they ought to look. Maybe, in hindsight, we should have made *our* drawings look like *his*. He drew very funny Mickeys; but when his test animation was screened later in the sweatbox,[3] the notes would always read, "Have Kelly clean these up and make sure they follow the model sheet."

Designing characters for a Disney picture was a difficult job, because you had to please so many people. You had to satisfy the directors, but more important, you had to satisfy Walt. After you got the okay on the sketches you made for a projected character, you also had to test-animate a few scenes, because the proof came when the character was seen in motion.

Kelly animated some of the crow scenes in Dumbo, didn't he?

He and Dave Swift[4] worked for me on the crow sequence. I was supervising and didn't animate every scene. I would draw the size of the figures, explain the business, and rough out a step or two. Kelly and the guys would bring in their test animation and put it on my Moviola, and without even getting up to look at the footage, I'd yell, "Cut it in!" We had a hell of a deadline; some of us were doing forty feet a week then, which was unheard of.

Did you originate that sequence?

No; it originated in the story department. I was given the sequence to animate because Walt had a notion that Kimball was good at dancing and music stuff, and because I had done an animated takeoff of Cab Calloway for the Silly Symphony *Woodland Cafe* when I first came to the Studio. I was half-assed musician and record collector, collecting old-time jazz records.

Did Walt have any problems with depicting the crows as blacks?

No. You have to realize that when *Dumbo* was released, Uncle Tom stereotypes were part of our American scene. There were Aunt Jemimas in MGM's Shirley Temple pictures, and a black maid in Disney's *Three Orphan Kittens*. You only saw her feet, big fat legs and slippers, saying "Dawggone stockin's! Down agin!" For the crows' song in *Dumbo*, we hired a black choir, so the voices would sound authentic behind Cliff Edwards, who did the voice of Jim Crow.

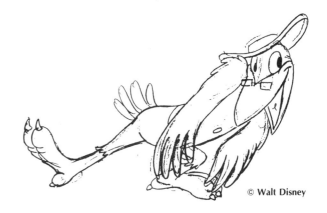

© Walt Disney

A Kelly animation drawing of a dancing crow from the Disney feature film *Dumbo*.

When we did this sequence, nobody talked much about it; but at the preview it got a big hand, and then everyone realized that the scene of the crows teaching Dumbo to fly was one of the highlights of the film. We didn't get any racial protests until later with *Song of the South*, which was picketed by the NAACP.

2. Moore is noted for the charm his animation brought to Disney characters; he helped set the look of the Seven Dwarfs and designed the cuter, more flexible Mickey of the late 1930s.

3. The projection room where test animation was screened while a secretary took down comments from the director and animators. The name "sweatbox" is a holdover from 1931, when the staff would pack themselves into the space below the stairwell to watch film on a Moviola viewer.

4. Swift was an assistant animator at the Disney Studio who went out on strike in 1941. He became a television writer and creator of the popular *Mr. Peepers* show, and later returned to Disney's to direct *Pollyanna* (1960) and *The Parent Trap* (1961).

Then, from the early fifties on, you never saw *Dumbo*. Because of the black crow sequence, the Studio was afraid to re-release that picture for years. It made its second debut at the Montreal Film Expo in 1967. This was after Walt's death. The Canadian Film Board was presenting awards to some of the old-time animators, and for the final night, out of all possible American films that could have been shown, they requested Walt Disney's *Dumbo*. The Studio was surprised and worried. There was a big discussion on whether we should send the film up there. "Look," I said, "this isn't an audience of your redneck, blue-collar, midwestern apple-pie people; these guys are film connoisseurs!" Finally Card Walker[5] reluctantly said okay. So there I was in Montreal, and they ran not the big live-action pictures that were winning awards at Cannes, but *Dumbo*. And it brought the house down. The whole place cheered when my crow sequence came on. I get goose bumps just thinking about it.

Did you work on any Mickey Mouse shorts with Kelly?

We did only one together. It was a terrible thing called *The Nifty Nineties* directed by Riley Thomson,[6] who didn't know one end of a director's chair from another. The animation I did on this cartoon was terrible. Kelly did a whole sequence illustrating the song "Father, Dear Father, Come Home with Me Now"—a takeoff on an old lantern-slide show. He drew a caricature of Lou Debney[7] wearing a little girl's blond wig and singing the song. Every time the film cut to this little girl on stage singing, she'd be crying a little harder, until at the end she had a complete breakdown, sobbing and standing knee-deep in gushes of tears. It was so funny that Fred Moore and I fell down laughing when we saw it. But Walt [Disney] thought the in-joke and little-girl animation were gross and decided to cut them out. Now you see only the lantern slides, with the singing voice offstage.

© Walt Disney

Kelly drew most of the preliminary storyboard sketches for the 1941 Mickey Mouse short *The Nifty Nineties*.

What was it like working with Kelly?

We found out we had a lot of things in common. For instance, he played the tin whistle—or six-hole flageolet, which I also played. And like me, he played a little harmonica. Our favorite pastime was when he and I would make our early morning trip to the men's john. When he felt the urge, he would stop by my room, tin whistle in hand, and ask, "Ready?" And my reply was always, "Ready!" I'd grab my tin whistle, and we'd walk to the room at the end of the hall and occupy the only two adjoining stalls. We'd sit down and play duets. We loved that men's room, because it was lined with tile, which gave our musical renditions Carnegie Hall reverberations. We'd play things like "Alabammy Bound" and "Tuck Me to Sleep in My Old Kentucky Home." Kelly loved all those Southern tunes. Even though he was very East Coast—and nothing is more eastern than Darien, Connecticut—he was enamored of the South and its music, with that "you-all" syndrome.

Well, we'd play these tunes, and if he was real knocked out with any of our improvisations, he'd yell, "Eatin' peanuts by the peck!" That meant it was real good. And we'd laugh like hell. Other guys would come in wanting to use the johns and plead, "All right, you guys, get your asses out and give somebody else a chance." After a concert we'd pack up and go back to my room, or go to Fred's room and try out some of the tunes on him. We'd say, "Listen to this,

5. E. Cardon Walker, Executive Vice President of Walt Disney Productions in the 1960s, is still on the Studio's board of directors.

6. Thomson was an animator who worked on Mickey Mouse.

7. Debney was an assistant producer who later worked on most of Disney's True Life Adventure films.

Fred!'' And he'd say, ''Oh Jesus, do I have to?''
Sometimes I would play drums on the wastepaper
basket, or Kelly would play rhythm. We also played a
zither. It was a terrible sound, but we enjoyed it for the
humor involved.

We had a lot of fun in those days. The gag
drawings flowed back and forth. We had Dave Swift
drawing gags, Kelly drawing gags, I was drawing
gags, Marc Davis was across the hall drawing gags,
Tom Oreb was doing it—everybody seemed to be
making funny drawings.[8] It was characteristic of
young employees at the Disney Studio then: if something that happened amused you, you drew a gag
about it, a little extension of it. Virgil Partch was
doing it, and Larry Clemmons; and Bill Peet in the
story department found time to join in.[9]

What sort of gags?

Caricatures mostly; there were all sorts of caricatures floating around. A little pornography, too, but
Kelly didn't indulge in that; he stuck with very
innocent, basic humor. His gags were exaggerated
illustrations of what really happened, but with a twist.
He would put situations in a different or impossible
setting, elevating his sketches above documentary
reporting. For instance, if we played touch football
during the noon hour, he'd come back and do a
drawing of our activities but would make himself the
coach. Because of all the hair on my chest, he would
draw a gag of me being expelled from the team for my
tacky appearance. Silly stuff like that.

When it rained, we played touch football in the
little narrow corridor that opened onto our various
rooms. Fred and I would team up against Tom Oreb or
Dave Swift or Kelly. We'd kick off in the middle of
the corridor. Everybody in the adjoining rooms would
shut his door in self-defense, because the football
might ricochet and knock over a lamp or a stack of
drawings. How we managed not to break the automatic

Kelly worked on the Lampwick sequence in Disney's *Pinocchio.* Here he caricatures Kimball and Fred Moore as Lampwick and Pinocchio.

ceiling sprinklers, I'll never know. Kelly used to
object to my playing because I wore these large orange
shoes with hard leather heels, which he thought were
dangerous to his health. I had metal taps on the front
and rear, and nobody wanted to be stepped on.

Is that how you spent your lunch hours?

Not always. Lots of times we'd go to the old Tam
O'Shanter restaurant for lunch. Fred, myself, Larry
Clemmons, Bill Cottrell,[10] and Kelly would sit and
gripe about the Studio over fish and chips. Kelly was
always the guy with the bow tie and dark suit. He was
very thin; he must not have weighed more than 145
pounds. He was the epitome of John Q. Public—five
foot eleven, little mustache, glasses—the character all
the old-time political cartoonists drew to symbolize
the common man, the guy the big trusts were always
leaning on.

Years later, in the early seventies, I was surprised
to see that he had ballooned way up to maybe two
hundred pounds or over. I had heard that Kelly was
hitting the sauce, but I personally wasn't there to see
it. I do know that when he was at the Studio he was
only a moderate drinker like the rest of us.

8. Davis is one of the Nine Old Men; he worked as a story
artist on *Bambi* and later specialized in animating villainesses like
Maleficent (*Sleeping Beauty*) and Cruella de Vil (*101 Dalma-
tions*). Oreb was a storyman who worked on *Make Mine Music,
Fun and Fancy Free,* and *Alice in Wonderland;* he later did
character styling for *Sleeping Beauty.*

9. Partch is best remembered for his *V.I.P.* and *Big George*
cartoons. Clemmons began at the Studio as an animator, left to
write for radio, and returned as a storyman. Peet was an accomplished sketch artist and storyman.

10. Cottrell began as Disney's first cameraman and eventually became a story director.

What's the story of your mutual interest in trains?

He was so damn amused that I had bought a full-size antique steam locomotive. It intrigued him, because anybody that didn't fit the regular mold was on his side. I would come back after a weekend railroad trip in the desert with Tom Oreb or Jesse Marsh,[11] and Kelly would say, "Let me know next time; I want to go along." One of the things I still feel bad about is that I didn't let him know about a couple of excursions before he left Disney's for good—because he just loved to ride behind a steam locomotive, he said.

Why did Kelly leave the Disney Studio?

When the strike happened in 1941, he liked the guys who were in the lower echelon, the inbetweeners and assistants who were the bulk of the strikers, and he had friends in the so-called "executive" branch: Fred, myself—we were supervising animators—and Bill Cottrell, who was a supervising storyman. So he refused to take sides, and instead of going out on strike, he simply resigned from the Studio.

Before he went east, he came back to the Studio one last time to get some of his personal stuff. I was working then on *Fun and Fancy Free*—we called it "the Mickey feature"—drawing a scene where Mickey, Goofy, and the duck are starving: all they have to eat is one little bean, which Mickey cuts into slices so thin they are transparent. The characters sing a song about food; my animation exposure sheet was titled "Goofy sings song." Kelly came into my room while I was away from my desk. He sat down at the desk and made a sketch of himself looking at my drawing of Goofy with a quizzical expression on his face. The caption says: "This ain't the Kimball we knew once and loved well." Later, when I found out that he had been in to say good-bye, I felt so sad that I had missed him.

Actually he had wanted to leave Disney's all along, because animation was a little hard for him: he was basically a comic-strip and gag man. The art of making things move, and the mechanics involved, seemed insurmountable to him. Not that he couldn't do it, but he wanted to have more fun doing his own

Kelly left this sketch on Kimball's drawing board when he visited the Disney Studio for the last time and failed to find his old friend in. It spoofs Kimball's animation of Goofy in *Fun and Fancy Free*, a film Kimball was working on at the time.

thing. This is a problem in any animation studio: you get a bunch of artists together who are various types of egocentrics, and they want to do things their own recognizable way. That's why you can never really organize a good, solid union among artists, because they don't seem to like being team players. That was one of the things I had to learn when I went to work at Disney's: I had to be a team player, and I had to subvert a lot of my creative instincts so I could conform and work with the other animators.

So Kelly went back east and did comic books. Sometimes he'd use his old friends as characters in his stories and send us the printed comics: Dave [Swift], Tom [Oreb], and all the guys. Then all of a sudden he took off on that southern cornpone swamp syndrome and became a success with his new *Pogo* comics.

What were your first impressions of Pogo?

At first I couldn't understand the southern dialect; it was like a foreign language. A lot of people wrote to the editors and complained about this, and as a result, he simplified the language. His first dialogue was authentic, I guess, spelled the way he thought the words sounded.

How did the southland atmosphere of Pogo *originate?*

As I said, he loved anything about the South. When he was at Disney's, if Edna Ferber's *Showboat* would come to town, or any show that had that old hokey southern stuff, he'd go to see it two or three

11. Marsh was a story artist during his tenure at the Studio; he is best remembered for the *Tarzan* comics he drew for Western Publishing's Dell series.

Kelly's gag drawing of himself, Kimball, Larry Clemmons, and Fred Moore performing as showboat entertainers.

Kelly was a fan of the Edna Ferber musical *Showboat*. In "Old Man Ribah" (Old Man River) he caricatures himself as the black retainer, Fred Moore as the heroine, Larry Clemmons as the riverboat gambler, and Kimball as the captain.

times. Then he'd draw gags about his friends based on his memories of the show. He'd cast Larry Clemmons as the gambler—the city slicker, the fast-talker. I was always the captain of the boat. Fred would be the girl or blond lady, and Kelly would take the part of the old colored retainer. He never talked in southern dialect, only wrote it; but he would remember all the lyrics from *Showboat* and use excerpts when he drew up a gag for us.

It must have been hard for you when he left the Studio.

It didn't hit me until a month later. Then I felt that I had lost a great friend, someone I really depended on for bouncing crazy things off of. And I think it was the same way with him. All of a sudden there was a big vacuum without Kelly around. I said many times later that he was the only friend who went out of my life that I missed terribly and felt bad about for two or three years afterwards. I just loved having him around; we got along great together. The common bond of being fellow tin-whistle players, and liking to sit around with a drink and grouse or laugh about conditions at the Studio, had suddenly evaporated. It was a sad event in my life.

I suppose we were both mavericks: our in-house gags and humor were not altogether the type of thing that fit into the Disney concept. I was always thinking up a new or unique way to treat a situation, and many times I would get shot down. I suppose my batting average was around five hundred. Kelly began to realize that he couldn't always design his own characters and situations; he had to conform to the team concept. So he did what was right for him: he became his own boss.

Every Disney artist has had to come to terms with those pressures.

That's why I sought outside hobbies and activities, so I wouldn't go crazy doing the same thing every day. That's why I took up the railroad hobby and why, even though I was at the Studio, I started doing gag pages for an antique-car magazine. I had been to art school for two and a half years and was trained to do oil and watercolor painting, as well as life drawing. Drawing with a pencil at Disney's, eight hours a day, fifty-two weeks a year—unless you got a vacation—was a discipline I wasn't used to. It became important

to me to break it up by following other artistic avenues on the side. Some made a little money and some didn't; but I kept it up.

I suppose the style of *Toot, Whistle, Plunk, and Boom* and *Melody Time* was my attempt to break away from the Disney look. Everybody said, ''You're crazy; he's going to shoot you down''—but Walt saw *Toot, Whistle* and loved it. There's where I came out batting a thousand.

Another time I was not so successful. When I saw the story sketches for *Alice in Wonderland*, I realized that every sequence in the picture was going to be mad, and how was I going to make a Mad Tea Party with all that competition? First I designed the characters, and they were approved; but then I decided to give the staging and timing a unique, surreal look. I even planned to have only the animation in color, with the backgrounds in the cross-hatched technique for John Tenniel. Mary Blair, who was designing backgrounds for the film, thought it was a great idea.

Not only did Walt shoot down my first scenes on the tea party, he N.G.'ed the idea of any change in the background style. His comment was, ''Ah, come on, give us that good old Kimball animation.'' So I redid the staging and timing to conform to the ''Disney look.'' As a result, the Mad Tea Party became just like everything else in the picture.

So, as I said, Kelly and I had that in common; we hated to be regimented into doing the same thing as everybody else. To this day I don't know how I survived my career at Disney's. People tell me I got away with more things than anyone else at the Studio, but that's because I tried to be *experimental* more. They don't realize how many times Walt said no.

How accurate is Richard Schickel's portrait of Disney in The Disney Version?[12]

Schickel's use of adjectives was his own, but it's not without a grain of truth. Walt did come back on Saturdays and Sundays and wander around the rooms to see what people were doing, to get ideas he could start thinking about; then he'd hit us Monday morning: ''I've been thinking; maybe the second sequence should have this . . .'' He'd been into our rooms, and that was an eerie feeling. Walt [Disney] always

12. Richard Schickel, *The Disney Version: The Life, Times, Art and Commerce of Walt Disney* (New York: Simon and Schuster, 1968).

seemed to know what was going on, but that was his nature. He was curious. He loved his studio. That's why he was a genius.

We'd criticize him lots of times and say he was a tyrant, but he was actually "fundamentally unorthodox" and ran the business the way he wanted to. A true rugged individualist. I can't criticize this, because he was successful. Look at the Disney Company today: they don't know what to do with their money.[13] Schickel had a lot of truths in his book—especially the financial figures, which he got pretty close—but a lot of the other stories he got second and third hand. I knew the source of a lot of them. If Schickel had asked me, I could have given him the truth, and it would have been more interesting and *funnier* than what he wrote. I'm not agreeing with him necessarily—even though he did say I was the "artistic conscience of Walt Disney" at the Studio.

That aside, there *were* a lot of things old Walt did that made people mad. Walt was a self-made man and —to use an old cliché—he was conservative in his politics, even though his folks were old-time socialists. The Disney Studio was Walt Disney; we were merely his tools. He created this thing; it was *his* stories, *his* gags, *his* conceptions, *his* decisions. He chose the people he felt would best carry out his ideas.

This has led me to the conclusion that the only great things in the world are done by individuals. All your great discoveries, new ideas, all your key achievements are made by individuals—not committees, not top-heavy corporations. Corporations are the worst thing that can happen, because nobody wants to be responsible and to say yes or no. When Walt was building Disneyland, he would see things that were wrong as they were starting to put the park together; and at great expense he would knock them out and put in something else. That seldom happens now. I ran into that problem of rigidity on the ride I designed for General Motors at EPCOT. Even on improvements that would cost little or no money, the response was, "Ah no, that's they way we okayed it." Walt had flexibility; he was always in the creative process. Right up to the end he was changing and fixing things to make them better.

13. This part of the interview was taped in 1981, before the new regime of Michael Eisner, Jeffrey Katzenberg, and Frank Wells had turned Disney's company around and made it into one of America's major film studios.

Schickel implies that Disney's workers were afraid of him.

We were all basically afraid of him. He had a habit of criticizing you in front of your co-workers; he was very bad about that. "Jesus Christ, that's a *dumb* idea," he'd say. And people felt embarrassed. He wasn't the type of employer who would wait until a meeting was over to call you into his office and say in private, "I didn't like your idea and I still don't like it, but maybe if you develop something out of it . . ." Instead he'd blurt right out. People got so they wouldn't speak up, and that was bad.

I told him this once when we were on a trip back to Chicago in 1948. The first vacation of his life, he took with me. The doctor had told him to relax, and he said to himself, "Who has more fun than Kimball? He likes railroads." Walt always liked them, too; so he called me up, and a week later we took the old Santa Fe Super Chief to Chicago to see the fair "Railroads on Parade." That was a long train ride: two and a half days. Walt would open a decanter of whiskey along about five o'clock, and we'd have a drink. One evening, as we were rolling across the plains, he said, "I can't understand it: people don't speak up in the story meetings. Why do the guys just sit around?" I said, "I'll tell you why: it's because you jump on them. If they make a suggestion that you don't like, you bawl them out."

"I don't do that!" he said. "Yes, you do," I replied. I told him a lot of things on that trip. But he would never admit he was wrong about anything. He would argue with me why he kept certain people at the head of their departments even though they were causing chaos and costing money. At first he would defend them; then maybe two months later they were gone.

On the good side, I'll always defend his genius for story, for staging, for gags, ideas, imagination, as against his habit of being a cross old bear at times. I always felt it was part of the game, and I didn't allow myself to be personally aggravated by the guy, as so many people did who quit. If one accepted his genius and wanted to work at the Studio—he paid well in most cases—one had to accept these idiosyncrasies. That's how I understood the situation. Consequently, I was able to survive; so were a lot of others. Those who were too egotistical about their work and who couldn't bend to the team operation, quit in a huff. He was a complex man; but we were afraid of him, basically. I don't think he had many close friends in the world, no buddy-buddy fishing buddies—never.

But he had a good sense of humor?

Well, humor was a serious business with Walt. Part of his genius was demanding that humor be part of the story line and endemic to the characters. He seemed to see things from an audience viewpoint. You couldn't tell Walt a dirty joke. He was pretty naïve about backroom humor.

Back to Kelly. Did you keep in contact with him after he left the Studio?

We kept in touch by letter. He lived in Darien, Connecticut, at Old King's Highway and Fairmead Road. I would send him résumés of what was happening during the strike, and he'd send me idiotic pictures—he'd find awful snapshots and talk about them. [Kimball starts to leaf through an album of letters.] This is one I love:

To Fred and Ward: Two Clever Boys from Illinois.

It is with the greatest of pleasure that I take pen in hand on this occasion to greet you and send kindest good wishes to you and yours. We have not had much rain here; the East is in fine shape, and crops are doing well. You will be glad to know this, I know. [This is a takeoff on those silly Christmas letters, I suppose.] In regard to other matters, to wit, health: I am fine—a little weary but fine, just as fine as fine is fine. You will doubtless be interested to learn that the train trip across these good Newnited States of ours was the longest sonofabitchin' trip that it has ever been my misfortune to endure in lo! these twenty-seven years, ten months of my existence. When you get tired of staring out the window, you stare at the dumb bastard across the aisle. The dumb bastard across the aisle was a splendid character, and we got to be fairly good friends. Of course, I was never able to persuade her to come into a berth with me, but if the train had gone on for another day or two, I am quite confident that a deal would have been worked with the conductor, who from the rear was as handsome a gentleman as these eyes have beheld in some, I might say, time.

So: to how are things, unquote—which we may safely assume you would ask me. Gentlemen, the answer to that one is—confidentially—stinko, with a capital STINK. Come plague, come strike, come pestilence, death, or five hundred feet with Bert Gillett,[14] nothing, good sirs, is as bad as neurotic acrobatics in the family. If worse comes to worst, I may be here for another month or more. Seriously,

it's not so good here like it's good where you are. However, the strike is probably doing nothing for your peace of mind, either. Sure hope one side or the other dies off or something before everything goes to pot. I've enough to worry about without fighting picket lines. I notice that a good many men in newspaper photographs of the picket line were amongst those sterling gentlemen who were canned a month or so ago after living on charity for a good many years. [He always thought a lot of guys on strike weren't worth a shit, anyway.] There's really a brisk undercurrent of war sentiment in the East. This section especially works in twenty-four-hour shifts on large armament orders. It indicates that a lot of these agitators would do well to keep their noses clean for the next few years, because there's already talk of slackers, reds, and spies. There are more cops and plainclothesmen in Bridgeport than in all of Warner's movies put together. There are a few more items to go through, but that's all the paper there is. Drop me a line—

Kelly [1941]

And here's his reply to a letter I sent him about the strike. He thought it was great, because I had written everything down as it happened.

Dear Fred and Ward:

Yours of some Goddamned date received and on hand. It may interesk both of you to know that a phew more days here and I hope to be heading back to the western frunk. Thanks for the firsthand account of the battle. To date we have had only scattered reports from men farting in empty beer bottles in back of the lines. Yours is the first on-the-scenes description. A native boy broke through last week and ran to the nearest outhouse to report that the ice is not yet saved. I thought this would be valuable information in the event you started to drive on the old third and fourth tees. Some skirmishing has been going on here in the bushes at Beardsley Park. Local authorities claim that these are unimportant uprisings that usually wear themselves out without too much trouble.

A giant pincher movement is being planned in the event I do not see my wife fairly soon. "Beat me, Daddy, over to the bar" is being used as a marching song, and I have the eye of an old serviceman looking around for a new recruit. The summer campaign slogan is "Into the wenches by Christmas!" I had hoped to arrange for an arbitrated piece before this, but my arbitration isn't what it used to be. Thanks again for the detailed report, Ward and Fred. I've written to Hal[15] telling him how I feel about the setup; that name-calling jamboree made my back hair rise. I can just see Williams[16] and Riley [Thomson] taking it with a smile.

14. Gillett was a Disney director; five hundred feet would be an amount of film to animate.

15. Hal Adelquist was the Studio's personnel director at this time; in the 1950s he became a producer on the Mickey Mouse Club television show.

16. Roy Williams was a prolific gag writer for the Disney films.

Undoubtedly the Guild has lost friends by their methods. I'm real hopeful of getting back to California in a few days. That depends on my sister's condition. But unless I tell you differently, I'll be around and be called a sommoner bitch along with the rest of you loyal bastards within a week or so. Things are different in the East. I don't believe that the unions could put on the act here that they can in the West. Business is tougher, and that condition may spread over the whole country. Best to Swift and Oreb and the rest of the best to the west of the best. Good luck—

Kelblat [1941]

Did you hear after that letter that he wasn't coming back to the Studio?

No; he was looking for any excuse to get out of there, because he didn't want to take sides in the strike. Later I heard he was looking for work, and then he started doing comic books:

Saw *The Gay Caballeros* [*The Three Caballeros*] the other day in a preview, since I must work on a book dealing with the—uh—thing.[17] It wasn't bad; and in wartimes, with shortages and stuff, you can't expect one hundred percent Moore, Kimball, et al. What I mean is—I would have liked more of it. Who got in there with the live action camera? The birds, which I suspect you had something to do with, and the little boy who changes his clothes à la Fred, were swell—as with the penguin stuff. Next time send us a can full of animation—no more dancers, sorry.

About the paper I'm using: I swiped it from my wife, who is getting old and can't keep an eye on things. She joins me in wishing you, Betty, and company Merry Christmas—

Kelly [1943]

When our Studio jazz band, the San Gabriel Valley Blue Blowers, was starting in 1947, if I had a little flyer that we printed for a dance, I'd send it to him. It would always get a reaction: "The world's record in low gear run: a new jazz band is born. These boys are fine." That's something Kid Ory[18] said about us. And then he would do a paste-up that had nothing to do with it:

Painter dies at seventy-four of infected herds. Servants slain and buried with . . . [Something fell off there.] Walt Kelly, who made art a part-time occupation during his forty years' employment as a post was destroyed by fire today after an explosion shattered a cupola atop the five-story

17. *The Three Caballeros* was published as Dell Four Color Comic No. 71 in 1944.

18. Kid Ory was a New Orleans jazz trombonist who occasionally played in Kimball's home jam sessions.

wood and sheet metal structure. Red Cross workers were ordered to the scene by Mrs. William Sawyers, chairman of the Patchahogie branch of the organization, and the car with the afghan, where his wife, Betty and Julius Filsenstein, of 820 West End Avenue. Walter C. Kelly, of Old King's Highway, who had not returned, turned up at the prison gates promptly on schedule the day after Christmas. Pulling his .45-caliber automatic pistol, Private Hill ran around the finance building, encountering two men with revolvers. They fired point-blank at him and missed. Walt Kelly struck a girder of the new bridge, moving it about a foot and affecting the rails above.

[Kimball produces another clipping.] This is when I was learning to fly; Lou Debney, Roy Williams, and I all got our solo permits at Whiteman Airport about the same time. This must be a picture out of *Fly* magazine with my instructor. So Kelly puts a joke underneath:

"Well, Dinah, I hear you are married."
"Yes'm," said the former cook, "I'se done got me a man now."
"Is he a good provider?"
"Yes'm. He's a mighty good provider, but I'se powerful skeered he's gwine to git kotched at it."

Then, since we were the San Gabriel Blue Blowers, Kelly calls these cars [in the picture] the Blue Blowers. Later I sent him some of our early albums. He liked the music so much, he wrote program notes for one record, *The Firehouse Five Goes South*.[19] He drew a picture of Pogo blowing a horn and titled the notes: "Why Pogo Does Not Endorse This Album."

In 1958, when the World's Fair was coming up in Brussels, Kelly had the idea of getting a few American cartoonists together to put on a big show. He wanted

19. The Blue Blowers became the Firehouse Five Plus Two in 1949. "We went from one name to another," Kimball comments. "When we began playing for little parties at the Studio, our band was called The Hugga-Jeedy Eight, because that was the sound my old Model T Ford made while idling. During the war and right after, we had lots of sessions here in my livingroom; that's when we became the San Gabriel Valley Blue Blowers. Sometimes bands from New Orleans would be in town, and they'd come out here for all-day jam sessions. We became the Firehouse Five in the late 1940s, when the Horseless Carriage Club organized its first national tour of old cars. I was program chairman, and I said, 'Why don't we have a little band to play along with the parade?' I had a year to find an old 1914 fire engine and restore it, and to talk the guys into wearing fire hats and red shirts. We called our band the Firehouse Five Plus Two to let people know that if they hired us, they got *seven* instruments. Sometimes we'd have eight, with George Bruns, the Studio composer, playing tuba."

our band to provide music; said he couldn't think of a more red, white, and blue organization than the Firehouse Five Plus Two. We said sure, and everyone on the Fair Committee thought it was a great idea. Then came an ominous letter from Kelly:

Dear Ward:
The accompanying copy of a letter to the Fair Committee will perhaps leave you somewhat surprised; but it is, in my estimation, a mild protest against the inept sort of treatment which this cartoonist's proposal has received.
[1958]

You see, Kelly's All American Cartoon Show had to be sponsored by the State Department; and somebody pointed out to John Foster Dulles, our leading brinksmanship Secretary of State, that the fellow producing the show was one of liberal mind who had once lampooned Joe McCarthy in *Pogo*. That ended Kelly's plans; he got the cold shoulder, and they wouldn't return his calls.

Of course, McCarthyism had been going on for some time. We had our own communist investigations committee here in California; they were after motion picture actors, writers, and everybody. I remember the day they had Les Koenig, the producer of our Firehouse Five Plus Two records, on television before the hearing committee. At that time he was a five-thousand-dollar-a-week writer for William Wyler,[20] with an office at the Paramount Studio; but as a hobby, he was also producing our jazz records. They got him on the stand and said, "Mr. Koenig, were you ever a member of a communist red organization, or have you ever associated with any red organization?" He said, "Yes," God! All the committee members sat bolt upright; they thought that they finally had a real witness (everyone else was taking the Fifth Amendment). "Tell us, Mr. Koenig, what is this red organization?" Les replied, "It's the Firehouse Five Plus Two. They all wear *red shirts*." There was pandemonium; the committee got real upset. So we don't know whether this all filtered back and got distorted when Kelly wanted our band to play at his World's Fair show.

Here's a song he wrote for us to sing good-bye to

20. Wyler was director of *Wuthering Heights, The Best Years of Our Lives,* and *Roman Holiday.*

Rod Johnson when he went into the army in 1941— one of the first guys to be drafted at Disney's. Kelly roughed out the words on paper and then sang the tune to us till we learned it.

My Daddy Is a Patriotic Man

[This starts off with a drum-like military cadence: *Tat*-tat-tat-ta! *Rat*-tat-tat-ta!]

If you wonder why I'm leaving,
Little girl, please stop your grieving,
For your Daddy is a drummer in the band;
With his sticks and cymbals clashing
Into battle he'll go dashing,
Just to serve his native land.

And perhaps I'll be a sentry,
For I love my dear old *ken*try,
And I know that I will show my stand,
And a rappa-kappa-tooey
On the old skebot 'n' blooey,
And the frizzle-frazzle-froozie frand.

[Then we would go into a legato for the bridge:]

For this is a land of beauty . . . [pause]
And I am a man of duty . . . [pause]
So I'll leave you, little cutie Gallo wine . . .
[Tempo picks up here:]
With the army men a-humming,
And I'm off to do my drumming,
For your Daddy is a patriotic man—from Pas-a-*dee*-na . . .
For your Daddy is a patriotic man! . . . Wham!

We all stood up in the Studio commissary at lunchtime and sang this without any warning to the people eating there. In those days, every table had a big bowl of hard dinner rolls that nobody dared eat; they looked and tasted like they had been shellacked. When we finished the song, hundreds of these missiles came flying toward us, as though at a prearranged signal, and they felt like rocks bouncing off our heads. Evidently everybody had the same gut reaction to our singing—as you no doubt had when you heard me do it. Of course, Kelly loved something like this mass reaction to our collective efforts!

What kind of music did he like?

Dixieland jazz, that old-time band sound. Our band sounded like that, because of the banjo and the tuba. He liked our Firehouse Five Plus Two because he could hear the melody, and it had a good rhythm.

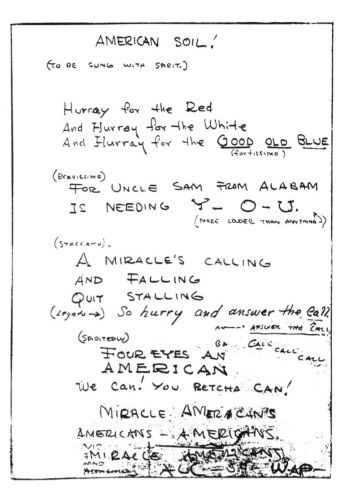

Sheet music for "American Zall," one of Kelly's mock-patriotic songs written during World War II, when many of Disney's employees were being drafted into the army. Kelly, Kimball, and Moore performed songs like this in the Studio commissary.

A panel from the *Pogo* Sunday page for April 16, 1950, in which Kimball appears as Kimbo Cat of the Firehouse Five Glee and Pilau Society (a takeoff on Kimball's jazz band, the Firehouse Five Plus Two).

Kelly loved to portray political confrontations. What were his own politics?

He was a liberal—he distrusted politicians. He was onto all of their tricks. He loved baseball: God, he loved baseball! He was a basic American; you know, he had that old Yankee suspicion of the city slicker. He was almost like a detective: suspicious of everybody and their motives. That's why, when he became very famous with *Pogo*, he never went into merchandising. I used to say, "Why don't we have Pogo dolls? You could make millions with them."

"No," he replied, "the sons of bitches never make the characters look like I want them to." Then I remembered that when Kay Kaymen, who was head of merchandising for the Walt Disney products, would make the rounds of the animation rooms with the latest Mickey Mouse toy or Disney character and hand out free samples to those who were raising kids, Kelly was very critical of the way they did Mickey. Of course, it's impossible to do Mickey in three dimensions. In those days, when we worked on a picture, the width of a line would vary the looks of a character. We all tried to draw alike. Then this stuff would come in from manufacturers who, lots of times, would be way off base. Kelly wouldn't think they did the character justice, and those experiences influenced him in not going into merchandising with Pogo. He *could* have made millions, as we all know.

When did you last talk with Kelly?

In 1969, right after the Pogo half-hour TV show that Chuck Jones directed,[21] which was a disaster. It was the last tragedy as far as Kelly's artwork was concerned. When I had lunch with him at Musso Frank's, I asked him, "How did you ever okay Chuck's Pogo story?" He said, "I didn't, for Godsake! The son of a bitch changed it after our last meeting!" I asked, "Who okayed giving the little skunk girl a humanized face?" Kelly's face turned red, and he bellowed, "Waiter! Bring me another bourbon!" Oh, that made him mad.

I said, "Chuck missed the whole satire of the piece, and your work is based on satire." He said, "That's not the way I wrote it. He took all the sharpness out of it and put in that sweet, saccharine stuff that Chuck Jones always thinks is Disney, but

isn't." He had come out to Hollywood for lots of meetings with Chuck to make sure that it would be a Walt Kelly story; and God! when he saw it, he wanted to kill—if not sue—Chuck. He said that when he left that final storyboard, it was the way it should have been on TV; he had gone over every little detail. I don't know how Chuck had the temerity to change it, but he did. That was the last time I saw Kelly—in a towering rage!

The following are excerpts which Ward Kimball read from his diary, made during Kelly's tenure at the Disney Studio:

November 18, 1939. Studio masquerade party. Walt Kelly and wife came to party as two goons wearing large hats.

February 15, 1940. Kelly tells me that he once imitated personnel director Herb Lamb's voice, chiding me about playing my trombone during working hours. [He'd called me up and bawled me out.]

February 22, 1940. After hearing Fred Moore and Ward trying to play slide whistle duets all afternoon, Kelly said we sounded like we were blowing into an empty toilet. [I was trying to teach Fred how to do it.]

January 25, 1941. Kelly remarks that he feels pretty discouraged about his future at the Disney Studio after Walt tells us all that we are running out of money and things look dark for Disney's.

February 8, 1941. Art Babbit,[22] who is trying to organize a union at the Studio, tells Walt Kelly in strict confidence that the trouble with Fred Moore and Ward Kimball is that they haven't grown up yet. They have a high school slant on things; they haven't had any problems to face yet.

February 18, 1941. Ben Sharpsteen walks in and catches Kelly and Kimball playing tin whistle duets.

March 17, 1941. Sterling Silliphant[23] approaches Fred Moore and Kimball to do chalk talk drawings for two kiddie afternoon shows at two theaters. We talk Kelly into being the MC. He okays the deal if he can have a few drinks before we go on.

March 22, 1941. Kelly, Fred, and Kimball meet

21. *The Pogo Special Birthday Special* aired on May 18, 1969.

22. Babbit was one of Disney's top animators; he drew the Queen in *Snow White* and designed Goofy's final look in the shorts.

23. Silliphant was publicity director at the Disney Studio; he later became a top screen writer.

at 11:30 A.M. at the Blue Evening for bourbon-and-sodas. We could hardly navigate when we left for the Stadium Theater on West Pico for the first show. Met Silliphant and theater manager. We went on after a Donald Duck short. Lots of kids in the house. Kelly droned on and on with unrehearsed doubletalk as Fred and I drew Disney characters. Kelly gave us a lot of asides which broke us up. Kelly at one point said to the audience, "I suppose you are wondering why Ward is wearing a railroad conductor's hat. Well, he's got a bald spot on the back of his head, and we told him to put black paint on it, but he refused and wore a hat instead." The kids clapped and liked our act.

We did the same routine again at the Fairfax Theater, to a better reaction. We were more sure of ourselves. The lights were hot, and I was sweating. [The kids would yell things like "Draw Donald the Duck! Draw Snow White!" We told Kelly that if the little bastards wanted us to draw Snow White, steer them away, because she was hard to draw. So when they'd yell for Snow White, Kelly would turn to us and say, "Gentlemen, we have another request for you to draw Donald the Duck." We got to laughing so hard that we would break our chalk, and I guess it became pretty obvious we were drunk.] Everything seemed to be going fine until a small bottle of gin fell out of Fred's pocket when he was rummaging around for a piece of chalk. This brought the act to a quick close, and I remember at the time, during the ensuing

excitement, the manager running out on the stage and saying, "You boys have got to get off! This is no good for the youth of America." Throughout it all, Kelly stuck to the mike telling Irish jokes.

March 24, 1941. At an emergency meeting of the key Disney people, while Walt explained the dire straits the place was in, and how everybody had to take a cut in salary and work hard, etc., Roy Disney praised Kelly, Fred, and me for taking our Saturday afternoon and doing drawings for the kiddies' matinees.

March 28, 1941. Article by Silliphant appears in *Studio Bulletin* about above chalk talks:

"Friday, March 28, 1941: *Kimball, Kelly, and Moore Wow 'Em at Theaters!* While MC Walt Kelly smiled glibly into the mike, troopers Ward Kimball and Fred Moore quick-sketched *Fantasia* characters for twelve hundred kiddies last weekend in two appearances at the Stadium and Fairfax Theaters' children's matinees. 'Well, we have to leave now,' Kelly archly said after a fifteen-minute period. Cries against departure went up from youngsters who flocked bug-eyed around the stage. The time was up, and leave they did. Agents of the Lyceum circuit are currently pressing contracts on the chalk talkers.'"

April 1, 1941. Ward handing out scenes to Kelly on "Dumbo" (the crow sequence).

April 29, 1941. Kelly and Ward make for laughs trying to do hula dance together.

Kimball, Fred Moore, and Kelly at the Fairfax Theater in Los Angeles, the day Moore brought their chalk talk to a sudden halt by dropping a bottle of gin.

A late 1930s photograph of Kimball, Kelly, and Moore playing instruments in what appears to be a jam session. In fact, this was only a pose for the camera; according to Kimball, Fred Moore was "very unmusical."

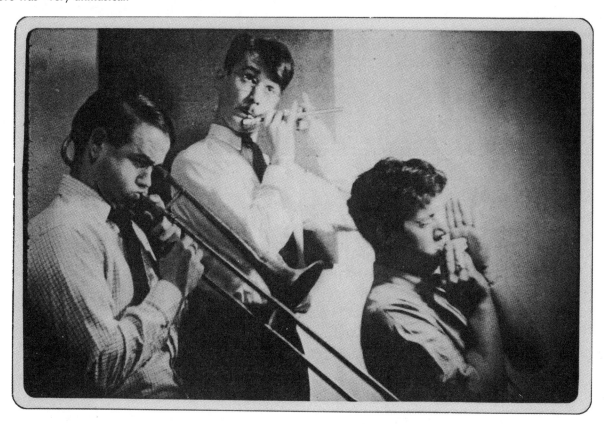

Ward Kimball's oil painting of himself, Kelly, and Moore based on the photograph.

Art Afterpieces

Ward Kimball and Walt Kelly maintained their friendship over the years. Therefore it was not surprising that Kelly wrote the introduction to Kimball's humor book on fine art masterpieces, Art Afterpieces, *which was published by Pocket Books (Simon & Schuster) in 1964. Kelly's intro is reprinted along with a few of Ward Kimball's "afterpieces," so you can see what Kelly was raving about.*

FOREWORD

✳

It is correct, we believe, to claim that Mr. Kimball's addenda, as they are collected in this volume, are original. The Parisian school of underground poster art says flatly, "Vive le moustache!" This group, claiming to be unique, has in fact produced nothing more than the additives of the mustache, the scrawl of eyeglasses, an occasional monocle (inevitably lopsided), and, if the viewer is lucky, he is treated to a blacked-out tooth in a creamy smile.

Then there are the hackneyed efforts of the imitative American alteration group, the so-called Subway Atelier in New York City. True, these monsters have made use of the added four-letter word across the faces of some of their subjects, but this is merely potential juvenile delinquency and to be classed with the accidental banjo-work of a messy monkey armed with a melting chocolate bar.

Now from the west rises a Lochinvar who is apparently a distinct cut above the messy monkey. In a talk with him this critic learned that Mr. Kimball, a youth of fifty, was disturbed about the publisher's estimate that his work was "unfailingly funny." According to Mr. Kimball, if his work is funny, it has failed. "Cheen Crimes!" exclaimed Mr. Kimball, his mouth full of melted chocolate bar, "this stuff is a lot deeper than they realize. It gets me right about here," he added, putting his hand to his throat.

For the fact of the matter is that Mr. Kimball is a master finisher. He finishes what others have started. Any bull can charge into a china shop, but the bull in this book ENDS the job.

Walt Kelly

AFTER THE HUNT

WILLIAM M. HARNETT

1848 · 1892

MISS WILLOUGHBY

GEORGE ROMNEY

1734 · 1802

THE WHITE GIRL

JAMES MC NEILL WHISTLER

1834 · 1903

Pogo Goes to College

No comic strip has yet surpassed Pogo in totally captivating two generations of American and Canadian college students. While other cartoon strips may have considerable popularity on campus today, Walt Kelly himself made the difference.

With endless energy Kelly traveled and lectured at campuses around the country. He didn't send out slick repro art to college publications. He drew them special art upon request. No present-day cartoonist has been willing to give of himself, his talent, and his time on a par with Walt Kelly.

This was not a one-shot deal. Kelly kept a killer lecture schedule for a good fifteen years. One wonders if the fact Kelly never himself attended college, in contrast with most of the newer syndicated cartoonists, was a factor in his enthusiasm for working hard at keeping Pogo Possum number one, the big possum on campus.

Tremendous research still needs to be done in the area of Pogo on campus. Sometimes luck plays a role. When I asked Jud Hurd for permission to reprint a piece by George J. Lockwood on Kelly, originally published in Cartoonist PROfiles, I had no idea I would discover photos from 1952 to illustrate the piece.

Kelly did so much on campuses that was undocumented by his syndicate or even himself that Pogophiles should delight in the "finds" for years.

Special thanks goes to Randy Shearer, Pogophile of note from California, who saved a number of Pogo-at-college photos from the move of the Field Syndicate. Traditionally syndicates are interested in one thing, money. When Selby Kelly decided to cease Pogo's syndication, Field Syndicate lost all interest in Pogo.

On orders of a senior executive in the late 1970s, when Field Syndicate was moving from New York City to Chicago, an entire bound run of Pogo daily and Sundays was destroyed. The syndicate didn't think it would ever make any more money from Pogo and didn't want to pay to ship the bound Pogo collection to Chicago. He could have donated it to the Museum of Cartoon Art or the Smithsonian Institution.

Field Syndicate had shown its true colors during the period Selby Kelly continued the strip by trying to sell other of its strips to replace Pogo. What they hadn't counted on was Pogo's many friends on newspapers calling Selby Kelly and tipping her off.

This digression serves a purpose as the Field Syndicate in a few years moved again from Chicago to the West Coast. There, somehow, Randy Shearer discovered a few Kelly and Pogo-at-college photos. It is also educational for those readers who think newspaper syndication is anything but extremely rough and tumble.

A promotion piece mailed to newspapers in the early 1950s had the headline "Pogo goes to college and enthralls the student body . . . and soul." The text of the promotion summed up Pogo's stature on campus.

"They ran him for President, voted him kingpin in popularity polls, picked up his catch phrases and made them bywords of the campus, started Pogo clubs, erected monuments in ice depicting the Pogo family of characters and have shown their admiration, loyalty and acclaim in a thousand enthusiastic mass activities across the length and breadth of the land."

The newspapers publishing Pogo were reminded that they shared in the advantages of Pogo partisan students. The promotion touted, "College students have a unique value as a vocal segment of your circulation who enthusiastically seek to share their pleasures with the World." Remember, this was the early 1950s.

As it is impossible to be even close to complete on Pogo's college presence, this is a visual presentation of some of the items that have surfaced. Thanks to Californians Tom Andrae and Geoffrey Blum for sending in a photocopy of "The 3ARS (Est Celare Artem)", a six-page comic-book-style Pogo story drawn in 1952 for The Pelican, the humor magazine of the University of California at Berkeley.

Kelly also didn't overlook his fans in high school. He made an absolutely charming drawing in 1952 in the spirit of The Belles of St. Trinian's by Ronald Searle for the yearbook of St. Ann's Academy, Victoria, British Columbia. The yearbook is dedicated to "Their Royal Highnesses, Princess Elizabeth and the Duke of Edinburgh." On October 22, 1951, the school had gone "on that cold, bleak, stormy day" to see the royal couple on their visit to Victoria.

Throughout his first years of syndication, Pogo was always very popular in Canada.

The selection here includes material from Cornell, Temple, Virginia Polytechnic Institute, the University of Illinois, Tufts, Dartmouth, the University of Arkansas and the University of Virginia, and this only scratches the surface.

B.C. JR.

One of Pogo's first successes in college publicity was in 1950 when he was awarded an entirely original honorary degree, Ow.L. (honoris causa) from Temple University.

Kelly drew special cover and inside artwork for the student magazine, The Owl. The story from the June 1, 1950, Philadelphia Bulletin *reprinted here shows the cover artwork. Joan Guerin's feature story, "Walt Kelly . . . Modern Aesop" is reprinted in its entirety.*

THE COVER

Copr. 1950,
Post-Hall
Syndicate, Inc.

(*Above*) The bluebird of happiness had to urge hesitant Pogo to uncoil his Bachelor of Arts degree when he received it for creating cartoonist Walt Kelly. But on the cover, Pogo, a veteran of hundreds of daily and Sunday cartoon strips, proudly takes his bows before madly applauding friends who are seated on the front row of Convention Hall, with lesser intellectuals behind them. He has just received an honorary degree of Ow.L. for "his outstanding accomplishments in bringing hilarious entertainment and profound satire to millions of chuckling readers."

Reprinted from the *Philadelphia Bulletin*
Thursday, June 1, 1950

Pogo Gets a Degree at Temple For 'Hilarious Entertainment'

By HARRISON W. FRY *Of The Bulletin Staff*

Pogo Possum—possum by trade—of the cartoon strips has received an exclusively new, entirely original degree Ow.L. (honoris causa) from Temple University's student magazine, The Owl.

The Commencement issue of the Owl is dedicated to Pogo and his pals—Albert, the alligator; Porky Pine, Howland Owl, Beauregard Bugleboy, man's best friend; Chug Chug Curtis, the Boll Weevil and the other forest folk who daily and Sunday appear in Bulletin comics.

Adorns Cover Page

The cover page of the magazine is devoted to Pogo wearing academic garb, taking a bow from his pals and a Convention Hall audience.

And The Owl, on its inside title page, notes that Pogo receives its honorary degree for "his outstanding accomplishments in bringing hilarious entertainment and profound satire to millions of chuckling readers."

With this issue the editors turn the magazine over to new editors for next year.

Pogo is to the comic strip readers of Temple—and elsewhere for that matter—what the "Perils of Pauline" were to the silent flicker audiences, Joan Guerin, of the Owl staff writes in a feature article on Walt Kelly, the creator of Pogo.

'Oldest Boy Artist'

Thirty-six-year-old Kelly, who describes himself as the oldest boy artist in the country, was an associate editor of a school magazine himself—and a writer of poetry, a cartoonist for it and a member of the school glee club.

The first two years of his life were spent in idleness but after a bit of migrating about to Hollywood and places of less glamor he finally settled for Bridgeport, Conn.

For a time he worked in the Walt Disney studios and the animal theme became an obsession.

Originally Kelly's animal parade was not the present lineup. It centered about a little Negro boy, Bumbazine, and his friends of the swamps and fields of the South—turtles, alligators, rabbits and the like. They were the forerunners of today's Pogo strip characters.

Characteristics Explained

Miss Guerin, in her feature article, quotes Kelly: "Albert, the alligator, is what we think of the other fellow. Pogo is the warm-hearted little guy we would like to think we are. Porky, the porcupine, sees the sour side and acts it, but underneath he has a heart of solid gold. Churchy La Femme, the turtle, is a reformed pirate captain who is having a lot of fun out of life. Howland Owl is a pseudo-scientist. Beauregard Bugleboy, the dog, is the sort of hound that always seems proud to be canine."

And Miss Guerin, in a final commencement tribute to Pogo, writes: "When neither aspirin nor your favorite psychiatrist can do a thing for you—remember—there's always Pogo."

Walt Kelly . . . Modern Aesop
by Joan Guerin

Strange undercurrents have been swirling through the hallowed halls of Temple University. Little comments have been heard here and there. "Did you read the latest *Pogo*?"; "Did the church mice get out of Albert?"; "Will Pogo save the 'Adams'?" For whipping up a near frenzy of enthusiasm, *Pogo* is to the comic strip readers of Temple—and elsewhere for that matter—what the "Perils of Pauline" was to the silent flicker audiences.

This being the case, there was nothing to do but thoroughly investigate *Pogo,* appearing daily and Sundays in the *Philadelphia Bulletin,* and its creator, appearing daily and Sundays in Darien, Connecticut, where he happens to live.

The man who ought to know the secret of *Pogo*'s success is the thirty-six-year-old artist and author, Walt Kelly, who very succinctly sums up the answer when he says he thinks people like *Pogo* because the characters in it are just plain friendly.

It is possible to enlarge on this and say that they're friendly because they have little on their little minds but being friendly. Does the atom bomb faze them? Of course not! They collect the "Adams" (atoms to you) in boxes and plan to use them for fish bait. Even the end of their pocket-size newspaper business didn't find Pogo with ulcers or the literal-minded Bookworm drowning himself in the swamp. These instances are enough to point out that the characters are completely imperturbable—not too bright, but charming enough to create a friendly atmosphere.

However, friendliness must have one particular ingredient if it is to be a success. It has to be warm and *Pogo* is that, if you want to call an occasional dash of honest sentiment, warmth. Who for example could resist the porcupine, or Porky as he is known. He's the prickly, seemingly antisocial character who, as any reader can guess in one minute flat, is secretly palpitating to be accepted as a friend by all. When the porcupine clutches a badly beaten-up flower to his chest and haltingly and awkwardly delivers it as a present to a friend—that, folks, is sentiment, and the way Mr. Kelly does it, it's warm, too.

But what about Kelly the man, who thinks up all these nice, though eccentric, characters and incidents, and who describes himself as ". . . the oldest boy-artist in the country . . ."?

In case our local Chamber of Commerce is listening and interested, Mr. Kelly writes: "The first years of Walt Kelly's life were spent in idleness. This statement is not to be confused with the statement: the first two years of Walt Kelly's life were spent in Philadelphia. Both are true but the first is regrettable and the second is not. If a man must squander his youth, it can be done in Philadelphia with dignity and thrift."

Nevertheless, Philadelphia palled on the youthful Kelly, and he ". . . his mother, sister and a bag of animal crackers . . ." soon hied themselves off to that bustling city of the bright lights—Bridgeport, Connecticut. The first World War was just under way at this time, and two-year-old Kelly, the slacker, refused to join up. Instead, he hung about, figuratively speaking, palling on Bridgeport until he discovered that that strange sound he'd been hearing recently was the school bell.

Eventually, he got to, and graduated from high school, having been, and we quote: ". . . an associate editor of the school paper, a writer of poetry, a cartoonist, a member of the glee club and the only man in the senior class who could take apart a ukulele blindfolded. Though no useful purpose has ever been discovered for blindfolding a ukulele (they are not skittish like horses) . . ."

Kelly was now on his own and panting to conquer the world—or at least Bridgeport. He was being particular about what jobs he was going to take and decided on, in rapid succession, a position wrapping scrap cloth in a factory and a job ". . . smashing faulty switches . . ." (when he wasn't smashing his fingers) in an electrical appliance plant.

Whether or not any light switches survived, miraculously Mr. Kelly's fingers did and he next took a fling at the newspaper world. Having flung himself into it, he was assigned to reporting and later to drawing, which he had done once for the paper at a youthful thirteen. According to Mr. Kelly: "A pen was thrust into his hand and for two long years and an extra five per week he drew and redrew daily strips based on the life of P. T. Barnum, another heroic figure in Bridgeport life. . . . Every time the writer got P. T. Barnum to the deathbed, old P. T. would get a flash and his entire life would pass again before his eyes to the tune of six months' additional copy. Nothing that Barnum exhibited ever equalled the Colossal Resurrectional Process exhibited by Kelly and the writer.''

After this came the call of the wild—the wild West, that is, but let Kelly tell it. ''With an empty stomach and a purse to match, the Voyager headed for California, reputedly a public garden spot full of breadfruit and plum. The Disney Studios offered shelter there and it was not long before Kelly was the envy of every one of the apprentices as the only man in the crowd with two shirts. He had found one stuffed in a desk, and, like its previous owner, had used it for some time as a dust cloth. It finally occurred to him that it could be worn when he was not using it to carry his lunch in, and so he became known as Beau Walt. From this point forward Kelly acquired worldly goods in rapid order. He acquired a wife, who came equipped with an automobile. He acquired a desk calendar which told him the date, 1937. And after a few years he had acquired sufficient knowledge of animation and story work so that he could look busy at the drop of a strange footfall outside his studio door. . . . In these years Kelly made the acquaintance of Walt Disney. . . . Disney showed Kelly many tricks . . . not the least of which was the art of sauntering unconcernedly through the gate when one had taken two hours for lunch. Kelly admired Disney's acting and story ability and learned so much about character projection that he was one of the first characters projected into outer space when the studio began its reconstruction rumblings in early 1941.''

When he finally came down to earth, Kelly looked around him and found, much to his surprise, that he was back in New York, shopping around once more for a paycheck and a desk on which to park his feet. A comic book concern that offered both quickly snapped up the Disney graduate. He should have been satisfied, but it gradually came to him that the bucket of blood type of comic was not his forte. ''Besides,'' he says, ''the editor said that as an adventure man, I had better stick to drawing mice. So I concentrated on puppies, kittens, mice and elves. . . .''

The animal theme pursued him and in 1942 Mr. Kelly got the idea of drawing a comic strip concerning life in the swamplands of the deep South.

This strip, when worked out, was not the *Pogo* of today. It was, rather, about a little colored boy, Bumbazine, who was surrounded by the forerunners of the characters in the present *Pogo,* among them: opossums, an alligator, turtles, rabbits, and so forth.

The alligator soon grew into Albert, but Bumbazine was discarded, though lovingly so. Mr. Kelly felt that Bumbazine presented several difficulties, among which was the fact that he would have to grow up someday. Therefore, Bumbazine's qualities of ''. . . innocence, naivete, friendliness and sturdy dependability . . .'' were transferred to the opossum who became—naturally—Pogo Possum.

Pogo first appeared in the New York *Star,* after a few difficult years in which Mr. Kelly couldn't convince potential buyers of *Pogo*'s true worth. Once the public had seen the comic strip, strange pieces of mail began coming in. Kelly eyed them suspiciously for a few months, finally took his courage in one hand and a sample letter in the other and opened it up. Great Heavens! It wasn't a subpoena, it was a fan letter! After the first flush of victory had subsided, it took him no time to read through the rest of the mountainous pile that was blocking all the exits. As Kelly tells it, ''The fan mail convinced the editors that either *Pogo* was popular or Kelly was very busy writing letters. Kelly managed to do a few political cartoons also in this period. Shortly after the presidential campaign of 1948, the New York *Star* ground to a halt. The carpetbaggers leapt from the smoking windows and with them went Kelly bearing in his arms the infant *Pogo.*

''Wandering about aimlessly on the sidewalk at the time was a street vendor named Robert M. Hall. As luck would have it, Kelly landed directly in Hall's arms, and Hall, taking one look at Pogo, Albert, Walt Kelly and the other animals in the strip, struck Kelly smartly across the skull with an ironbound contract. *Pogo* then went into the syndicate business and Hall followed him in, leaving his pushcart to Kelly.

''Kelly is still allowed to draw and write the strip and he admits that Hall does not make him pay very much for the privilege.''

This brings the Kelly saga up to the present moment.

When properly pinned down, Mr. Kelly will divulge some of the secrets to the true characters of the star players in *Pogo*.

"Albert," he says, "is what we think of the other fellow. Pogo is the warmhearted little guy we would like to think we are. Porky the porcupine sees the sour side and he acts it, but underneath he has a heart of solid gold. Churchy La Femme (the turtle) is a reformed Pirate Captain who is having a lot of fun out of life. Howland Owl is a pseudo-scientist. He is convinced that he knows everything so he plunges into every experience with the confidence of ignorance. Beauregard Bugleboy (the dog) is the sort of Hound that always seems proud to be canine. Although he talks about himself all the time, actually he possesses many of the qualities he boasts about. . . ."

Mr. Kelly says that he has always been fond of drawing but feels that art should serve a definite purpose. Actually he likes writing the strip as much as doing the artwork. All those who think comic strip work looks too easy to call for much effort on the part of the creator should heed Mr. Kelly who says: "I work hard. Inspiration is only the result of long concentrated thought." He adds, "It's fun though. I enjoy doing every strip—this is unusual perhaps."

Unusual perhaps, but this obvious enjoyment of his work comes through in sparkling fashion in *Pogo*. Nothing quite as zestful has turned up in a long time.

When neither aspirin nor your favorite psychiatrist can do a thing for you—remember—there's always *Pogo*.

by JOAN GUERIN

George Lockwood on Walt Kelly

George J. Lockwood was managing editor of the Syracuse University (NY) Daily Orange *when he first met Walt Kelly in May 1952. They became friends and when Lockwood was in the U.S. Navy after college, Kelly would send him autographed copies of new* Pogo *books.*

In the 1960s, George Lockwood became magazine editor of the Milwaukee Journal's *Sunday magazine,* Wisconsin Insight. *The article by Kelly for the February 22, 1970,* Insight, *"The quizzical Kids: An understanding cartoonist appraises the youth of today and finds*

them NOT wanting," was reprinted with special artwork drawn by Kelly in Pluperfect Pogo (1987).

When Kelly died in fall 1973, George Lockwood wrote in an editorial, "When Walt Kelly pointed out the hypocrisy and sham in our [political] system, he did it with a sense of purpose; he was a cartoonist with a conscience."

Our thanks to George Lockwood and to Jud Hurd, publisher of Cartoonist PROfiles *magazine, for letting this piece be reprinted.*

It was the spring of 1952. Negotiators were trying to resolve the war in Korea. Dwight D. Eisenhower was on his way to the Republican presidential nomination and on the campus of Syracuse University, where I was a junior and newly named to the senior staff of the college newspaper, the smell of lilacs and apple blossoms was in the air in nearby Thornton Park.

The senior staff had invited Walt Kelly, the cartoonist, to visit the university to address the student body and judge the parade of floats during Spring Weekend, the last big college blast before final exams.

Kelly had become the darling of the college students of the fifties. Every afternoon in the Acacia fraternity house there was a tug-of-war over the *Syracuse Herald-Journal.* Everyone wanted to read *Pogo,* the most sophisticated comic strip of its time and perhaps the finest cartoon ever to appear in American newspapers.

I can still remember, vividly, John Lake, a fraternity brother and the sports editor of the college daily, rolling on the living room rug and laughing his heart out over Pogo and Porkypine or Albert the Alligator and the other characters that paraded through Kelly's wonderful strip.

And so on that warm spring afternoon, when a bunch of us drove down to the New York Central train depot on Erie Boulevard to meet Kelly and his wife, Stephanie, I was in a state of euphoria. Up until that day about the only person of consequence I had ever met was the early morning farm announcer on station WGY in Schenectady, N.Y.

Kelly was everything I had hoped for. Gregari-

ous, fun-loving, open, friendly and best of all, a first-rate conversationalist. Years later he would describe himself as "the last of the great barroom talkers."

And he brought with him several hundred "I Go Pogo" buttons which were devoured in a matter of hours by students on their way to class. One of the story lines in Kelly's strip that year had Pogo running for the presidency (presumably of the United States), a campaign that was ill-suited to the bashful marsupial who wished only to escape the tumult and the shouting of a boisterous political campaign. But the comic strip

Mimi Hannon of Syracuse University presents Walt Kelly the key to the university and the student body's heart during his spring 1952 visit.

Walt Kelly loads a cannon owned by Alpha Tau Omega fraternity at Syracuse University in May 1952. The cannon was fired to announce the arrival of Pogo at the university's campus. Alpha Tau Omega brothers Bradley Deed and Richard Kemp look on.

campaign was all in good fun; it provided Kelly with a platform for his college appearances (he loved college kids and for that matter everybody else, too) and provided Pogo with nationwide exposure, a fact not overlooked by his newspaper syndicate which distributed the strip to some 400 newspapers in the fifties.

For the next two days Kelly was omnipresent on campus. At an open house in the student union, he gave a chalk talk to an enthralled audience that wouldn't let him leave until every last *Pogo* character had been drawn on butcher paper, appropriately autographed and handed out as a memento which, I am sure, is treasured to this very day.

Kelly's biggest test on campus was a guest appearance in Archbold Stadium, the football field where most of the student body of eight thousand turned out for a variety show to help raise money for a new fieldhouse. He shared billing with Charles A. Noble, dean of college chapel, and the most popular personality on campus.

There was some apprehension on my part that Kelly could hold his own, let alone match quips with Dean Noble who was famous in central New York for his after-dinner talks and his inspirational sermons Sunday mornings in Hendricks Chapel.

I had no need to worry. Kelly and Noble were instant hits, tossing out one-liners and teasing each other to the positive delight of the student body. It has

been thirty-one years since they performed on that makeshift stage and I have long forgotten their jokes. But I will never forget Noble, a Methodist minister, and Kelly, an Irish cartoonist, holding the spotlight that night while students held their stomachs laughing.

That's what made Kelly such a special person. He had both the gift of gab and the gift of humor. He was a gentle man who could find something entertaining about the worst of the characters in the real world. And he could also be as indignant as hell over some human stupidity.

In later years, when business took me to New York City, where Kelly lived, I never neglected to telephone him and arrange a meeting. He was always available for his newspaper friends and generally we would arrange a lunch. It seldom lasted more than four hours.

By the time the sixties rolled around, Milwaukee was making headlines with open-housing marches and Kelly would pump me for information on the details. He was never satisfied with a sketchy outline of what he considered important news. Injustice, racial prejudice, political demagoguery, or cultural hypocrisy were red flags to Walt Kelly. He was a liberal in the

Walt Kelly shakes hands with his verbal sparring partner Charles A. Noble, dean of the Syracuse University college chapel. The two passed friendly quips before eight thousand students in early May 1952, as described in George Lockwood's piece from *Cartoonist PROfiles* magazine.

truest sense of the meaning and could not, would not, understand why some Americans like to belittle their less fortunate brothers.

Once during a long and sometimes heated dinner conversation over civil protest, I tried playing the devil's advocate with Kelly. He was in no mood for my arguments and dismissed them—and me—out of hand. The conversation came to an abrupt halt, Kelly paid the check (he always paid the check) and he stomped off into the night, angry as a wet hen that I would even consider that injustice had a flip side.

But he never stayed angry. The next time I saw him he was as cheerful as ever.

Walt was generous to a fault with his time and his talent. He might charge *Newsweek* magazine, for instance, several thousand dollars for an original drawing, but when I asked him to prepare a full-color cover for *The Journal's* Sunday magazine in 1964, he wouldn't charge me a cent. He asked that I donate the paper's customary rate for such work to a charity of my choice. And in the name of *The Journal,* not his own.

As a habitué of a number of mid-Manhattan bars, he was known and loved by a wide aassortment of patrons and characters. On one of my annual visits to the Big Apple, he invited my wife, Eileen, and me to join him and Stephanie Kelly for dinner and drinks at his favorite watering hole—Moriarity's on Third Avenue.

Not only did Kelly know the bartender and the assistant bartender, but he greeted just about everyone in P. J. Moriarity's by name, including patrons, the stock clerk, several hangers-on, the flower lady, the waiters and, of course, the busboys. He, like Will Rogers, never met a man he didn't like.

He was particularly fond of newspaper reporters. Jimmy Breslin, newspaperman and bon vivant, was one of Walt's frequent barroom companions. After Kelly's death in 1973, Breslin wrote the kindest words about Walt that I have ever encountered:

"Kelly probably made a lot of money over the years, but he didn't care about money, he just gave it away. He took care of everybody but himself—that he wouldn't do.

"He always told me that it did not matter how long you lived; the important thing was how far you got. Well, he got far enough; the pity is that he did not live very long (only 60 years). In this he was very thoughtless, because original minds arrive in our midst only every quarter of a century or so, and if they leave us too soon, as Kelly did, we are in trouble."

What Kelly did leave us was a legacy of graphic humor unmatched by any American cartoonist, before or since his death.

His political satire paved the way for such popular comic strips as *Doonesbury* and, more recently, *Bloom County.* His nonsensical verse, like "Deck Us All with Boston Charlie," compared favorably with that of Lewis Carroll. And his whimsy, generally unrecognized at the time he produced it, will some day be valued for its intelligence and for its cultural accuracy.

Walt Kelly was an original. Whenever I think about him my thoughts inevitably turn to a Christmas card he sent me in 1967. It was a reproduction of one of his daily strips and featured several of his cartoon characters looking over a huge inscription which read "God is not dead—He is merely unemployed." He signed the card "For Eileen (also George)—Steffie and Walt K."

You were right, Walt. Absolutely right.

Kelly Visits the University of Illinois

In mid-February 1960, eighteen years after his Syracuse University triumph, Kelly was still on the college lecture circuit. Reprinted here for the first time is the coverage in The Daily Illini *of Kelly's speech at the seventh annual Baldwin Human Relations Conference. Also reprinted is the* Pogo *daily published in* The Daily Illini *which subscribed to* Pogo *and a special drawing Kelly did for the editor of the campus newspaper. Quick sketches of* Pogo *were Kelly's stock-in-trade on these trips and many are no doubt framed and hanging in the homes of Pogophiles across the country.*

To Rich
Happy Day After
St. Valentine's Day.
from Pogo & Walt Kelly

WALT KELLY TOOK TIME OUT from his busy schedule on campus Tuesday to draw a quick cartoon for Daily Illini editor, Rich Archbold. Kelly, the creator of the nationally-syndicated Pogo comic strip, delighted an Auditorium crowd Tuesday night with his illustrated talk.

"Know Yourself" Is Pogo's Message Told by Walt Kelly in Baldwin Talk

"Know yourself," was the essence of the message cartoonist and Pogo father Walt Kelly instilled in an hour of lively but subtle humor which he gave a responsive audience Tuesday in the Auditorium.

"Our problem is that we don't understand ourselves," stated Kelly, the featured speaker of the seventh annual Baldwin Human Relations Conference. Without self-understanding it is impossible to comprehend the political and social problems of today, he believes.

However, he feels that, "if you can find out who you are and if you can talk to yourself," the problems will be solved. Language will be unnecessary and love important.

Optimism For Future

Kelly showed considerable optimism about the future of the United States along this line. He thinks the U.S. is well on the road to self-understanding.

Right now, Kelly said, we are in a doldrums with no driving aim or purpose.

In a news conference before his speech he said that the feeling of conservatism that he found among college students, "pretty well summed up the attitudes of the entire republic." He contrasted present views to those held by students in the late 40s or early 50s.

The human relations message of Kelly's speech was light and easy.

About the message of Pogo, Kelly said, "Cartoons can't teach you anything. They can only try to make you see what you already know."

He said that his "know yourself" was the same as the one reflected in his cartoons. "Each character in Pogo represents a different facet of one person—of every person," said Kelly.

The round-faced cartoonist, balding and with graying hair, then told what parts each of the Pogo characters play in our personalities.

Sketching as he talked, he told of the family in the Okefenokee swamp.

Can't Draw Possum

Pogo, of course, was first. "He started out to be a possum," said Kelly, "but I can't draw a possum." So he ended up looking more like a little boy.

"It was a good thing too," quipped Kelly. "We found out that far more little boys read the strip than possums."

Pogo represents that good, but often naive section of our nature.

"The politician type is represented by Pogo's friend Albert Alligator—he has a thick skin and a head to match."

Everything But Answers

"The Owl is like a college math professor—he has the answers to everything but the questions."

Both during the speech and at an earlier conference Kelly predicted political doom for his current figure, Fremouth. The boy bug candidate, supported by his mother and sister in the comic strip because he is a "good candidate," represents to Kelly many of our current politicians. "They don't know much about politics, the other candidates or even about themselves." Kelly dismissed the conversation about Fremouth by saying, "He'll never make the election."

The Puppy Dog in the strip was there because somebody told me that we needed a "cute" element, said Kelly. "But we don't use him much any more. I had enough of drawing red and blue pants on mice at Walt Disney."

Never did Kelly say things were Jes' fine.

THE VIRGINIA
Spectator

Vol. CXII, No.5   February Pogo Issue   25c

(*Opposite*) The cover of this February *Pogo* issue of *The Virginia Spectator* was printed in such strong dark colors that Albert's tone on the original is the shade of British racing green. Most of the detail lines are obscure on the original cover. The copyright notice says 1951 but this might be a February 1952 issue, given the time needed to print a magazine.

The serpentine wall in the background is a University of Virginia landmark designed by Thomas Jefferson.

THANKS,

Walt Kelly,

(creator of Pogo) . . .

. . . for being our

guest cartoonist.

Walt Kelly was guest cartoonist for the 1953 *Sentinel* of Virginia Polytechnic Institute. The publication was 5¼" x 7½" in size.

Kelly used his years of comic book experience to create this six page special story for a 1952 issue of The Pelican, *the humor magazine of the University of California at Berkeley.*

I IS BEEN SHOT AT AN' *STABBED AT*...... THE RABBLE HAS ARIZ

A STUDENT *REE-VOLT.* *HELP!* *HELP!*

NOW, OF COURSE THERE IS THE LI'L' MATTER OF THE *LUNCH!*

HEY! THAT'S *REALLY* NOT LUNCH.

YOU MIGHT BE ABLE TO FOOL THE *FACULTY*, SON, BUT STUDENTS LIKE ME IS THE SOUL OF *PERSPI-CASSIDY.*

AWRK!

RAT-A-TAT TAT...

I'M GONNA SUE SOME-BODY.

I BRUNGED OL' WOODPINKER AS A *NATURE* EXHIBIT.

A CERTAIN PERCENT OF THE STUDENT BODY IS GITTIN' NEW HOLES FOR ITS HEAD.

TAKE IT ONCE OVER LIGHTLY, POGO---- ♫ UH-ONE UH-TWO-- ♫ OUR MEM'RY IS A SHALLOW LASS, HER FACULTY IS SMALL --- ♪ -----OUR COLLEGE HAS A SCENE I'LL ADVISE HER TO RECALL ---♪

♫ WOONIP GAUMP

COPR 1952 WALT KELLY

Possum at Cornell

The Cornell Widow *of November 1953 sold for 25¢ and the price was well worth the charming drawing of Pogo as a football player that graced the cover. Inside is a play, "Anybody Here Seen Kelly?" The dramatis personae include Walt Kelly, Albert the Alligator, Beauregard Bugleboy, Churchy La Femme, and Howland Owl.*

Kelly also drew special artwork for the short comedy including Albert as a fraternity gator.

At this time Pogo was available in 4- or 5-column size daily. Comics aren't printed that large anymore. On Sundays, Pogo was published in one-third page, one-half standard or full-page tabloid sizes.

Kelly cover artwork for *Cornell Widow* showed Pogo as a quarterback.

ANYBODY HERE SEEN KELLY?

DRAMATIS PERSONAE:

ALBERT ALLIGATOR, president of CIA, a member of Delta Alpha Rho (fraternity men run everything). He is a true-blue Cornellian. He is drinking beer. He is wearing a gold fraternity pin. There is an IFC Houseparty Watchbird watching him. Was an IFC Houseparty Watchbird watching you?

BEAUREGARD BUGLEBOY, M.B.F. (A.A.), T.N.D., treasurer of CIA, a dog of outstanding virtue and unsurpassed charity. Already he has provided funds to buy Redheart for some of the more unfortunate independents. He is wearing a gold CIA pin.

HOWLAND OWL, secretary, a collegetown apartment man, owner of 15 shingles and a mummy pin.

CHURCHY LA FEMME, director of Research and chairman of the committee to investigate houseparties. A shy, retiring native Ithacan, who has worked his shell to the bone for CIA.

WALT KELLY: A freshman newly arrived at Cornell from the Okefenokee swamp. He is plumpish, looking rather like a smaller version of Paul Whiteman, complete with mustache. He is fortyish, and wears glasses. Under one arm he clutches a bundle containing 226 newspapers and a copy of the Cornell Daily Sun. *His demeanor bespeaks intelligence, breeding, and financial stability.*

THE SCENE: A dimly lit room in the basement of Morrill Hall. At the rear hangs a Scotchlite banner bearing the letters ''CIA,'' and a tattered poster reading ''Syracuse Block Seating Here.'' Seated at a table are Albert, Beauregard, Churchy, and Owl. Enter Walt Kelly.

AL: Don't interrupt us'n right now bein' as how we is conciliation' (*Envelopes Kelly in cigar smoke*).

KELLY: But I was told . . .

OWL: (*Staring at Walt.*) Sho' nuff. We is intervening for the Cornell Independence Association of nineteen hunnert fifty-four p.m.

CHURCHY: Amen.

KELLY: But that's why I'm . . .

(*Noble ears of noble Beauregard etc. etc. suddenly go straight up in a position of rigid attention.*)

BEAU: Whuffo were that?

CHURCHY: Wuffo were what?

BEAU: I heerd a drapsome sound.

(*All listen. A drapsome sound is heard.*)

AL: Wal, I swom. I is lost my frater-nifty pin!

KELLY: Say, I was supposed to . . .

BEAU: Ne'mind that now. I, Beauregard Bugleboy, Man's Best Friend (Also Alligators). The Noble Dog, gone find it.

OWL: (*Still staring at Walt.*) LOOKEE! (*All crowd around except B.B., M.B.F., A.A., T.N.D., who sniffs eagerly under the table.*)

BEAU: I, the noble dog, will trace the wherefores of that badge of liberty, equality, and paternity, the symbol of good followship.

AL: Whuffo you lookin' at, Owl?

(*A muffled choking sound is heard.*)

CHURCHY: It's a rooch clamberin' down the wall. Cute li'l rascal, ain't he?

KELLY: You mean a cockroach, of the family Orthoptera blattidae.

BEAU (*Suddenly becoming interested.*) I used to

know a family, name of Malott. I was his best friend.

OWL: (*Peering out from under Albert's tail.*) *Oof!* That's a genius of another speechies.

AL: Did you distract our distention all the way over here jes' to gaze at a measly rooch?

CHURCHY: Look: it say "CURW" on his back.

AL: A union bug, by jing!

OWL: Obiousmently it stand up for "Cornell Unfair to Rooches-of-the-Wall."

CHURCHY: He ain't no yellowdog.

OWL: Well, mebbe he's a goldbug!

BEAU: (*Nose a-quiver.*) Has he got pearls on?

AL: He don't look familiar to me.

KELLY: Look, I came here for an interview.

OWL: Is you this feller on the wall, which is what I was lookin' at previousment?

AL: He's bigger'n a rooch.

CHURCHY: Besides, he's got mustages on.

OWL: I is refirming to this here name writ on the wall. It say: "Al Thwapp—class of nineteen-hunnert-ought-seventeen." Is this you?

AL: Mebbe it's Porky's Uncle Baldwin.

CHURCHY: I use to know a gummint perfesser named Rossinger, but he gone religious.

AL: (*Blowing beer foam into Kelly's face.*) Whuffo you here for, Uncle Baldwin?

KELLY: My name in Kelly, Walter Kelly. I came for an interview. I want to be a CIA man.

AL: (*Taken aback, takes a long draught of beer.*) *Hummmmm.*

CHURCHY: Go ahead, Albert, say sumthin' interviewerful.

OWL: Sho' nuff. It's yore Solomon duty to ax him a question.

BEAU: As Ganges Kahin once said, duty is as duty does, duty never strikes twice, at least not in the same place, duty is jes' a bowl of sour grapes, and rather poorly ones at that, we have nothing to be duty-full about but duty itself, on my honor I will do my best to do my duty . . .

AL: (*Recovering, glancing surreptitiously at notes stuffed under his vest.*) Why do you want to be on the CIA?

KELLY: Well, you see . . .

OWL: How come you startin' off with the tough ones?

CHURCHY: Ax him whuffo he's wearin' glasses, Albert.

OWL: Stop interompting, Churchy, mebbe he's shy. Prob'ly an interwort.

KELLY: To me the CIA means . . .

OWL: Defermently he don't relapse easy in company. He prob'ly has a difficultsome time coming outa his shell.

CHURCHY: Me too. Does that make me an intervenous too? (*tapping his shell nonchalantly under the armhole.*)

BEAU: Age before duty, but save the wimmen an' chitlins first. I FOUND IT! Man's Best Friend, The Noble Dog, has once again proven . . . Oh, Balderdash! It's another rooch.

CHURCHY: (*Tapping shell curiously.*) I once knew a feller named Isingshower, who bought out a hat store . . .

BEAU: I was his best friend.

AL: Well, since you don't seem to be partickly brainful on that subjeck . . .

OWL: Ax him if he wants a co-edification froshman campus, Albert. That's a jim-doodley. It always Burfaloes 'em.

CHURCHY: (*Tapping shell anxiously.*) You gone leave him on the horns of a dilenema, Albert.

KELLY: Well it seems to me . . .

BEAU: I 'member oncit back in Abalony, he says to me, "Beau," he say . . .

CHURCHY: Whuffo a feller want to come out of his shell for anyhow?

AL: Shesh! (*Turns to Kelly.*) How come you isn't affixiated wif a flatternitty-club?

KELLY: Well, you might say . . .

BEAU: "Beau," he say, "I came, I saw, I did my duty."

OWL: Don't embarraface him. Mebbe he ain't the brotherin' sort.

AL: Well, whuffo is yo' good for, anyhow?

OWL: Can you perambulance a bus?

KELLY: Well, I . . .

AL: You is hydramatically electered!

OWL: Many happy returns, yo' is in!

CHURCHY: I once knew a bus driver named Dew-pell . . .

(*The Noble Dog, steadfast in his devotion, points.*)

BEAU: I is found it!

AL: Wh-wh-wh-wh-whuf*fo!*

CHURCHY: Gesundheit!

BEAU: Shecks, another rooch.

. . . holcomb

During World War I, the famed Black Watch regiment from Scotland earned the nickname ''Ladies from Hell.'' Kelly's 1952 drawing for St. Ann's Academy, Victoria, British Columbia, makes one laugh and feel good just looking at it. These marauders in school uniforms from the deep South are guided by pirate Captain Churchy La Femme and a road map as they navigate the waters of the northwest coast. These ''Ladies from the Okefenokee'' would make quite a scene should they ever find St. Ann's Academy.

Out of the Okefenokee swamplands and into "The Aquinian" comes Pogo, the 'possum! Mr. Walt Kelly, originator of the astoundingly popular comic strip which specializes in making gentle fun of its many avid readers, answered our earnest request for an original cartoon with almost incredible generosity. To our readers, most of whom are already friends of Pogo and his swampland friends, we proudly offer this page. To Mr. Kelly, our heartfelt thanks.

Pogo and his pals were favorite subjects for ice sculptures at college winter festivals. Pogo primed for winter sports and Albert fishing are from a Dartmouth Winter Festival. The sculpture of Pogo and Albert, similar to the drawing used on the cover of Outrageously Pogo, is autographed to Kelly by Zeta Eta chapter of Sigma Nu fraternity, Tufts College.

Kelly must have marveled at what great legs Pogo had when he lined up with some cheerleaders from the University of Arkansas at a football game halftime. It was a scene he would repeat at colleges across the country.

Pogofest in Georgia

This official "Waycross Wants You" Pogo artwork was used on T-shirts, ball hats, plastic mugs, letterhead and news releases for the first and second annual Waycross Pogofest and Homecoming.

Tucked away in the southeastern corner of Georgia, the town of Waycross is the northern entrance to the Okefenokee Swamp. Its Chamber of Commerce will tell you that it is the largest town (population 20,000) in the largest county east of the Mississippi River. Ware County is spread out over 912 square miles.

In recent years farming in the area declined, railroads merged and laid off workers, and local industry stagnated. Waycross's population remained about the same as that of a hundred years ago.

Some residents say Waycross was so named because of the many churches in the area—"Way of the Cross." Others suggest that the name came into being from the railroad tracks that crisscross the town's streets and surrounding landscape.

As a rail center, Waycross is home to CSX's Rice Yard, the most sophisticated classification yard in North America. The $40 million terminal has 145 miles of track on an 850-acre site. About 60 freight trains move through and are resorted and assembled in the yard daily.

"We have many of the same economic problems that five hundred or so small towns from here to New Orleans have," notes Bart Thigpen, Human Resources Director for Waycross.

Seeking to unite the people of Waycross and dispel the creeping feeling of pessimism that started to surface, the local government launched its "Waycross Wants You" campaign on January 17, 1987.

A key element of the campaign was the permission granted by the Walt Kelly Estate to make Pogo Possum Waycross's Goodwill Ambassador.

"Pogo is this area's most famous son. Having his home in the Okefenokee Swamp put us on the map nationally," said Bart Thigpen.

What follows is a composite of articles about the first Pogofest and Homecoming (July 2–4, 1987) written by Bill Maher, city editor of The Waycross Journal-Herald.

The celebration is slated to be an annual event and Selby Kelly, who was made an honorary citizen of Waycross, returned for the second Pogofest in July 1988.

Among other famous people born or raised in Waycross who it is hoped will return for their "homecoming" are: Pernell Roberts (Trapper John, M.D.), Burt Reynolds, and Ossie Davis.

This was a down-home event with swamp fries (catfish, hush puppies, grits with gravy) served from morning to night.

The debut event in 1987 received national television coverage on ABC's Nightly News and was featured in the special July 4 holiday pull-out section of the Atlanta Constitution.

Our thanks to Bill Maher for being the Pogophiles' man on the scene.

This wonderful portrait of Walt Kelly sketching scenes of the Okefenokee Swamp during his 1955 visit was taken by the late Liston Elkins. Our thanks to Jimmy Walker, who succeeded Mr. Elkins as manager of the Okefenokee Swamp Park, for providing this photo.

Pogofest in Georgia
by Bill Maher

WAYCROSS, GA.—It's been a dozen years since Pogo Possum and his pals from the nearby Okefenokee Swamp last graced the nation's funny pages, but people along the Georgia-Florida line still pay homage to the snub-nosed cartoon character and to the man who created him—cartoonist Walt Kelly.

When Pogo made his triumphant return July 1, 1987, for an Okefenokee Homecoming, Pogophiles young and old turned out by the thousands—and television cameras rolled—for the five-day celebration.

More than four thousand people filled city streets for an outdoor dance in his honor, and another twelve thousand packed Waycross's Memorial Stadium to watch the warm-hearted swamp philosopher unveil a twenty-foot likeness of himself.

There were Pogo buttons, Pogo cups, Pogo hats, Pogo T-shirts and Pogo money everywhere. Some fans replaced the alligator trademark on their Izod knit shirts with—you got it—Pogo.

Kelly's widow, Mrs. Selby Kelly, who recently approved Waycross's use of the copyrighted character as its ambassador of goodwill—to promote rural southern Georgia and the 450,000-acre Okefenokee National Wildlife Refuge—explained Pogo's lasting popularity.

"He's kind of shy, sort of an 'aw shucks' character," she said during her first visit to the famous swamp. "Kelly used to call him the cement that held everything else together."

Kelly created the comic strip *Pogo* in 1942 and for more than a quarter century used the character, and his "enchanting troupe of anthropomorphic critters," to comment on the political, social and moral ills of the twentieth century.

Pogo reached his zenith in the 1950s when he launched his first two spirited bids as write-in candidate for President. The comic strip was carried daily by more than four hundred newspapers and the Okefenokee—an old Indian term meaning "Land of Trembling Earth"—became a household word around the globe.

Mrs. Kelly, herself an accomplished cartoonist and animator, continued the comic strip for more than a year after her husband's death in 1973, but finally discontinued it. "Nobody could do it the way Kelly did it," she admitted.

When Waycross officials asked Mrs. Kelly last winter for permission to use *Pogo*, she readily agreed. She also accepted the town's invitation to visit the swamp as guest of honor for the Okefenokee Homecoming.

Kelly himself had visited the swamp either two or three times—depending on the recall of the old-timer one may ask—but it was Selby's first trip. (The two were married only one year before his death.)

A large crowd of sign-waving Waycross residents and reporters greeted her incoming flight at nearby Jacksonville (Florida) International Airport. Pogo, too, was there to make her welcome. Waycross officials had commissioned a costume maker to construct a likeness of the lovable possum, and a city hall employee had spent a week at Walt Disney World learning to play, uh, possum.

"That's a good Pogo strut," Mrs. Kelly said while watching the costumed actor. "His ears are just right. His nose is just right. Well, he's Pogo."

With Pogo at her side, Mrs. Kelly floated into the Okefenokee for her first glimpse of the swamp.

"It's more beautiful than I thought," Mrs. Kelly said as she was steered down boat trails deep in the 650,000-acre swamp by guides Johnny Hickox and Lamar Hall, along with Okefenokee Swamp Park manager Jimmy Walker.

"I've wanted to come here for a long time, but I didn't expect to come as a celebrity," Mrs. Kelly laughingly admitted as she was followed through the swamp by a boatload of television and newspaper reporters.

"I love it," she said. "My brother used to go out when I was a child in Florida and catch baby alligators and bring them back to me."

After the two-hour boat tour, Mrs. Kelly joined Pogo for a television interview using Pogo's home for

Selby Kelly and Pogo Possum wave to fans during Selby's first visit to the Okefenokee Swamp in July 1987. (Photo by Bill Maher)

a backdrop. The friendly opossum provided the antics while she did all the talking.

Walt Kelly had first come across Waycross and the Okefenokee by accident. While working for the old New York *Star* in 1948, Kelly cast about in his library for a suitable swamp setting for the comic strip, but it was January 1955 before he first visited the place, tried the swamp stew and saw his first live opossum.

Roy Moore, former manager of the Okefenokee National Wildlife Refuge and Kelly's guide on the trip, said the cartoonist was looking for background for the comic strip. "I took Kelly and Pat Lahatte, an Atlanta newspaperwoman, in my boat to Jones Island," Moore said. "Kelly talked Pat into jumping out of the boat to what looked like dry land. We ended up pulling her out of waist-deep water and mud. Later on, Kelly referred to 'Bog-hopping Pat' in several strips."

Moore, now retired and living in Waycross, said Kelly, an avid conservationist, was concerned at the time about plans to drill for oil in the middle of the swamp and about the drought of the previous year that had lowered the water table throughout the Okefenokee. "After he returned home he did several drawings pertaining to those subjects. He sent me three of his originals, and one of them had my name on Pogo's boat."

Kelly often added the names of special friends to the stern of the flat-bottomed skiff that Pogo and his pals poled through the swamp. It was his way of saying thanks.

Moore said the swamp's water table later returned to normal and the drillers never got permission from the U.S. Department of the Interior. Nature took care of the former, Moore said, but Kelly was probably responsible for the latter.

Mrs. Kelly, who now lives in Santa Barbara, California, was the guest of the City of Waycross for the three-day Okefenokee Homecoming event that featured her late husband's troupe of animal caricatures. Her hosts were Dr. and Mrs. Ray S. Eleazer.

Mrs. Kelly grew up in Winter Park, Florida, but attended high school in California where she studied art. Mrs. Kelly said her own marriage to the late cartoonist was worthy of Pogo's gentle humor.

She and Kelly almost met in the 1930s when they both worked on animated films for Walt Disney Productions in Anaheim, California. Disney kept his male and female employees segregated in separate buildings; they never met each other then.

"Kelly told me years later that he had wanted to date me then and had asked someone about me," Mrs. Kelly said. "They told him I was dating someone else."

She went on to become president of the Screen Cartoonists Guild, and Kelly met and married someone else. In 1968, while Kelly's second wife was dying, Kelly met Selby when she helped animate a Pogo film. They were married in 1972, a year before his death.

Pogo took his sabbatical from the funny pages 18 months after Kelly's death.

Mrs. Kelly was asked by reporters if *Pogo* could be a successful comic strip in the 1980s if she decided to revive the snub-nosed possum and his swamp pals, like the cigar-chomping Albert Alligator, the happy-

go-lucky turtle named Churchy La Femme and the sourpuss philosopher named Porkypine.

"I think so," she said, "and some of the syndicates have asked me to put him in. They must know something."

Mrs. Kelly said she has seriously considered the idea of reviving *Pogo*. So far, she said, contractural arrangements have been a major stumbling block.

"We're checking to see if there's someone who can take care of the business end of it," she said. "I don't want to get back into that. I'm 70 years old and I think I should be allowed to retire."

The comic strips that attempted to follow in *Pogo's* tradition—such as *Doonesbury* and *Bloom County*—lack the gentle humor that made Kelly's

Pogo a famous character. A revived *Pogo* comic strip would require an artist "with a satirical vein who can treat everything lightheartedly and not be vengeful," according to Mrs. Kelly. Also, she said the characters in the strip should help decide if it is to be revived. "That's something that would have to be voted on. After all, the swamp's a democracy too."

Mrs. Kelly found that her wit was matched by the men of the Okefenokee Swamp. "We had a typing teacher come through here a couple of years ago, and she put her hand out of the boat," guide Johnny Hickox told Mrs. Kelly when she was about to reach into the water. "The next year she was teaching shorthand."

BILL MAHER

Tales of Pogo's Campaign Trail in 1988

This artwork was printed in red and blue on the outside of white 6″ x 9″ and 9″ x 12″ envelopes used to send out news releases.

In a phone conversation with Selby Kelly in spring 1988 we discussed whether or not a ''Pogo for President'' campaign should be mounted. At the time I didn't know that plans were afoot to have *Walt Kelly's Pogo* syndicated with a new creative team already in place.

Although Selby didn't enlighten me regarding Pogo's return to the comics page, she did agree it would be good for Pogo to be in the presidential arena. She also mentioned she'd be attending the second annual Pogofest in Waycross, Georgia, over July 4 and we agreed it was the perfect opportunity for Pogo's hat to be tossed into the ring whether he was ready or not.

. Initially it was hoped that Iris Hitt and Bart Thigpen of the city of Waycross would be able to manage the campaign. This soon appeared to be impossible because of their heavy responsibilities managing the Pogofest. So I became press secretary and Pogo's political theorist by default.

The first news release, ''Strange Noises Heard in Okefenokee Swamp,'' was released just prior to Selby's arrival in Waycross. It had an Okefenokee Swamp dateline and carried the following news.

''Jimmy Walker, manager of the Okefenokee Swamp Park, Waycross, Georgia, reported today that his guides who take tourists through the swamp had heard strange chanting.

''Deep in the swamp, past the furthest point guides normally take visitors, they heard an eerie rumbling that sounded like: 'Run Pogo run. Run Pogo run. Run Pogo run.'

''Fortunately, Mrs. Walt Kelly arrives in Waycross June 30 in preparation for the second annual Pogofest/Homecoming held July 1–4. . . . Mrs. Kelly has the unique ability of being able to converse with Pogo Possum, Albert the Alligator, and the other swamp critters.

''Some Waycross old-timers have speculated that Pogo's new book, full of 'new ideas,' strange chants in the swamp, and several sightings of the bear P. T. Bridgeport, might have something to do with both the Republican and Democratic national conventions being in the South.

''Ever skeptical, they proclaimed these noises from the swamp to be 'monkey business.' ''

The news release received some local attention in Georgia and set the style for releases that would parody the politicians of the campaign.

The Pogo candidacy, however, was not announced at the July 4 Pogofest. Instead, the release ''Pogo Throws Hat (and himself) Into Presidential Race'' was dated Bastille Day, July 14, and had a Waycross, Georgia, dateline.

This chance French connection proved prophetic when Mam'selle Hepzibah joined the Pogo Party ticket in early August.

Pogo's National Campaign Headquarters became my Bridgeport post office box and my mother's kitchen table, the creative nucleus of my life. Soon news releases were crisscrossing the country. I used the mailing list I'd developed for the ''Boston Charlie'' releases of former *Pogo* subscribers and newspapers with over 100,000 circulation. I expanded the list to include all papers over 50,000 circulation and zeroed in on geographical areas. About every daily and weekly newspaper in Georgia and Northern Florida received Pogo material.

The ''hat into presidential race'' news release was built around a Kelly release from 1956 but updated to include references current for the 1988 campaign. It is published here in its entirety.

It had been hoped that Waycross's costumed Pogo would be able to appear at least outside the Democratic National Convention in Atlanta. The July heat and intense security prevented this, however.

Instead "Pogo" and some Waycross boosters stumped in an Atlanta shopping mall. There, in air-conditioned comfort, they heralded the joys of Waycross and the Okefenokee.

Prior to the Republican National Convention in New Orleans in mid-August, there was speculation over whether George Bush would select a woman to be his vice-presidential running mate. Elizabeth Dole was considered a front runner.

Although Pogo had never really had a running mate before, this was too good an opportunity to miss. Two news releases were sent out.

"Pogo Possum Indignant Over Working Conditions of Political Symbols" again reworked a Kelly release from 1956.

"A mad 'stampede' of elephants headed for New Orleans was viewed today by Pogo, presidential dark-possum, as only the first sign of growing unrest among animals in general and elephants in particular. 'Elephants,' said the Pogo Party candidate, 'should have rights as equal as anybody. Maybe even equaller.' "

A kitchen table in a house is not the most photogenic of national campaign headquarters. Enter Dan Makara, a Bridgeport, Connecticut artist and arts promoter.

As a sideline Dan was organizing a series of concerts for Bridgeport's Austin Street Cafe, a trendy bar-restaurant just off the University of Bridgeport campus and Bridgeport's oldest saloon. Would I consider Austin Street Cafe for Pogo's campaign headquarters?

Inasmuch as Kelly had been no stranger to saloons, and since Pogo's ad hoc headquarters in 1952 had been a bar in Chicago, I knew it would be perfect. Besides, I had been dodging the press who were clamoring to photograph the current campaign headquarters—my mother's kitchen. Now Pogo would have a wonderfully theatrical set.

Things got better. The cafe ordered a banner for about $150 proclaiming "POGO FOR PREZ.—NAT'L HDQTS," and hung it prominently across the front of the building. Dan Makara painted a beautiful four-foot-high likeness of Pogo on foamboard which was placed over the bar.

Once again the French connection kicked in. Makara had booked Grammy winner Queen Ida, the

Dan Makara's drawing of Queen Ida is from the newspaper ad for her concert.

"missionary of zydeco," and her Bon Temps Zydeco Band to perform.

The stage was set for the August 11 news release: "Pogo Possum Names a Lady Skunk as His Vice Presidential Running Mate." A news conference was called to announce Mam'selle Hepzibah's selection.

In the tradition of great Bridgeport promotion Makara had assembled three key elements that would get "Pogo for President" in the newspaper with a photo and on local television: Mayor Thomas Bucci of Bridgeport, a guy in a bear costume, and a live alligator.

I wrote the Pogo Party platform and read it at the conference. Mayor Bucci duly proclaimed August 25, 1988 (which would have been Kelly's 75th birthday), Walt Kelly Day. The guy in the bear suit wore a campaign hat with the top cut out so it would fit over his furry ears.

Bridgeport has the only zoo in Connecticut, and Gregg Dancho, director of the Beardsley Park Zoo, displayed a live alligator dubbed Albert, Jr. The Austin Street Cafe, knowing the proclivities of reporters, provided free food and drink. This was real old-time all-American politicking.

The campaign gained momentum when Linda Stowell of the Associated Press office in Connecticut did a story with photo that went out on the national wire. It was published in the *New York News* on Sunday, October 1, 1988. This is America's largest circulation tabloid, with a readership of about 1,270,000.

Happily the Pogo campaign broke in the *Daily News* with three nice stories, including one by the mysterious Lounge Lizard saloon reviewer who keyed in on Austin Street's patriotic fervor. (I personally think the Lizard had done some serious partying with

Back here in the real world, meanwhile, Lounge Lizard reminds you that Mr. Pogo Possum is running for President again this year and reports that National Campaign Headquarters, which is an outfit in Bridgeport, Conn., called Austin St. Cafe, has invented an Official Campaign Drink called an "Okefenokee Mud" or something like that. Lounge Lizard has not yet personally tasted same, but he intends to do so very soon.

Pogo's campaign headquarters gets in the *New York Daily News* thanks to a pal of Albert the Alligator.

Albert the Alligator some time back.)

Alligators had presented the campaign with a chance for Pogo Possum publicity. The *New York News* had published a story, "Gator's Game: Swamp Beast Turns Tables," about a New Yorker who took part in the Florida alligator hunt. This prompted a letter sent out to thirty Florida newspapers.

Hopes were high in the home stretch. Mam'selle Hepzibah said, "Ze elephant frightens me not, nor the donkey. The possum and ze skunk will win this election by a nose."

The last weeks of the election were spent blanketing college newspapers with *Pogo* news releases, along with states such as California, Ohio, and Texas that were considered key.

This was a national campaign. Pogo for President

material went out to every state in the union plus Guam, Puerto Rico, and the Virgin Islands. The campaign was enhanced because Pogo was a positive campaigner in a year when the negative campaign gained ascendancy for the Republicans and Democrats.

The major parties dealt in "sound bites," but they can be disillusioning about how the media actually works.

I had a call from a woman representing WOR Radio's drive-time morning show "Rambling With Gambling," which is extremely popular in the New York market. The next day a different woman called and we did a telephone interview about Pogo for President.

Three days later, when the interview aired, everything had been spliced together. It sounded as if I was in the studio one-on-one with John Gambling. Yet I had never spoken to the guy.

It was great publicity for *Pogo*. The show has a major market share. But if this can happen to a casual campaign by a comic-strip character, think of the manipulations possible in legitimate political campaigns where candidates work eighteen-hour days and seek any opportunity for air time.

Midway through the Pogo campaign all hell broke loose for a time when the lawyer was negotiating for the Kelly family with the Los Angeles Times Syndicate. The syndicate wanted to know, "Who is this guy Crouch and why is he running a Pogo for President campaign?" It seemed Selby Kelly and Peter Kelly had neglected to tell them what was afoot.

Ultimately the presidential campaign and the publicity for the projected *Walt Kelly's Pogo* dovetailed nicely. Pogo stayed in and out of media on a regular basis from July through the end of 1988.

BILL CROUCH, JR.
Press Secretary,
Pogo for President, 1988

This artwork went out to over 500 college newspapers along with news releases and posters.

National Campaign Headquarters
Pogo Possum for President 1988
P.O. Box 2311
Bridgeport, CT 06608

FOR IMMEDIATE RELEASE

Press Release

Pogo Throws Hat (and Himself) Into Presidential Race

WAYCROSS, GA, July 14—The campaign hat of Pogo Possum was thrown into the presidential ring today by a group of political well-wishers who unfortunately forgot to remove the candidate from his lid. The comic-strip character whose first bid for the presidency was in 1952 was not noticeably disturbed.

"I've been thrown before," he remarked to a cheering throng at Waycross's Okefenokee Swamp Park.

Critters in the Okefenokee Swamp drafted Pogo to enter the presidential race in a raucous convention deep in the swamp. Guides from the Okefenokee Swamp Park had their first inkling of today's announcement when they heard the chant, "Run Pogo Run. Run Pogo Run."

"I don't even jog," said Pogo today and immediately changed his campaign chant to the tried-and-true "I GO POGO." The candidate admitted it had been his slogan for several unsuccessful campaigns but said, "It's a winner."

The ursine political strategist P. T. Bridgeport has usurped the position of campaign manager.

Pressed for ideas on his platform, Pogo indicated he was for a regular old-fashioned flat-bottomed-type platform for use on land or sea.

Pogo noted he would be leaving Waycross, a major railroad center, on a fast freight for a whirlwind tour of the nation. But he stated he was sharp enough to steer clear of the Mason-Maddox line.

Asked by reporters to comment on the other candidates, Pogo noted that his candidacy would add zest to the campaign. "I'm the only presidential hopeful with a prehensile tail," said Pogo, who claimed it helped him get a firm grip on political affairs.

Pogo refused comment on the Meadow Party's candidate Bill the Cat from the comic strip *Bloom County*. He did say, however, that vice-presidential hopeful Opus the Penguin might have a problem if

rumors proved true that he had been born in Antarctica.

Pogo also autographed copies of his new trade paperback *Pluperfect Pogo*, which has an introduction by Jim (*Garfield*) Davis. When questioned by reporters, the candidate said that he must have made the wrong type of deal with Simon & Schuster, as his royalties were well south of the 55 percent that Speaker of the U.S. House Jim Wright is earning from a different publisher. "What's right for Wright is wrong for Pogo," he said.

Although too young to vote, a number of Waycross children visiting the Okefenokee Swamp Park proclaimed Pogo Possum to be "good, kind, thrifty, honest, clean, decent, concerned and tolerant."

The Pogo Party claims its possum is "the best nontoxic alternative to the human beans already in the race."

Pogo challenged the other candidates to "bring on their truth squads," and claimed he was the only candidate that could tell the American public the real truth as he had so little chance of winning.

"It's self-evident," said Pogo, "that if elected I would have to raise taxes to combat our nation's number one problem, the federal deficit."

It is widely rumored that Pogo will visit both the Democratic National Convention in Atlanta next week and the Republican National Convention in New Orleans in August.

POGO'S HAT THROWN INTO RING

National Campaign Headquarters
Pogo Possum for President 1988
P.O. Box 2311
Bridgeport, CT 06608

FOR IMMEDIATE RELEASE

There's no campaign jet for Pogo Possum as America's most frugal candidate heads out on the campaign trail.

Press Release

Pogo Possum's Presidential Prospects Peak

WAYCROSS, GA, Sept.—Presidential candidate Pogo Possum claimed that he's the ''best nontoxic alternative to the human beans already in the race'' at a recent press conference held at Waycross's Okefenokee Swamp Park.

The comic-strip character whose first bid for the presidency was in 1952 has just returned from a campaign swing to the headwaters of America.

The Pogo Party is the only major or minor national political party with a female vice-presidential candidate. Mam'selle Hepzibah, a feisty lady skunk with a French accent, is given credit for energizing the Pogo campaign.

''Lloyd Bentsen, ze Democrats' vice-presidential candidate, claims he'll speak up if the Duke slips up in the Oval Office,'' said Hepzibah at the press conference. ''Ze Republicans boast of an ethics committee in the White House. In the unlikely chance Pogo runs amuck, I'll not only verbally berate him, I'll raise a stink.''

Pogo, not known as a dynamic stump speaker even with his Okefenokee Swamp background, prefers to advance his philosophy for America with his books. *Pluperfect Pogo*, with an introduction by Jim (*Garfield*) Davis, was recently published by Fireside/Simon & Schuster. Pogo is pictured on the cover in a Roman toga.

The candidate's garb on his latest book's cover has prompted the media to question if Pogo's White House style would be more imperial than the current administration's.

Heading off what he referred to as a media ''feeding frenzy,'' Pogo's ursine campaign manager and former circus performer P. T. Bridgeport stated that Pogo was so attired because he supports legislation to mandate a toga party per semester at every college in America.

The Toga Party theme allowed for promotion of *Pluperfect Pogo* published in Fall 1987.

''One columnist has called this year's campaign a television miniseries, 'The Patrician and the Plebian,' '' said Pogo. ''I'm amending that to 'The Patrician, the Plebian and the Possum.' ''

Noting that Michael Dukakis was recently referred to as ''Wilsonian,'' Pogo reminded reporters that he himself was often referred to as ''marsupial.''

''I may not know beans about brown bread,'' said Pogo, ''but does Michael Dukakis know okra from collard greens?''

In campaigning against Republican candidate George Bush, Pogo said that he'd rely on skills learned on the baseball field. ''It will be a picture's duel,'' predicted Pogo. ''Which candidate will get his picture in front of the public the most.''

Pogo and Mam'selle Hepzibah.

Pogo credits running mate Mam'selle Hepzibah with the concept of jump-starting the campaign through music. Early in the campaign the Charlie Daniels Band played at Waycross, Georgia's second annual Pogofest on July 2. Then in August, Grammy winner Queen Ida, the "missionary of zydeco," and her Bon Temps Zydeco Band brought their marvelous gumbo of Creole, Black, Cajun and Acadian-French music to Bridgeport, Connecticut, in honor of the Pogo Party ticket. Bridgeport was hometown to Pogo's creator, the late Walt Kelly.

"I decided we had to spice up ze campaign if we are to win," said Mam'selle Hepzibah. "Zydeco music is HOT, danceable and uniquely American ethnic family music. Ze college students and baby boomers will dance into the polls for us in November."

The Pogo Party claims to be the only political movement to turn mere political rallies into danceathons.

"Unlike other political parties where harmony is only a truce," said P. T. Bridgeport, "the Pogo Party is fully united behind the Pogo–Hepzibah ticket. Low voter registration and low voter turnout is a national shame. Our goal is to alert the public and college students in particular to exercise their civic duty to register and then VOTE."

"Our family trees may be undocumented,"said Pogo. "But I defy any candidate to call either Hepzibah or myself unpatriotic. Our ancestors said hello to the Pilgrims in Massachusetts, the English in Virginia, and the Spanish and French in Florida. Our platform addresses environmental problems, voter awareness, the strength of my prehensile tail in foreign affairs, and most importantly the fight against the dopers. I strongly advocate the word 'dope' be used instead of drugs."

"Jesse Jackson may be the 'General of the War on Drugs,' " chimed in Hepzibah. "But the Okefenokee's own Albert the Alligator has declared himself ze 'Admiral of the War on Dope.' Of course he will not enter the state of Florida until the alligator hunting season is over."

Jump-started by zydeco and country rock, the Pogo Party urges concerned citizens to rally to the traditional cry, "I GO POGO."

Pogo and "Admiral of the Dope War," Albert the Alligator.

FOR IMMEDIATE RELEASE

"I'm for a regular old-fashioned flat-bottomed-type platform for use on land or sea. Nobody takes party platforms seriously anyway. The platform always sinks whichever political party is elected."

Pogo Possum, presidential candidate.

(POGO PARTY PLATFORM for 1988)

The Greenhouse Effect, Trash and Pollution:

Mother Earth is giving the United States and the rest of the world the message to wake up and change their ways. Pogo's most famous saying, "We have met the enemy and he is us" is more relevant today than ever. Pogo is no George- or Michael-come-lately to environmental issues. His statement goes back to Earth Day 1971. The efforts to insure a clean environment are a top priority of the Pogo Party.

Foreign Affairs:

Pogo Possum is the only presidential candidate with a prehensile tail. While Pogo's experience in foreign affairs is limited, he feels his tail will allow him a firm grip on all issues both foreign and domestic.

Drugs:

Illegal drugs are a terrible threat to our great country. The Pogo Party is in favor of pushing the use of the word "dope" instead of "drugs." Dope is dope. The word has a completely negative meaning. Drugs have both a positive and negative side. Serious disease is often cured with drugs.

Albert the Alligator, who's more at home in the water than on land, has volunteered to become the "Admiral of the Dope War." The Pogo Party pledges to mobilize both public and private efforts to mount a crusade against the doper scum that threaten our life, liberty and pursuit of happiness.

Registering to Vote and then Voting:

The Pogo Party believes it is a national shame that more citizens, especially younger ones who are eligible, do not exercise their civic rights and duties. Pogo is pledged to greater voter education.

Letter to the Editor
New York Daily News
220 E. 42nd St.
New York, NY 10017

HIGH BLOOD
PRESSURE?

Albert the Alligator
Okefenokee Swamp
Okefenokee, GA 31501

Sept. 28, 1988

Dear Editor:

Thanks to a traveling salesman I happened to see your front page coverage and large article about the New Yorker who participated in the Florida alligator hunt in the September 25 Sunday *News*. Frankly, I was appalled.

My fellow alligators were described as "the monster" or "swamp beast." Mr. Alpern, the author/hunter, describes "two angry bull alligators." I'd be angry too if I had just had a harpoon stuck in me. I say bravo to my fellow gators who tipped those hunters' air boat over in the murky water of Lake Okeechobee, Florida, and gave them the scare of their lives.

The American alligator (Alligator *mississippiensis*) is a noble creature and much maligned. How often I think of my fellow gators exiled as mere babes by New York tourists to the sewers of the Big Apple. Some claim it's only a rumor but I know the truth in my heart.

As an important member of the Pogo Possum for President election team, I've found this gator hunt to be a major inconvenience. I'm a virtual prisoner in the federal wildlife refuge of the Okefenokee Swamp. I sure can't campaign for Pogo in Florida.

Pogo advocates the word "dope" be used instead of the paradoxical word "drugs." As the "Admiral of the Dope War," my cold reptilian blood is boiling with frustration. I need to be out in the front lines fighting the dope dealers, not reading about the glorification of icing the official mascot of the University of Florida.

ALBERT

© 1988 OGPI

FOR IMMEDIATE RELEASE

The creative team for Walt Kelly's Pogo *and the Los Angeles Times Syndicate mailed out the following promotion just prior to the November 1988 presidential election. This promotion and the Pogo for President 1988 National Campaign Headquarters had no knowledge of each other.*

POGO TO THE PEOPLE: "GO POGO, GO VOTE"

(Fort Mudge, Ga., Oct. 33) — Pogo Possum, beloved comic strip character and perennial presidential involunteer, confirmed denials Tuesday that he had launched a voter registration drive in a last ditch effort to get his name placed on the Nov. 8 ballot.

"I is only tryin' to *get* a ballot," Pogo said. "I was just registerin' myself, so *I* could vote."

The denouncement marked the 10th straight Pogo-for-President campaign in which Pogo refused to participate, leading to speculation the possum was positioning himself for a 1992 bid. Further, in a move widely viewed as an attempt to keep his constituency on the voting rolls, Pogo actively encouraged his followers to cast ballots for any of the official candidates in the upcoming election.

"If you want to go Pogo," he said, "go vote."

In an uncharacteristically angry outburst, the typically mellifluous marsupial also accused the media of invading his privacy, beating that old dead horse.

Speaking to a crowd of reporters gathered around his washbasin, Pogo splashed out at his questioners. "Unless one of you is gonna do my back," he said, "I'd appreciate you turn yours."

Earlier in the day, Pogo's campaign manager P. T. Bridgeport released a series of candidate statements that seemed to contradict statements made by the candidate himself.

"Of course, Pogo's running," Bridgeport said. "And he will win, spectacularly."

With so much negative campaigning and so much of the electorate voting against one candidate or another, Bridgeport said Pogo cannot lose. "A vote against somebody is a vote for nobody," he explained. "And Pogo *is* about as nobody as they come."

"We're running a clean campaign," Bridgeport added. "Just go look around back."

House ads for publication

Selby Kelly, Walt Kelly, and Pogo Possum: 1968–1975

After Walt Kelly's death, his widow Selby Kelly, with the help of Kelly's son Steve and Kelly's longtime assistant Henry Shikuma, took over production of the syndicated Pogo comic strip. It was her debut in syndicated comics although she'd worked all her adult life in animation.

It was indeed a baptism by fire. Walt Kelly had one of the best of all deals in syndicated comics. He had a 70/30 split with the syndicate. Not only did he get 70 percent, but the syndicate paid all the expenses. Traditionally syndicates and cartoonists often split 50/50 and share the expenses.

Immediately following Kelly's death the syndicate changed the contract on Pogo. It would now be a 40/60 split with the Kelly Estate receiving 40 percent and getting to pay all expenses. Still, Pogo remained profitable enough for Selby Kelly to pay off all the debts from Kelly's final illness. Then she ended Pogo's first run of syndication.

Through the kindness of Jud Hurd, publisher and editor of Cartoonist PROfiles magazine, we are able to reprint two interviews with Selby Kelly. One was published in 1974 and the other in 1984. They discuss the continuation by Selby, Steve and Henry of the Pogo strip and aspects of Kelly's animation of Pogo.

This section concludes with an interview in which Selby covers the period from fall 1968 through summer 1975. It contains some heartrending details of Kelly's last days. But in lieu of any biography of Kelly, it has always been the mission of The Okefenokee Star to gather as much primary research as possible about Walt Kelly. As sick as he was, the amount of work that Kelly produced is totally amazing. Even when his ability to draw the daily Pogo properly failed him, his writing was still top drawer. The daily strips that are reprinted for the first time from Kelly's period of ill health in late 1972, show the torment of the great talent unable to let go and find a crew of assistants to help him. However, he did regain his form for part of 1973.

Considering the amount of minimal art in current comic strips and the use of ants by Johnny Hart in B.C. the minimalist Pogo's might have been viewed in a different light if Kelly had not already spoiled his readers with his brilliance for so many many years.

I would like to thank Selby Kelly for her trust and openness in sharing this information with Walt Kelly's many fans. The interview was tape recorded in 1985 at a time when she and I had tremendous empathy. I had just gone through helping a good friend through viral encephilitis and was very familiar with comatose loved ones, intensive care units, and the rigors of hospital life. I think our empathy was responsible for the resulting good interview.

For anyone interested in cartooning, I must recommend the quarterly periodical, Cartoonist PROfiles. Please write P.O. Box 325, Fairfield, CT 06430 for more information.

B.C. JR.

Cartoonist PROfiles Interviews Selby Kelly

October 7, 1974

SELBY KELLY, the widow of the famed WALT KELLY, is carrying on the writing and the drawing of the Sunday POGO page for the PUBLISHERS-HALL SYNDICATE. Here, in this conversation with your editor, she talks about her career in animation, about Pogo, and shares some of her thoughts about Walt with our readers. I think we should add a few biographical facts about him at this point. Walt and his first wife, Helen, had 3 children—Kathy, Carolyn, and Peter. His second wife, Stephanie, who died of cancer a little over 4½ years ago, and Walt, were parents of Andrew, John, and Stephen. Steve, who's 22, currently writes the POGO dailies which are drawn by Don Morgan who also works for the Ralph Bakshi Studios in California.

Reader Believes Pogo "As Satirical And Enjoyable As Ever"

Tom Hill, Publisher

The Oak Ridger

EVERY EVENING MONDAY THROUGH FRIDAY

P.O. BOX 3446   •   (615) 482 1021   •   OAK RIDGE, TENNESSEE 37830

April 2, 1974

President
Publishers-Hall Syndicate
401 N. Wabash Ave.
Chicago, Illinois 60611

Dear Sir:

Could you tell me who is drawing the Pogo comic
strip since the death of Walt Kelly? We have
had the following question sent to our Action
Line column:

"How does the Oak Ridger still print the cartoon
strip "Pogo"? I read that Walt Kelly died last
year. I was wondering if someone else is writing
it now. The strip is still as satirical and enjoyable as ever."

Thank you.

Yours truly,

Mary Smyser
Action Line

Publishers-Hall Syndicate
401 NORTH WABASH, CHICAGO, ILLINOIS 60611

Promotion sent out by the syndicate in spring 1974 to support the *Pogo*
being done by the team of Selby Kelly, Steve Kelly and Henry Shikuma.

Selby and Stephen both live and work in the family brownstone in New York City on East 89th Street.

JUD HURD

Q: You started in animation didn't you, Selby?

A: Yes, and that's all I've ever done since I went with Disney's in 1936. I began there as an inker, worked in the paint lab making the paint, eventually was head of it. I've shot camera, done cutting, in fact was involved in every phase of the business except playing musical instruments.

Q: In the beginning women didn't have a very wide range of opportunities in animation, did they?

A: I'll say they didn't! Soon after high school I read an ad in *Popular Science* reading "MEN—we need you at Disney's if you can draw!" It had happened that I always seemed to win all the art contests in high school—in fact, they made me stop entering them because it looked rigged. I answered the ad, and here's a "Women's Lib" story I tell often: The girl at the studio laughed rudely in my face and finally said, "Well, if you insist on trying to get a job here, go across the street—that's where the girls are—this is for men." They looked down their noses at me and asked, "Have you ever done anything commercial? We don't hire anybody unless they're real artists." Thinking they meant something like magazine work, I said, "No." But my mother, who had driven me down from our home in Pasadena, piped up with, "You've done a series of children's books and you've sold float designs for the Rose Parade." The contest for the Pasadena float always involved everybody in the city school district, and for four years I won those. So they did accept me for the Disney School, and started me at $10 a week. At this point I quit a job in the dime store where I'd been getting $15.

Q: How did you eventually manage to get beyond the inking which girls were assigned to?

A: When we went out on strike in 1941, I met a lot of the men at the studio and they taught me to do in-betweens and assistant work. Then during World War II there was a shortage of men of course, and the studios started hiring girls as in-betweeners, and finally allowed them to go into "breakdown" and then into "assistant" work. After the war the guys came back, and although several of us had made it into animation, they pushed us back down again.

Q: Isn't it true that Walt Kelly first saw you when you were both working at Disney's in 1936, but that you didn't meet until years later?

A: Right. Disney had a rule that if a woman was caught in the men's building, she'd be fired immediately—he allowed no fraternization whatever. In later years Kelly told me that he used to look out the animation building windows and watch me walk from the parking lot to where I worked. But there was no occasion for us to meet. He wanted to meet me apparently but the other men kidded him either by saying they were going with me, or some other guy was, so nothing came of it at that time. Finally, in 1968, we did meet when he came out to California to do a TV Pogo special at MGM. I had been asked to come over and work at MGM and one day Kelly came into a room where I was picking up some work from an animator. When he started to leave I said to the animator, "Benny, I've never met Mr. Kelly." Walt turned around and Benny introduced me as Selby Daley. Kelly looked at me and said, "That wasn't your name!" That feat of memory really bowled me over. I guess a little explanation is in order at this point. I was Margaret Selby when I first started at Disney's but there were so many Margarets that I decided to go by my last name—Selby. (In fact at the time I was in charge of the paint lab, 9 of the 18 girls under me were named Margaret). Later I married Roger Daley and discovered that his former wife's name was also Margaret. At that point I changed my name officially to Selby Daley. Kelly had not only remembered my real name for over 30 years but recalled that I wore red shoes at the time he first saw me!

Q: Will you tell us about some of the problems you've faced in writing and drawing the Sunday POGO?

A: The drawing has been easier than the story for me. I'm surrounded by Kelly originals and when I want to draw Pogo, for instance, I look through Kelly's things and find a Pogo that's in the position I want. If I can't find one, I take two or three that are *almost* in that position and study them to get the full flavor. It's not tracing or copying exactly but trying to be sure that it looks the way he used to draw him.

I really got acquainted with the Pogo characters after I met Kelly at MGM in 1968 and became his assistant. My duty was to check on all the people who

were drawing the characters for the Pogo TV special and to make sure that they wre all drawing them the same because we didn't have model sheets. I had worked up some model sheets but Kelly was a little against the idea because his characters are very fluid and they were never planned for a whole bunch of people to draw them. If you look at Churchy, for instance, you'll notice that his head sometimes is perfectly round on the back of it, and that at other times it's almost square—according to the mood and what he's doing. Kelly didn't want the characters pinned down. I got the essence of what Kelly wanted from him and I was the liaison between him and the staff.

Incidentally, when this special was completed and we saw it on TV, Kelly was very disappointed with it. Stephanie was dying at the time and he couldn't spend as much time as he would have liked on the picture. He had to be back in New York with her and it got out of his control. It was so unlike a real Kelly product that he decided after Stephanie's death that he and I would make another film of our own. We then made a 15-minute full-animation picture which

we completed but which so far has never been shown. Kelly reanimated a lot of the scenes several times to get just what he wanted—he was a fantastic worker—so fast!

Q: Your method was different from the usual one, wasn't it?

A: Yes—we didn't work on cels. We didn't like the look of solid color paint applied to characters drawn on cels, when backgrounds etc. were done with colored pencils on paper which had a tooth to it. For instance, let's say we had a bird flying through a background which had been drawn and colored on paper. After Kelly had drawn the bird's various actions on paper, I'd ink them, color them, cut them out and then paste them on the number of cels required. In that way the handling and appearance of the character which was moving would be in harmony with the background drawing. Kelly did most of the drawing—I did some of the assistant work—and I did all the coloring, the cutting and the editing.

Kelly hastened his death in completing this picture because at this point he should have gone into the hospital for a checkup and rehabilitation. He had heart trouble and diabetes, and everything was deteriorating, but he insisted on staying in California to finish the picture—he could hardly walk, he was so ill. He worked just in his room—didn't even leave it. Then he came back to New York and went into the hospital. From then on, for the next two years, he was an invalid. For all his health problems, he was a phenomenal man. He could do a great deal of work at any time and could always do what it would take 6 other people to accomplish. Finally Kelly realized that he would be pretty weak from then on, so at this point he hired Don Morgan to be his artist. Kelly figured that he himself would write the strip, that Morgan would do the drawing on the dailies, and that Kelly and I would do the Sunday page together, with him doing the penciling and me the inking. Don, incidentally, now draws the dailies which Kelly's son, Stephen, writes. Don works for animator Ralph Bakshi in California. Steve writes the dailies here in New York and mails them out to the coast after the lettering has been done here.

Q: You and Walt were married under very unusual circumstances, weren't you?

A: We were all ready to get married—had had all our blood tests, license, etc., but he developed gangrene in one of his legs at the time of his amputation. I wasn't going to be allowed to visit him in ''intensive care'' unless I was a member of the family, so it was arranged that a judge friend of his, Sam Silverman, the Supreme Court judge, came over and performed the ceremony here in New York. After a while Walt recovered and came home.

Q: You mentioned earlier that the drawing part of the Sunday Pogo *was easier for you than the story. Can you say something about that?*

A: You might think that by reading and rereading some of Kelly's cartoons that maybe you could pick up a clue here and there, and possibly redo them—but it's impossible.

I *can* say that Kelly and I had a similar sense of humor. Of course his was much better and more developed but we laughed at the same things. Talking back and forth about some situation, we'd often come out with the same conclusion. We were so in tune in most ways that I can imagine, to some degree, what he would do with a certain idea. If I succeed in any manner in making the strip seem like Kelly, I'm very happy. I used to tease him by the way, and remind him that *I'm* actually a swamp person. I was raised in the swamps of Florida—we lived way out in the country, we were surrounded by them, and my brother and I used to go out and catch little alligators, whereas Kelly never even saw a swamp till Pogo was several years old.

I was asked by the syndicate not to deal in politics on the Sunday page because Sunday should be more for the children, and more fanciful things, fairy tales and pratfalls etc. should be worked into the page. I do try and emphasize big words once in a while—it's an educational thing and something different. Sometimes when I'm really dry on ideas, I sit down and go through a bunch of Kelly's things and take notes about some kind of a twist I might give them. Or I might even note exactly how he handled an idea, hoping to do a twist of it later.

Q: Walt Kelly often seemed to have a gruff exterior. What was he really like?

A: He was the softest-hearted guy inside that gruff exterior, but he could scare people silly. He'd be sitting in his room when he and I were making that 15-minute animated film I told you about a little while ago, and no one would dare come into that room. He could just turn around and glare at them for interrupting him and they'd melt. I remember that the guy who operated a studio where we were working at one point was afraid to talk to Kelly. He'd come to me and ask me to speak to Kelly for him. But if anybody needed anything, Kelly would always be the first to try and help them with it. And he was always trying to help somebody get a job. He was always a big tipper. Never small-talked and particularly didn't like anybody to fawn over him. When anybody came up and said, ''Oh, Mr. Kelly, I think you're marvelous!'' he would just withdraw completely and wilt back down inside himself. As a result, he'd be gruff toward these people because he was embarrassed and ill-at-ease with them, and wanted them to just go away and leave him alone.

As I said, he didn't like small-talk. Maybe he was more of a lecturer than a conversationalist. When we first started going together, he almost always asked someone else to come with us, thinking that I'd like to be entertained with the third person's small-talk which he didn't want to indulge in. After he found out that I didn't talk much either, and preferred to listen, and didn't mind his silence, we'd just go out by ourselves. My friends used to kid me by saying, ''You make a remark to Kelly one day and he answers you the next!'' He was a very intelligent man and knew so much about so many things. He read a great deal and retained everything he read. He could give you accurate information about almost anything you'd mention. At times when somebody would be talking on some subject, he'd sit quietly for a while till he couldn't stand their inaccuracies anymore, and then he'd say, ''Well, here's how the situation *really* is.'' But he wouldn't always put you down. Politics, history, geology, all these things and more interested him. He had toured the world several times and knew what was going on in politics in any country. He seemed to be able to predict what was going to happen so often, and I think he could have been a top-notch economist if he hadn't been a cartoonist.

He didn't want anybody to know who he was personally—wanted to be known only as Walt in a bar, for instance. Didn't want people to say, ''That's *the* Walt Kelly.'' This made him very self-conscious. Steve tells of an occasion when Walt was at P. J. Moriarty's and some guy came up to the bartender and said, ''I understand Walt Kelly comes in here.'' Walt himself was sitting down at the other end of the bar and overheard the bartender reply, ''Aw, he used to—I don't see much of him anymore.'' Afterwards, according to Steve, Walt slipped the bartender a $20 and said, ''Boy, that was a close call!'' We used to search out places where he wouldn't be known.

Q: I'd like you to add a few words about your own son if you will.

A: I'm delighted to—Scott Daley attends college in Santa Barbara, he's 26, and he's worked a good deal in the studios during summers and holidays. He composed the music for the animation film Kelly and I did, and played all the parts himself with various instruments.

Interview by Nancy Beiman

Nancy Beiman, the animator whom we PROfiled in Issue #54, for June 1982, recently talked with SELBY KELLY, the widow of Walt (Pogo) Kelly, and came up with the following very interesting conversation.

Q: What was Kelly's job at Disney?

SELBY KELLY: He started as a story man. One day he went to Walt Disney and said, ''I think I would be able to write better for the animation if I knew more *about* animation. I'd like to try animating.'' Disney said, ''Sure, go right ahead.'' He wound up doing the ringmaster in *Dumbo*, among other things.

Q: I'd like to ask whether you ever met Walt Kelly at the Disney Studios, since you were there at the same time (in the 1930s).

SELBY KELLY: No, I didn't meet Kelly there. In fact, while I was there I didn't even hear of him. After the strike (of 1940), when I got to know a bunch of the people who worked there, I heard about him; particularly when he put out the *Pogo* comic books.

They would say, ''Have you seen this? He's one of us.''

Q: So it was the people at the MGM studio who first brought his work to your attention?

SELBY KELLY: Mostly Disney people who had gotten together during the strike. We had little groups. In California, you lived so far apart from each other that you didn't fraternize once you moved to a different studio unless you lived *somewhere* close.

My first husband, Roger Daley, and I used to get together with Pat Matthews, Frank Smith and others and read the *Pogo* books. We'd have ''*Pogo* Evenings.'' We'd all get together, have spaghetti and meatballs, and sit around—each one of us would be assigned a character—and we would ''read'' our characters, saying what they were saying in the books.

Q: I'd like a little background on the film, We Have Met the Enemy and He Is Us. *How did you get involved in the project?*

SELBY KELLY: Well, first there was the MGM

Pogo special directed by Chuck Jones. At that time, I was President of the Cartoonist's Guild, and I was working as a freelancer out of the Guild office. Frank Braxton, the first Negro animator, called me up and asked me why I didn't work in the studio instead of freelancing. I said okay, that sounded like fun; I'd been in my ivory tower for quite a while. So I went to MGM, to the Chuck Jones unit. I worked as an assistant animator to Frank Braxton, but he had cancer. They thought they had it in remission, but shortly after I got there he had to go back into the hospital. So I was at MGM without any particular person to work with. Kelly and I met and he asked that I be his assistant.

Q: Was Kelly actually animating on the picture?

SELBY KELLY: Yes. He did the layouts; of course he wrote the story; and he animated a lot of scenes.

Now, MGM had three different films in production at the same time. On the same day, sometimes, the animators would work on *"Phantom Tollbooth"* and *"Horton Hears a Who"* and the *Pogo* Birthday Special. So they didn't draw Pogo the way Kelly did it. They're very subtle characters, anyhow. There's another problem because of the amount of footage that has to be put out (on a television special).

The animators didn't add any "extra" little things. If you're working at home, and you want to cut in on to your own time, you can take as much time as you want to and you're paid by footage. But when you're working in a studio, you have to put out a certain amount of footage per day, or per week. If you stop, and juice it up a little and add a lot of extra personality bits so that it makes a nice scene, you're not getting your footage in. So most of the action in the scenes was down to the bedrock. They just did *exactly* what was called for. Kelly was very disappointed in the picture.

So he said to me one day as we were sitting at the bar upstairs: "What do you say that *we* do a picture ourselves, and show them how it *should* look?" I said, "Fine, wonderful, I'd like that." I didn't know it at that time, but Kelly had already talked to a producer, who wanted to do this pollution thing. Kelly decided that this would be the perfect opportunity; he would have total control; so we did it ourselves. But the producer had a partner who was enamored of live action, and who talked him into getting involved in a

production with the "Burtons" (Elizabeth and Richard). They went over to England to see them, and what with this, that, and the other they used up all the money. It left Kelly and me without a studio to work for, although we used the offices where we had already established ourselves. We finished the picture under shoestring operating conditions because Kelly didn't have a great deal of money at that time to invest in anything. His wife Stephanie had just died after prolonged, expensive illness.

Q: Was that why the film was cut from 30 minutes to 15? (A reel shot from storyboard drawings, a "Leica reel" still exists in the 30-minute form.)

SELBY KELLY: Originally the storyboard was for a full half hour. The man who was to sell it to the networks said he could sell it better if it were two 15-minute lengths, so that it could be shown on different days, or could subsequently be shown with other films if they wanted to. Kelly rewrote the story a bit, and did the first fifteen minutes, but never did get around to doing the second. It is a complete picture, but it leaves out a lot that was in the original half-hour. At first Kelly did the film storyboard fashion. Then, as we had time on our hands, he'd add a little more to the scenes as they were trying to sell it. He was waiting for the money so that we could do it in really *full* animation. He'd redo scenes; some of them were redone six times, adding more action each time. We never did get full animation in the whole picture.

Q: Did you assist on the drawing of the comic strip?

SELBY KELLY: Not while Kelly was alive. I drew the strip for a year and a half after Kelly died. That wasn't meant to be the case. In 1973 Kelly had been too ill to draw for some time, and the syndicate was after him to get a "crew" together. He didn't know anybody in New York who could draw the characters (it turned out later that one of his assistants, Henry Shikuma, could do them quite well), but Kelly hired a guy from California who had worked on the MGM special. He did a few dailies to stories that Kelly had already written when suddenly there was a week's work that was indescribably awful. It seems that due to personal problems the artist had farmed it out to someone else who did it in a very Japanese style. I couldn't continue using his work if it was going to be farmed out, so I started doing it myself.

Q: I've heard about the "legendary" speed at

These dailies cover the period from Selby and Walt Kelly's wedding day, October 23, 1972, when he was very ill, through December 2, 1972. All of these dailies were lettered by Henry Shikuma. Kelly's mind remained nimble despite his infirmities. While Kelly's ability to draw was somewhat impaired at this time, his writing stayed crisp and funny.

which Kelly worked. While cataloguing some work, I checked the dates: he was simultaneously *drawing a comic strip, doing political cartoons, writing a political column, illustrating books, writing and illustrating five different comic books,* and *taking trips with John Lardner to report for magazines on issues in different parts of the world! Did he draw with his hands and feet? How did he manage to do all this?*

SELBY KELLY: He was very fast. But, if you really stop to think about it, a drawing originates in your mind. And if you don't have it in your mind, you can't expect it to flow out of your fingers. Kelly had a very fast, brilliant mind, and he was thinking all the time and making little notes about what he was going to do. When it came time to put it on paper he already had it "drawn" in his mind, so he would just sit down and whip it out. He didn't have to hesitate, or stop and ponder. He had so many story ideas that he would have two or three of them going at once.

He asked me once when he was starting to get back into the work after a trip to the hospital, to go through some of the more recent proofs and try to find some story that he had discarded and not "carried on." With so many characters in the strip, you could have two or three doing one thing, and two or three

doing another, and they would branch out and go their own way. Sometimes he wouldn't go back to see what they were doing, follow them up.

John Horn, a man who worked with Kelly in many of his escapades with television, newspapers, and magazines, once said that he and Kelly were going to go out to lunch. Kelly batted out his political column, handed his week's worth of strips to someone to carry to the printer's, and started to go out the door. Suddenly he said, "Oh, just a minute!" went back to his desk without even taking his coat or hat off, sat at the typewriter and batted out a sheet of words. John looked over his shoulder, and saw that it was a fairy story, one that he wasn't even going to illustrate. It was being done for a breakfast food company, to go on the back of a cereal box.

Q: He wrote those too?

SELBY KELLY: Yes, and in addition to all that he did a lot of charity work. At the National Cartoonists Society's Reuben dinners, he used to do beautiful drawings for Pan Am airlines. Pan Am would buy a page in the Reuben dinner book, and donate the money to the cartoonists' welfare fund. Kelly would illustrate them, and they never paid him for it.

Q: I've heard that Kelly never actually visited the

Okefenokee Swamp until years after starting Pogo. *What made him decide to go with the southern animal strip instead of developing the African animal strip* (Goozy) *that appears in some of the same issues of the comics as* Pogo?

SELBY KELLY: Kelly grew up in Bridgeport, which had a large amount of people from different countries. He liked to say that he and all his buddies "had more foreign languages that they could say that no one *else* had any use for." I guess he must have meant swear words. He was interested in languages because of that.

His health wouldn't allow him to be in the service during the Second World War, so he went into a branch of Government work that had him illustrating dictionaries. He traveled with various USO groups, and he was interested in talking to the people from different parts of the United States, compare their accents, etc. He liked the Southern accent. Also, his father used to read him things like *Uncle Remus*, and he picked up a lot of the Southern accent and the "fun talk" from his dad.

Q: That would also explain the "playing" with the language in the strip, where one word is meant but a similar one used in its place. You once mentioned that he would "think like a child."

SELBY KELLY: When people are very old and can't hear well, or very young and all words are new to them, they misinterpret them a lot. You *think* you hear something you don't hear, and you get a lot of fun out of those by twisting things round.

Q: A little talk about politics would be in order. How did political caricatures start going into Pogo? *The early strips are "funny animals" gags, and then all of a sudden you have McCarthy as a major character.*

SELBY KELLY: He was enough to make *anybody* political. People were really frightened of him. This was the first time that any comic strip had political comment in it. Comic strips were just meant to be funny and amusing. People pretended that they were for children, although the adults read them more than the kids did. Having lived through that era, I must say that it was a really, really terrible time. Anybody who did anything against the establishment was harassed.

Q: Did Kelly have any threats made or actions taken against him?

SELBY KELLY: Kelly's phone was tapped. He was threatened with all sorts of things, mostly with removal of his livelihood. Many papers dropped the strip. (Note: [documents obtained under] the Freedom

of Information Act recently revealed that the Government was corresponding with a civilian reporter who was sure that the ''lingo'' used in *Pogo* was a secret Russian code.) To prevent the papers dropping *Pogo*, Kelly used to do *two* strips. They are a lot of fun to look at. One set is called the ''Bunny Strips'' and most of them really were about bunnies; though some were also about the Okefenokee people. Kelly would send the ''Bunny Strips,'' along with the regular dailies, to papers that expressed disapproval of the politics. This way, they didn't have a big hole in the paper where *Pogo* usually was. Some newspapers had the guts to print *both* strips at the same time. On their editorial

page, they would say something like ''certain parts of the country won't print one of these strips,'' and made it into a good filler for themselves.

Q: Did the political harassment discontinue as the strip got older; say, when he was doing Johnson as a steer?

SELBY KELLY: There was a lot of pro-Wallace papers that didn't like what Kelly had to say about him. He drew him a little rooster, the Prince of Pompadoodle. Everything in life is politics, you can't just ''stay out of it.'' That's pretty much the way the ''political'' part of the strip was; instead of doing just a ''gag-a-day'' kind of thing, Kelly did poke fun at

LOOK, DUMBKOFF, YOU GOTTA BE AT *LEAST EIGHTEEN* BEFORE YOU CAN VOTE...SO FROM NOW ON YOU'RE 18.

EIGHTEEN IT IS.

11-9 PUBLISHERS-HALL SYNDICATE, INC.

NOW GET OUT THERE AND *REE*-CRUIT.

REE CRUIT, IT IS.

HOWDY, MIZ FROG... THIS IS THE YEAR FOR *WOMEN'S LIB*... ALL US GIRL VOTERS GONNA DRIVE THEM MEN OUT OF *OFFICE*.

GOOD FOR US, MIZ FLEA.

YEP, THEY GOT A NEW *VOTIN' AGE*...IT'S SEVENTEEN OR NINE-TEEN, OR *ONE* OF THEM.

WELL, LET'S SEE, I BEEN MARRIED SIX TIMES, GOT A THIRTY YEAR OLD BOY AN' A TWENTY-TWO YEAR OLD GRAN'CHILE ...HOW OLD'S THAT MAKE *ME*?

LESSEE, MIZ FROG, YOU GOT A 30 YEAR OLD SON AN' A 22 YEAR OLD GRANDCHILD, ...HOW OLD DO THAT MAKE YOU?

IT GIVES ME A LEG UP ON *THIRTY* AT LEAST...

11-10 PUBLISHERS-HALL SYNDICATE INC.

THEN YOU CAN VOTE...THE MINIMUM AGE IS UM...

THE MINIMUM AGE OF *ANY* THING IS *ONE* YEARS OLD.

THEN YOU CAN VOTE ALL THE YEARS AFTER BEING ONE YEARS OLD.

MY GOODNESS! S'POSE I LIVE TO BE A HUNDRED... I CAN VOTE *ONE HUNDRED* TIMES.

JUST IMAGINE YOU COULD LIVE SUCH A CLEAN LIFE YOU MIGHT LIVE FOR A HUNDRED, TWO HUNDRED, *FOUR HUNDRED* YEAR.

IF I PUT MY MIND TO IT, I COULD MAKE A *EVEN* FIVE HUNDRED.

11-11 PUBLISHERS-HALL SYNDICATE, INC.

PROPERLY TRAINED YOU'D MAKE A *THOUSAND* EASY.

YOU GOES ON A DIET OF GROUN' NUTS AN' PUNKIN' SEEDS....RUNS AROUND THE BLOCK 126 TIMES EVERY MORNING AND DO 57 PUSH-UPS EVERY DAWN.

WHAT'S THE TROUBLE?

DOIN' ALL *LIKE THAT THERE,* I FEEL OVER A THOUSAND ALREADY.

IT'S FUN TO BE A FLEA AN' WORKIN' FOR WOMEN'S LIB.... 'SPECIALLY IF YOU'RE A GIRL.

11-13 PUBLISHERS-HALL SYNDICATE INC.

'COURSE, IF I WAS A *GENTLEMAN FLEA*

I WOULDN'T TOUCH THE ASSIGNMENT WITH A TEN FOOT *HAIR-PIN*.

MY SAKES, WHO'S *THEM*?

what he knew best, because he was a reporter. He started out as a reporter long before he became a cartoonist, and was very proud of the fact.

Q: Pogo *first started in* Animal Comics *comic books, didn't he?*

SELBY KELLY: Kelly did quite a few comics, actually. There was *Our Gang* comics, *Brownies, Animal Comics* and many others. He would get more money if he wrote a story in addition to illustrating it, as he was paid for two different jobs. He started this little group of characters in the swamp. Because what he wanted to do was have his own little town, a microcosm of the whole world. The swamp is surre-

alistic, away from everything, a little mysterious. In a way, the animals did have a town. They had a store, a newspaper, and a variety of things. At first Kelly's Okefenokee Swamp bunch of animals were friends with a little boy named Bumbazine. The comic book was called *Bumbazine and his friend Albert* and then it was just *Albert*; and then it was *Albert and Pogo*; then it was *Pogo and Albert*; finally just *Pogo*. Kelly dropped Bumbazine rather early because he decided that while it is possible to imagine animals talking to each other, you know they don't really say things that a human being can understand when "talking" to them. The animal might understand the human being,

11-17 PUBLISHERS-HALL SYNDICATE, INC.

© 1972 WALT KELLY

11-18 PUBLISHERS-HALL SYNDICATE INC.

© 1972 WALT KELLY

11-20 PUBLISHERS-HALL SYNDICATE INC.

© 1972 WALT KELLY

11-21 PUBLISHERS-HALL SYNDICATE, INC.

© 1972 WALT KELLY

but a human can't really have a conversation with the animals. Bumbazine also looked very realistic and the animals were drawn like cartoons. Pogo was in from either the first or the second story, and he sure looked different from how he looks now. He looked like a potbellied rat. Long pointy nose with little pieces of wire sticking out of it.

Q: He actually looked a lot like the Deacon Mushrat character he did later on. What made Kelly decide to put Pogo *into a daily strip?*

SELBY KELLY: Kelly just got really going on the comic stories. He was doing reporting, but needed more money, so he kept doing comic books on the side. He was just going into high gear on *Pogo* when they stopped publishing *Animal Comics*. At the same time Kelly was given the opportunity to take over a post in management of the *New York Star*, which is what *PM* magazine turned into after it folded. Kelly was Art Editor, and he had to buy artwork for the paper from various people, so he decided to put the strip in there.

Q: Very clever.

SELBY KELLY: Well, it was clever, but the newspaper didn't last very long. When the *Star* folded, *Pogo* was out of business again. It was then picked up by the Post-Hall syndicate, but eventually

WHAT WE *GOTTA* DO THIS YEAR IS MAKE UP A NEW CHRISTMAS CAROL.

IF WE KNEW ANYBODY NAMED MADELINE, WE COULD WRITE *PADDLIN' MADELINE HOME.*

I'D RUTHER PADDLE HER OVER TO *FORT MUDGE LUNA PARK.*

HOW ABOUT "*UP JOSEPHINE IN YOUR FLYIN' MACHINE*..."

THAT'S IT.... THE KIND OF THING THAT WRITES ITSELF.

11-25 PUBLISHERS-HALL SYNDICATE INC.

©1972 WALT KELLY

ARE YOU FIGHTIN' BY THE MARQUIS OF QUEENSBURY RULES...?

NO! THE MARQUIS OF *KINGSBURY'S* RULES--- OTHERWISE A CERTAIN AMOUNT OF CHEATIN' SETS IN.

OKAY NOW, *STAND BACK!*

HOW CAN *EITHER* ONE OF 'EM BE FOR WOMEN'S LIB WHEN *NEITHER* KNOWS IF THEY DRESS ON THE RIGHT OR THE LEFT?

11-27 PUBLISHERS-HALL SYNDICATE INC.

©1972 WALT KELLY

AIN'T YOU GONNA GIT INTO THE MELEE?

I BEEN *THINKIN'* ABOUT IT.

THERE'S YOUR CHANCE... GRAB THAT *STICK.*

I WOULDN'T *DO* THAT IF I WAS YOU, SIS.

NO?

NO, YOU SEE I'M A *LADY ANGLEWORM* WHAT BEEN COLD KONKED AN' MY MISTER DON'T FANCY ME BEIN' IN *PUBLIC FRACASES.*

VERY WELL.

11-28 PUBLISHERS-HALL SYNDICATE INC.

©1972 WALT KELLY

MARTHA, LOOKS LIKE THAT'S YOU...YOU MIND IF I TAKE MY WIFE *HOME* MADAM?

HELP YERSELF.

SHE GOT KINDA COLD KONKED IN THE WOMEN'S LIB BRAWL.

IF THERE WAS A HALF-OUNCE CATEGORY, SHE'D BE A WORLD CHAMP.

I'D CARRY HER OVER MY SHOULDER IF I HAD ANY *SHOULDERS.*

ROLL HER UP IN A BALL AN' BOUNCE HER HOME.

. GREAT, I CAN DRIBBLE HER ALL THE WAY.

11-29 PUBLISHERS-HALL SYNDICATE INC.

©1972 WALT KELLY

Kelly held all copyright to the strip himself.

Q: He would have been one of the first artists to own his own strip. Could you tell me if there were any other comic strips that Kelly developed at any time?

SELBY KELLY: There are a few Sunday strips featuring a little puppy dog. I don't remember its name. He started to do an advertising comic book designed to go in magazines, for Ma Bell, featuring an octopus-conglomerate. He showed it saving children, putting out fires, and so on with all its octopus arms. He did some pretty color sketches, and some finished ink drawings, but I don't think it ever got anywhere.

He also planned to do a science fiction strip. He knew two or three good writers, including a lady named Betsy Curtis who had been a *Pogo* fan for a while. She was going to write the strip. The syndicate told Kelly, when he was going to start it, that "the world was in such a turmoil" (this was during the Korean War) that people didn't want a "stressful" thing. Stick to the funny animals and forget science fiction. Later, a section of *Pogo* strips had them going to Mars and winding up in Australia. He also had some fantastic settings in the strip in the '60's.

He never did the science fiction strip, never even

designed the characters, but I do have a paper analyzing all major stars and planets, determining which would and which would not be plausible as points of origin for various characters.

Q: I'd love to know the reasons for discontinuing the strip. Was there a decline in syndication?

SELBY KELLY: The strip declined a little after Kelly died. But a lot of strips had started weathering that. It was formerly the ''kiss of death'' if the original artist was no longer doing the strip. In this case, it didn't decline immediately. The newspapers started giving less and less space for the comics. If you remember *Pogo*, it's got a lot of words and lines, and every bit of space was taken up with the design of the strip itself. So when they got smaller and smaller, down to the size of a postage stamp, people couldn't really read it. A lot of the ''dramatic'' continuing strips have fallen off too, because of this. The News-

paper Comics Council had a meeting, where it was revealed that the papers had no intention of giving more space to the comics (even though the ''paper crisis'' that had precipitated the shrinkage was over); and I said that there was no way I was going to continue *Pogo* then. The quality would eventually fall off too far. However, now that I've started to do comic strip *books*, there's plenty of space in them. We design the pages the way we want to, with nobody tampering with them and making them small, nonreadable.

Q: We are all looking forward to seeing the new Pogo comic books. Thank you very much.

NOTE: A Walt Kelly Pogo *retrospective was mounted at the Graham Galleries in New York City from September 27 through October 1983, commemorating the* 40th *anniversary of the starting of the* Pogo *strip and the 10th anniversary of Walt Kelly's death.*

These are daily strips done by Selby and Henry Shikuma after Walt's death.

HEY, CHURCHY, WHY'S WE RUNNIN' FROM THE **ETERNAL REVENUE SERVICE** MAN FOR?

WE DON'T PAY NO INKUM TAX 'CAUSE WE DON'T GOT **NO INKUM.**

I DUNNO 'BOUT YOU BUT **I** WAS AFEERD HE WAS GONNA ASK ME 'BOUT THE **53¢** I WON OFFA MR. MIGGLE IN A **PINOCHLE GAME** BACK IN '71····

3-26 Field Newspaper Syndicate, 1975

I DUNNO WHY EVER'BODY'S SO SKEERED OF THE **ETERNAL REVENUE SERVICE** MAN···· ALL ONE'S GOTTA DO IS TELL THE **TRUTH**····

3-27

'SIDES, NOBODY IN THE SWAMP PAYS **INKUM TAX** 'CAUSE NOBODY'S GOT NO INKUM.

IT'S ALL RIGHT FOR **YOU** TO TALK, POG', BUT **I** IS STILL IN THE **50% TAX BRACKET.**

50% OF NOTHING IS ······?

★WELL★ Hello, THERE!

HELLO, SIR!

3-28

❥*I*❤ don't believe ★**I** have SEEN ☞**YOU** before, *my* **GOOD MAN**≈

I'VE BEEN HERE BEFORE AS A REPORTER FOR **NEWSLIFE** MAGAZINE BUT NOW I'M WITH THE **INTERNAL REVENUE SERVICE.**

Um ☞ I just REMEMBERED, *I'm* due in ➤**GREENWICH**★ CONN., for the MUSEUM≈ of CARTOON ART *Show* ◀🔲

?

HEARD THAT A **REVENUE SERVICE** MAN IS IN THE SWAMP ASKIN' QUESTIONS····

UM?

3-29 Field Newspaper Syndicate, 1975

WHAT!? A GUMMINT **REVENOOR** IN THE SWAMP!? I GOTTA GIT BACK HOME!

EASY, EASY···· IT'S THE **ETERNAL REVENUE SERVICE** MAN···· NOT THE *LIKKER* KIND.

WHOOSH! YOU HAD ME SCAIRT! I HAD VISIONS OF ALL MY BOTTLES OF **SNAKE-BITE CURE** BEIN' SMASHED····

SORRY

An Interview with Selby Kelly

On June 8, 1985, I recorded the following interview with Selby Kelly in her New York City apartment. It has never been published before.

B.C. Jr.

A self-portrait by Selby Kelly on a business card (about 1978).

Q: Would you tell me about your memories of making the Pogo Special Birthday Special, *the half-hour animated cartoon show that aired on NBC-TV, May 18, 1969?*

SELBY KELLY: That's the name of the MGM picture that Chuck Jones did at Sunset and Vine. That's where the studio was in Hollywood. I know that Kelly wanted to do some animation and he shied off from having it done at Disney because he was afraid it would become a Disney product instead of a Kelly product. I don't know if he knew Chuck before or not. I really don't know the intimate details. But he decided to do it and Chuck Jones was a good way to go.

Q: Did Kelly approach Chuck Jones or vice versa?

SELBY KELLY: I really don't know that, either. I know there were a lot of people involved, including Proctor and Gamble who were underwriting the production. Maybe they suggested Jones.

Q: How were you hired to work on the film?

SELBY KELLY: I was working in Hollywood at that time as a freelancer. I was president of the Screen Cartoonists Guild. It's the original union that went out on strike against Disney in the 1940s and the reason it was called a guild was that a lot of people wouldn't join a union. But Michelangelo belonged to a guild, so that made it all right for them to join a guild. Unions weren't aristocratic. After all, you're an artist. Anyway, I was working out of the Guild's office.

I received a phone call from a black animator, one of only two in the business at that time. His name was Frank Braxton. He told me that I should be his assistant at the Chuck Jones unit of MGM. I told him that it sounded good, as I wanted a steady income instead of the feast-and-famine of freelancing. So I became Frank's assistant.

At this time they were working on three pictures and I didn't know that they had the *Pogo* film to do. They were doing a picture from the children's book, *The Phantom Toll Booth* and they were doing one of Dr. Suess's books, *Horton Hears a Who*. And then the third one was a *Pogo* picture with Walt Kelly supervising it. I had never met Walt Kelly, but I admired him and certainly admired his work on *Pogo*. So I was very thrilled that the *Pogo* project was going to be there. This would have been September 1968, because I met Kelly in October 1968.

Frank Braxton, unbeknownst to me, was ill. He had Hodgkins disease. He told me about it after we started working side by side. He had to take pills, so he told me why he was taking pills. He thought it was in remission but within a couple of weeks, Frank was in the hospital again. And sadly, this time he succumbed. Chuck Jones wanted me to stay on . . . and that got me into the MGM unit. I should add that Frank Braxton was the first black man ever elected president of any union in Hollywood.

I had worked for Chuck Jones before and had a good reputation as an animator. I had worked for him at Warner Brothers on *Looney Tunes* and *Merry Melodies* and those types of things—Bugs Bunny, the Roadrunner.

So after Frank died and I stayed on at MGM, I would at first just get the overflow from other animators. I continued working as an assistant. An animator does the emotional action. He interprets it in pencil—not every drawing, but he does the main part of it. He may leave out three or four drawings in between his own drawings. In those days the animators' drawings were done roughly. This was also the time photocopying instead of inking was first being used by some people.

As an assistant I would be cleaning up the animator's drawing. I'd put the drawing on my light board and a clean piece of paper on top and then redraw it, using his rough as a structural guide, drawing a neat line.

Q: How were you assigned to the Pogo *project?*

SELBY KELLY: I was picking up work from various animators one day and I went into Benny Washam's one noon to say I was about out of work. He was having lunch and offered me some fruit. I was sitting munching on it when Kelly walked in. He tried to excuse himself and back out and Ben told him to come on in. Kelly was at that time doing the layouts on the *Pogo* picture. So he showed Benny some things and handed him a section of layouts that Benny was to work on.

As Kelly turned to leave, I did something I'd never done in my life before. I asked for an introduction. I'd seen Kelly in the hall but I'd never met him. I knew who he was. So I said to Benny, "I have never met Mr. Kelly."

Walt stopped, turned around and came back in. Benny apologized and said that he thought I knew everybody. "Walt, this is Selby Daley," said Benny.

Walt looked at me and said, "That wasn't your name."

I responded, "What do you mean, that wasn't my name?"

"When you worked at Disney's, that wasn't your name," said Kelly.

"Well, that's true, but how did you know?"

"What was your name then?"

"I was Margaret Selby then."

"Yes, that's right. I knew that because that was my mother's name," he said. Well, it wasn't his

mother's name at all, but he remembered me from Disney's back in the late 1930s, even though we had never met.

Q: How did he remember you?

SELBY KELLY: Well he used to stand at the window of the men's building. Disney's was segregated by gender then. Women were not allowed in the men's building and vice versa. A woman who entered the men's building would be fired immediately. I was hired [there] in 1936. I had a job in the dime store to hold me after I'd put in my application at Disney's, but this was my first animation job. The extent of my art training had been during high school in Pasadena, California. I was born in Colorado, raised in Florida until the ninth grade, and then graduated high school in California. At that time they only allowed women to do inking and painting at Disney's. They put me into training and I learned to ink and paint in the Disney style. They were hiring lots of people and I inked and painted part of *Snow White*.

Q: Do you remember which sections of Snow White *you worked on?*

SELBY KELLY: No, no, no. They broke up scenes into such small bits that you'd never know. We didn't do like the men and have one character you'd work on. They would hand you a small scene or portion of a scene, a stack of drawings that you would then trace off onto celluloid. You'd use the pegboards with the little registration pegs to hold the art in place. I worked on all the characters in *Snow White* but I don't know what scenes they're in.

Q: At Disney's, were you in one big room working with a group of other women?

SELBY KELLY: In a way, it was a series of halls more than rooms. As you entered the women's building, on the right were a couple of offices that the woman in charge of the the women had, and then on the left of the entrance was the ink and paint department, where they made all the paint. Then off the main hall were four or five more hallways. There were two desks each in a long row down the halls, about 10 deep.

I practiced inking and painting and I liked painting much better. Then, while I was painting, my brother was about to move away to Florida for four years. We were very close. He was driving to Florida and he came to the studio on the day he was leaving to say goodbye. They would not allow me to walk out to the gate and say goodbye to him. I was so heartbroken it caught the attention of a number of people there. Even though they were bosses and semi-bosses, they were angry about it. One of them, Mary Wiser, who was in charge of the paint lab, was very angry about the treatment I had received from Disney management. She needed somebody in the paint lab, so she asked for me. Eventually I became in charge of it. I started out by delivering the pigments and ended up in charge of mixing them and supervising the department.

You'd take the major jar of a color, about a quart mason jar, and scoop it off into a half ounce or an ounce jar. Mary had a big stone mill and she'd get pounds and pounds of different pigments. In the summer the formula for colors was a little different from the formula used in winter. At the time gum arabic was the main base of the binder and we'd put a little extra glycerin in it during the dry weather, and a little extra alcohol in it during wet weather. This was to try and keep the cels from sticking when they were put together.

Q: Returning to Kelly, how did he know you there?

SELBY KELLY: He had visually known me. In those days nothing was as brilliantly colored as [the colors] we have now. Cars were dull colors. Clothes were dull colors. Shoes were black or brown. My father had bought me a pair of red shoes. Kelly remembered my red shoes. I wore those red pumps and he had asked somebody who I was. At the old Disney Studio on Hyperion, most of the girls had to park out on the street if they drove a car to work. The men got the parking lot. So you had to walk through the front gate and pass the men's building before getting to the women's building. Later on, when the studio moved out to Buena Vista, we had to walk past even more of the men's building. The women's building was clear in the back corner of the lot.

As part of their fun of the morning, Kelly and all the other guys used to watch all the women walk by. He asked somebody my name and when they told him, they also told him I was going with somebody.

He either was married or just about to get married at that time. Kelly liked to tell the story and he told it different ways different times, that he thought I was interesting and would have liked to meet me, but his life was involved. I know his first wife held him off a little before they were married and this might have been during that period.

So at MGM he asked me what I was doing and where my desk was. He came over later that afternoon and stood by my desk and asked me who I was working with and I told him the circumstances of Frank Braxton's death. He then asked if I'd like to be his assistant and I said, ''Of course.'' Then he cleared it with Chuck Jones.

Q: At that point, how far along was the film?

SELBY KELLY: I guess maybe one-third through the physical animation of the story.

Q: Did making the film go pretty smoothly?

SELBY KELLY: Well, in animation in the old Disney times they would assign different men to each character. You would study the personality of the character and by a Mickey Mouse guy or a Donald Duck guy and you wouldn't draw the other ones. You had to really feel it and put yourself into it because animators are really actors. In the modern way of drawing, particularly in a studio that had three films going on at the same time, different animators would have to work on all three features simultaneously to keep up with production schedules and deadlines to get the pictures out.

Q: Did Kelly ever verbalize frustration over this?

SELBY KELLY: Afterwards. During this period his wife Stephanie was ill with cancer. When I first met Kelly, she had not yet been diagnosed as having cancer. She was only 45 years old when she died in 1970. According to a story her sister told me, she had said as a child that she wouldn't live past 45. Where she got that idea I don't know. Kelly was under a great deal of pressure and stress. He was on the West Coast and he had this crisis on the East Coast. He had to get the *Pogo* strip out. He had to spend time with his family and Stephanie. And he had publicity to get out on the *Pogo* film as well as doing layouts and guiding it.

Q: I assume he had a drawing board and did the Pogo *strip at the MGM studio. Is that right?*

SELBY KELLY: Kelly worked on the twelfth floor of the building at the corner of Sunset and Vine in Hollywood. Chuck Jones called it Tower 12. I think Chuck had a studio of his own there before he hooked up with MGM and then they moved the contract work there. There was a room with two desks in it that Kelly and I had and Kelly often did the syndicated strip there during this period. He would alternate between the East and West Coasts, spending one or two weeks in each place. On the West Coast he stayed at the

Hollywood Roosevelt Hotel. He would just work, work, work. He would come to the studio early in the morning and stay until late at night.

Q: Kelly did storyboards and layouts. Did he also do model sheets?

SELBY KELLY: No, he didn't do model sheets to guide the other animators, which seemed odd to me. He had distributed a lot of *Pogo* books, so maybe he expected Chuck Jones to take care of that matter. As a production person I looked for model sheets, and when I discovered there weren't any, I asked Kelly's permission to do them. Of course I didn't do the drawing myself. I took a bunch of Kelly's drawings, including some *Pogo* books, photocopied them, cut them out, and made the model sheets that way.

When you're drawing a character in motion you change its shape. You should have a basic shape to start and then elongate it, squash it, or manipulate it to fit the action. This is particularly true of Churchy. His head is mostly nose and it changes into all sorts of shapes. Production on the picture was half over before I distributed the model sheet.

Q: Would this be prior to the cel being inked and painted?

Model sheet of *Pogo* made by Selby for MGM film in 1969.

SELBY KELLY: That's right. When the assistant had finished cleaning up the animator's work and had done the in between drawings, Kelly would clasp the drawings together with one hand and flip them with the other.

Q: Here's a theory about why Kelly became involved with the animation of Pogo *in 1968. The syndicated comic strip had been successful since the late 1940s. Kelly wasn't getting any younger. His health wasn't getting any better. He had all these problems with his wife's health. It certainly wasn't for the money that he agreed to do this film and work like a dog. Did he feel it was now or never? Did he ever talk to you about why he became interested in animation again?*

SELBY KELLY: He had a feeling he wasn't going to live much longer. He did mention that to me a couple of times—that he wasn't in the best of health, wouldn't live forever, little remarks like that—so I think that had a lot to do with his interest in animating *Pogo*. He's also said that when he first designed the characters he had animation in mind. He had waited all these years to animate *Pogo*. It was almost a last hurrah.

Every time he started to do something extracurricular with *Pogo*, such as merchandising, something happened. Before the film he started to do merchandising with Wade Pottery in Ireland. He designed wonderful model sheets for them to do Pogo figurines. He cut up the one he had done for Albert. He did things like that sometimes. If he needed a piece of paper, he'd grab an old drawing or old original and use the back of the paper and cut it up in pieces. He drew the Pogo one, Albert was cut up and turned into a template, and he made some starts on others.

When he did the Pogo model sheet for Wade Pottery, Stephanie was pregnant. They went to England and met with the people at the pottery. Kelly made friends all around. Then they came back to the States and Wade Pottery went ahead and made the Pogo figurine. I guess in a way Kelly was testing them out. If they made Pogo right, he'd go ahead with others. They made some prototype figurines and forwarded them to Kelly.

Stephanie then had her child. No one was sure what the problem was at first, but the baby wasn't reacting the way a baby should. The child was mentally retarded and remains so. It was a devastating emotional blow to Kelly. I've seen Kelly's correspondence with Wade Pottery telling them his personal problems about having the baby tested and how it would prevent pursual of the project. Kelly did a phenomenal amount of work but he really had his hands full.

Q: Returning to the Pogo *film, how did Kelly lay out the scenes?*

SELBY KELLY: A layout is made to block out the action of the scene. Kelly had written the script and done the storyboard, which is like a long comic-strip breakdown of the script. Each one of these scenes from the storyboard must be drawn up in the proper size for the animator. Kelly would do the first and last drawings and the animator would take it from there.

Q: Were you there when Kelly saw the first showing of the completed film?

SELBY KELLY: Yes, I was. We had seen bits and pieces in what used to be called the sweatbox, a small room with a projector and a whole lot of people. I don't think he was really happy with anything. Kelly had spent a great deal of time on drawings to be used for point-of-sale displays in stores, but no one came to pick them up. I just know he gestured to some stuff on his desk once and complained that there'd been such a hurry for it and now it was laying around for months. I never questioned him closely on anything. He didn't like to go into a lot of detail about anything. He'd make his remarks, say what he wanted to say, and I'd listen.

Q: The plastic figures of Pogo and friends packaged in Proctor and Gample soap came out at this time. Do you know the story behind them?

SELBY KELLY: A company that was a licensing group did the plastic figures. I don't know if that company did the initial sculpting or sent it to Japan. The initial three-dimensional Pogo and Albert were absolutely laughable—they didn't resemble the characters much at all. Albert the Alligator wore a turtleneck sweater with an eiderdown ruff at the bottom around his hips. Kelly refused to use them. He took some plasticine clay and sculpted the characters himself—Pogo, Albert, Beauregard, Churchy, Howland Owl, and Porkypine. They were all done in the size to be reproduced. Then the mold was made, maybe in Japan, I'm not sure, but I know the figurines were made in Japan. They also did some plastic mugs with decals on them, but Kelly wanted them to be like

Toby mugs and even did some sculpting for them. He created a bunch of those in plasticine. I saw them there at Tower 12/MGM and then I never saw them again. I think that after the picture was done and he left that room, lots of things disappeared. The rooms were not locked. Anybody could get in and out.

There were a number of layouts where each character had a full page of heads drawn by Kelly and those disappeared from his bulletin board while he was on vacation. So he had an awful time with things. He'd come back from New York, walk into his animation office, stand there awhile, and say, "Somebody's moved one of my pencils."

Q: When was the work on Pogo Special Birthday Special *finished?*

SELBY KELLY: I honestly don't remember. It was televised on May 18, 1969. I believe they had originally planned a series, because one of the guys at the studio was collecting information from Kelly books, ideas that Chuck Jones thought would make a good picture. And Kelly did two or three more storyboards also.

Kelly didn't like the way the picture looked. When Kelly worked at Disney's every animator would throw in personality things of their own. If they were asked to have a character walk from left to right across the screen, they would try to do something special with little bits of actions. But given today's working speed, nobody can take time to do any extra things, especially when working on three films simultaneously.

Q. Is it fair to say that the animated Pogo *wasn't as much fun as anticipated?*

SELBY KELLY: It wasn't as successful as Kelly thought it would be. I'm talking about the film artistically. I know he was unhappy—he didn't like it. We were sitting at a bar called The Room at the Top located in the same building as the animation studio. He said, "Selby, what would you think if we did a picture, just you and I? And we'll show them what *Pogo*'s supposed to be like."

I told him I thought that would be wonderful. It turned out he'd already been thinking about it and had made arrangements with a producer who wanted to do an ecology film. And so we started working on *We Have Met the Enemy and He Is Us*. That was in 1970. I also worked at two or three small studios. I worked at Jay Ward part of the time, also at Graphic Films and

Churchill Films, making educational animated pictures. It was a time when freelancers moved around a lot.

Q: Where did you and Kelly have your studio?

SELBY KELLY: In another office building on Sunset about three blocks from Vine. Now both he and I didn't like the idea of celluloid animation technology for *Pogo*, with the characters painted a solid color. The idea of a solid-color figure placed in front of a finely noodled background didn't appeal. The techniques are so different. We felt it was a flaw in animation in general. Kelly wanted an effect more like a flip book.

To do a background he would draw a vignette. The background would actually be a foreground—a tree or a table or a something—and it would be held under the camera with the characters moving behind it. Now, with only one character to animate it was fine as we did every drawing on each page. We didn't break it up the way Hanna-Barbera does, the body held in place and legs and arms moving on separate cels. But when Kelly had two characters, one standing and listening while the second character did something, the listening character would jiggle a bit on the page because there was no way to attain perfect registration. So we started doing the old-fashioned thing of cutting the paper.

We didn't much use blue pencil underneath as by then I was familiar with the characters. Mostly we'd do the black line on regular animation bond and then color it in with Prismacolor pencils. Kelly selected the colors he felt most suitable for the characters. The #911 green was Albert the Alligator. To color the artwork I would feather it on, holding the pencil almost horizontal, going back and forth, back and forth, and then maybe turning it a little.

Q: Was there a specific division of labor?

SELBY KELLY: He did the animation and I did the assistant work in the original drawings. Then I did the coloring of the characters. Kelly did all the backgrounds, doing them in colored pencils directly.

Q: Were other people helping you?

SELBY KELLY: For a while we tried to hire a couple of people but we didn't have much cash flow. It was not supposed to be, but it ended up that Kelly was paying most of the cost of the production. This was tough on Kelly, coming immediately after Stephanie's long illness and death. He hired two other people but their technique was different and it didn't work out. Then there was one woman who did the editing and read the sound track. For some reason or other when Kelly did his lip sync animation to her track reading, it turned out wrong. At that time there was some question about whether to do the reading before or after the lip sync and how it related with the sound reaching the ears. I don't know what the theory was, but anyhow, her track reading didn't work with his lip sync. So I reread the track and eventually I did all the track reading, the rough editing of the audio, and the video of the picture after the camera had shot what we'd drawn.

Q: What was the planned length of the film?

SELBY KELLY: It started out as a half-hour film, but as it developed, it was decided by the man who was going to distribute it, and possibly sell it to TV and syndicate it, that it should be in fifteen-minute segments. Kelly reworked it so that the first fifteen minutes was a story in itself. He could easily have made a second fifteen-minute segment, but he had taken parts of the whole thing to create the first segment.

The film ended up being thirteen and three-quarter minutes long. The plan was to have the mayor of a town or some such official first make a speech; then the film would be shown, filling a half-hour segment.

Q: Was the end product of We Have Met the Enemy and He Is Us *a working print of the film?*

SELBY KELLY: Well, the original soundtrack was done just after the storyboard was finished, before we had done the animation, and the production people wanted to send the storyboard out on the road. However, they didn't want to send out the actual very cumbersome storyboard. The man who was head of production and who was going to do the selling said he thought it would be better if Kelly would do the sound effects with it. So they put the storyboard on film and Kelly went to a recording studio and talked the film through.

So now Pogo walks into a scene, sees Albert, and says to him, ''Albert, is that you making all that stench?'' And Albert turns to him and says, ''No it isn't me—it's that pig over there.'' Kelly did the whole picture like that, doing the voices and describing the action. That was the sound track we finally ended up with. On Kelly's instructions I edited it down to

where only the sounds needed for the characters were used and all of Kelly's descriptions were left out. It didn't turn out too satisfactorily because the guy in the sound booth when Kelly did the original didn't give him any cues. Kelly came out of there saying, ''I didn't know how I was sounding. They didn't give me any feedback or anything.''

Q: Do you think the problems that Kelly had in those situations were due to his lack of experience in animation for many years?

SELBY KELLY: Well, it was frustrating because the people producing it with him, or for him, ran out of money. They were trying to do two projects at once. They decided to go into live action. The producer bought a story and went to England to woo Richard Burton and Elizabeth Taylor to act in it. Well, by the time he'd received a maybe from them he didn't have any money left and he couldn't get anybody else to back him.

This meant we were not able to have anybody else work with us to finish the film. Kelly couldn't just stand back and direct—he had to do the physical work. By then he had put about $75,000 of his own money into the film, and that didn't include the lab costs.

Q: Who owns the film?

SELBY KELLY: The original producer folded as a company, but the man who was going to distribute the film paid the lab costs. I have no idea what the costs were. The film was never commercially released. It was shown for the first time at the Springfield Museum of Fine Arts in the fall of 1974, after Kelly died.

The thing that complicated it was that when the film was ready for the final mixing of sound and visuals, a problem arose. You put the soundtrack on and tell the guy to raise the sound a little here, lower it there, put in the sound effects there. But because there are separate tracks of sound a very complicated sheet of instructions must be followed. Kelly and I spent hours working on these instructions, and he was so sick at the time he could hardly stay out of bed. But we finally got it ready for the dubbing session. Kelly got on an airplane and went to New York to enter a hospital. I went to the dubbing session aremd with the written instructions.

The man who paid the lab costs and who was going to merchandise and release *We Have Met the Enemy and He Is Us* also came to the dubbing session and arbitrarily countermanded many of our instructions. The lab, of course, heeded him, unaware that these other instructions were Kelly's and that I was representing him. They treated me as if I were some upstart employee and the sound track turned out badly.

Q: Theoretically, couldn't the sound track always be redone?

SELBY KELLY: Well, I hope so. I don't know where all the sound tracks and things are now. My son Scott did the music for the film. He and Kelly had composed it, played it and recorded it.

Q: Again, theoretically, if all the parties involved could come to an agreement, couldn't the film be released?

SELBY KELLY: Yes. But when Kelly went to New York that time he was very ill. Some scenes were reshot up to six times. He was waiting for the miracle of getting enough money to do it fully animated, but he knew he'd have to have a crew to do it. So when on either side of a scene there was something hardly animated at all, he'd animate that himself.

Q: During 1970 and 1971, his artwork on the Pogo *comic strip was quite ornate. Do you think there was a relationship between what he drew for the strip and his work on the film? His assistant on the comic strip, Henry Shikuma, told me he used to ask Kelly, "Why are you doing all this extra work?"*

SELBY KELLY: I don't know, maybe Kelly did feel more artistic at that time. He wasn't going out and doing lectures or anything. In a way, he had more time to work on things. He was still having one book a year published.

Q: What happened after the dubbing and Kelly's return?

SELBY KELLY: When he returned to New York I didn't hear from him for a long time except for phone calls while he was in Lenox Hill Hospital. At that time we had agreed that we would marry, but we hadn't announced it or anything like that. Finally I decided to find out what was going on with his health. He'd say things like, "Oh, I'm doing pretty good." But he was still in the hospital.

So I came east to check up on him. He was very close to being dead. His feet and legs were quite swollen—they looked like they would burst if you touched them with a pin. He had edema from the knees down. This was from his diabetes. The sheet was propped up so it wouldn't touch his feet. Anyway,

he gradually got better and the hospital said they would release him home if I'd take care of him. I said that of course I would.

I learned how to give hypodermic injections so he could receive his insulin. I still can't believe that I could do that—stick a needle into anybody, much less Walt Kelly. He was released from the hospital in 1972 and could walk around the house a bit or take a short walk around the corner to Francesco's, a restaurant he liked. He enjoyed chatting with people he knew there.

Then he got to feeling fairly good. He was up and around and starting to do the strip again. *Time* magazine wanted to know if he would do a cover. He said yes, he would. We set a date for a conference.

Kelly and I went out and caught a taxi that cold and blustery day. He had to stand quite awhile because some young thing ran out and grabbed the taxi that we were about to get into. He was using two canes but she didn't care—she jumped in and away she went. Eventually another taxicab came but he was kind of chilled.

Kelly told the cab driver where to go. I didn't pay any attention because I didn't know where *Time* magazine had its offices. Well, the taxi let us out on the wrong corner. I was surprised when Kelly said, "This isn't the right place." We were on Fifth Avenue instead of Sixth Avenue, where *Time* was. I wanted to get another taxi but Kelly insisted he could walk one block. But it's a long block. He immediately got tired, of course, so he agreed to take another taxi.

I stepped out into the street to hail a taxi. Then another young gal came running down the sidewalk, zigzagging in between people. She was in a big hurry. She bumped into Kelly. Here he's standing there waiting, using two canes, and she knocked him down flat. He wrenched himself so badly trying to catch his fall that he was a bit shook up.

We did get a taxi and did go to the meeting at *Time*. However, during the meeting they called me out into the hall and asked me if I thought Kelly could really do the assignment. I don't remember it exactly but it called for caricaturing some political people from England or Europe.

I told the *Time* magazine people that if Kelly says he can do it, he can do it. But I promised to keep an eye on him and if anything happened I'd let them know. So we went home and Kelly went to bed. The next day he was still badly off, quite stiff from that

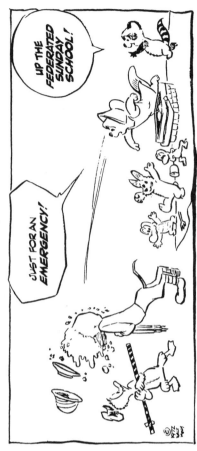

Sunday pages from the period of Kelly's ill health in Fall 1972 show how he struggled to keep the action in his slapstick comedy. Kelly always felt Sundays were for kids and rarely made political comment on those pages.

11-19   PUBLISHERS-HALL SYNDICATE INC.

fall. I had to call *Time* and tell them Kelly wouldn't be able to do the cover drawing.

When I called he seemed all right, but then Kelly went into a coma. I called the ambulance and they took him to the hospital but a room wasn't available, so they put him in a ward.

We weren't married at this time because he said that he wanted to be able to stand up for me so I could walk down the aisle. We had our marriage license and everything and then this incident happened.

In the hospital he nearly died before he got to intensive care. Some student nurse was supposed to prepare all patients being admitted. She bathed their faces and hands and scrubbed their teeth. Here's Kelly, comatose, and she filled his mouth with water, and said, "Just roll over and spit it out."

I stayed with him every second and that's probably how he lived through the experience. I screamed. I grabbed him by his shoulders and rolled him over on his side. The student nurse started hitting me and shoving me, saying, "Get away—this is my patient." It was a struggle. He was a big man. But I got Kelly turned over so he didn't choke and she ran down for the head nurse.

The head nurse threatened to evict me, but I would not be evicted. So she called the doctor, found out what was going on, and I was allowed to stay. Then they finally got Kelly into intensive care.

There the doctor decided one of Kelly's legs had developed gangrene. There was no choice but to amputate his left leg above the knee. His right leg was saved.

The day that the leg was amputated we had decided to get married. I wasn't a relative and wasn't supposed to be in the intensive care unit at all. The doctor allowed me to come in, but it was against all the rules.

Judge Sam Silverman, a good friend of Kelly's, came to visit him for three days in a row to make sure Kelly was of sound mind. Of course, we already had our marriage license and everything which showed Kelly's intent. So the judge married us. Steve Kelly was also present. Within half an hour of the ceremony, Kelly was on the operating table and they took his leg. The doctor told me Kelly had less than a 50/50 chance of recuperating, but Kelly had the spirit then. I believed he was going to get well and so did he. Then Kelly went back to intensive care. The date was October 23, 1972.

Q: But Kelly did recover after that?

SELBY KELLY: Yes, he came home and got better. We installed a chairlift so he didn't have to climb any stairs in the brownstone. The bedroom was on the second floor.

Q: At that time did Steve Kelly begin to work on the Pogo *comic strip?*

SELBY KELLY: No, none of us worked on it while Kelly was alive.

Q: When Kelly was physically unable to do the strip, who decided that the old Pogo *strips would be rerun?*

SELBY KELLY: The president of the syndicate, Mr. Cole, made the decision. Bob Reed was head of the New York office and he worked with the group on this. Then there was a woman editor whose name escapes me who made the selections. She hired George Ward to retouch the lines on the enlarged photostats.

Once in a while they would change the words in the balloons. I didn't become involved with the syndicate distributing *Pogo* until after Kelly died. I just stayed with Kelly. It was a full-time job taking care of him.

I know one time Bob Reed came over after Kelly was able to get up and around. Kelly met him downstairs. Bob strongly urged Kelly to get a crew together to take over production of the *Pogo* strip. The syndicate had rerun a lot of Kelly material. Almost all of the 1973 material was old strips. Bob told Kelly that they couldn't continue to print reruns because many editors had discovered what was going on, didn't like it, and were pulling out. *Pogo* was losing readership.

Kelly said okay and called Don Morgan on the West Coast. Morgan had done the backgrounds on the MGM picture, *Pogo Special Birthday Special*. Don Morgan and his wife came to New York and spent a weekend or more with us. He spoke with Kelly about doing *Pogo*. Kelly gave him a bunch of artwork and a few *Pogo* strips, then told Morgan to go back to the West Coast and study them.

Then Kelly started to write strips for Don to do. But Don didn't start doing them at that time. In fact, Kelly tried to draw some of his own but he would draw the characters smaller and smaller and smaller. Some of these strips were published. There were no backgrounds, just little tiny figures in the center. Well, the syndicate did the best they could with them. Actually, it seemed to me that if they'd taken photostats and blown them up they would have worked better but the time limit was short.

He did try to get caught up. Kelly tried to get George Ward to do some drawing. He gave him a Sunday page and asked him to do it in blue pencil. He told Ward to bring it back and show him as he wasn't sure of the storyline. After George went away, Kelly said, "I'm not sure he can draw it and I want to see what it looks like."

When George brought it back he looked at it and told George, "I've changed my mind—I'm not going to use this." Kelly was a perfectionist and he wasn't totally happy with the results. For one thing, George had no animation background.

Q: Did Don Morgan actually draw Pogo?

SELBY KELLY: Not at that time. Don went back to California. This guy from California with the film *We Have Met the Enemy and He Is Us* was calling up saying I don't like this and I don't like that. Kelly said, "You're not to make any changes." So the guy said, "If you won't change it, tell me who to have do it; or if you don't appoint somebody, I will change it." He was aware of Kelly's health. Kelly told him, "You have no right to change the film. If there are any changes to be made, I will see to it when I come out next time."

Q: So right up until Kelly's death, this film for which he had such high hopes was a muddle full of frustration and stress?

SELBY KELLY: Well, you usually see an answer print and make corrections. The guy sent us an answer print and Kelly projected it at home. Generally, he liked it. There might have been some things he'd have changed if he'd been in high health, but he said it was all right. Because he was feeling better, we went to California. He was in a wheelchair. This was in August, 1973.

Kelly was sick and tired of being confined to the New York house. The feeling was, if he were up and out maybe he would be up and out with a change of pace.

So we went out to Hollywood and met with the lawyer to deal with the film. We had spoken with a doctor on the West Coast prior to leaving New York City. Kelly hadn't been allowed to smoke or drink for some time.

Q: Regarding the smoking and drinking, did Kelly know he should have stopped long before he did?

SELBY KELLY: Oh, yes. In fact, after he stopped smoking I didn't know he had stopped. It was Christmas of 1971. I gave him a box of cigars and he told me that the doctor had just told him to quit cigars. Later, apparently he lit one. The next day he came to me and said, "What are you trying to do, kill me?" The cigar had made him ill. He never even tried to smoke any more.

As for drinking, the doctors said when we left the hospital after the amputation, that if Kelly took a drop of any kind of drink he'd die immediately. It was a slight exaggeration, but it did the trick. He was an obstinate guy and when he wanted to do something he did it. Eventually his doctor in New York did tell him that if he was very careful, some moderate drinking might not hurt him.

So when we got on the airplane and the attendant came around with beverages, Kelly took a glass of champagne. He immediately tested the rules. And when we got to California he told the people in the hotel that he was allowed to have a little to drink. The California doctor also agreed that some very moderate drinking couldn't hurt. So Kelly had a beer with dinner and maybe a glass of wine. But it was too much. He should have really had maybe half a glass of wine every other day or someting along those lines.

We had been in California less than a week. What he had drunk was relatively little, but it was too much. He became ill. He went to bed and had a very bad night. I became very sick too. I don't know if we'd both eaten something bad or if I was just tense. I called for the house doctor, thinking there was a doctor in residence at the hotel. It turned out their house doctor was farther away than if I'd called the one we'd been going to.

So this doctor for the hotel came in and started to treat me. I said, "Forget it. I'm not the one who's sick. It's my husband."

Even though the room was going around in circles for me I didn't feel I could be sick. The doctor went over and looked at Kelly. Kelly was saying, "Leave me alone. That's my wife. Go take care of her." The doctor told him, "You ought to be in the hospital." So then the doctor gave me something to quiet my tummy and he left.

In the morning I woke up and as usual I tapped Kelly on the hip and said, "Honey, it's time for your shot." I would never just give him his insulin shot. He hated that. At the hospital they'd sneak in on you when you were asleep. So I would always whack him on the hip. Then I injected him. I had ordered orange juice and his breakfast came. But he didn't wake up. I couldn't get him to wake up. I called the doctor.

Q: Was he in a coma?

SELBY KELLY: He was in a coma, but I didn't know it. He was always logy in the morning. The doctor told me to force some orange juice down his throat and I tried. The ambulance was called but it didn't come for almost two hours. When we'd called the hospital the third time they said the ambulance was on its way but they didn't have a bed ready. Can you believe it? It was Cedars Sinai Hospital—big, brand-new. Well, they finally got him there and he was placed in intensive care. Then he went to a different hospital later.

Q: He never returned to the East Coast?

SELBY KELLY: No, he died in the Motion Picture and Television Hospital, Woodland Hills, California. I was eligible for that hospitalization because of my long involvement making animated films. As my spouse, Kelly was also eligible.

Kelly did have Blue Cross and Blue Shield but the length of his illness and hospital stays had already eroded his benefits.

Cedars Sinai Hospital called me over to their office one day. I thought the medical insurance was paying Kelly's bill. I had turned in our identification cards and never heard a word from the hospital. They asked me to come to their office immediately. So I went.

A young man behind a desk said, ''Mrs. Kelly,'' and then proceeded to dress me down for neglecting to pay the hospital bill. I told him that nobody had given me a bill. He said, ''The insurance is no longer good. You owe us a lot of money. You haven't made any payments. We find it very difficult to keep your husband in this hospital.''

I replied, ''My husband is finding it very difficult to stay in your hospital.''

He became very embarrassed. He got up and left the room and I never saw him again. He sent a woman back in and she started talking to me and I said, ''Nobody has given me any kind of a bill. I have no idea what we owe.'' I was really irritated.

So they told me that if I didn't remove Kelly or pay the bill, Cedars Sinai Hospital would send him to the county hospital. At that particular time there was no way I could pay a $25,000 hospital bill.

Q: That's when you found you could place Kelly in what's sometimes called the Actors Hospital?

SELBY KELLY: I called the union (the Screen Cartoonists Guild) and asked about the hospital. They looked up my work history and were a tremendous help. I had contributed to the Actors Hospital over the years.

Also, at Cedars Sinai Hospital the doctor was telling me that Kelly was totally brain dead.

Q: Kelly never came out of the coma?

SELBY KELLY: Not officially, but I told that doctor I disagreed and that I saw reactions in Kelly. One day I was sitting beside the bed and I said to Kelly, ''Honey, I'm going to be gone for a little while. I'm going to go down and have a cup of coffee.'' I always treated him as though he was awake. And he said, ''I wish I could go with you.'' Well, the nurse who was in the room at the time almost fell out the window.

Then I didn't want to go, but he would feel better if I did, so I did.

I left and came back and the doctor came in. ''Hello, Mrs. Kelly, has your husband been doing anything today?'' I said, ''Yes, he spoke to me earlier.'' The doctor didn't believe me. Then the nurse said, ''I was here. I heard him.'' They were astounded. That was the last time before the hospitals were changed. He died on October 18, 1973.

Q: You went out to the West Coast in August. What month did Kelly enter the hospital?

SELBY KELLY: It was in late August. He was comatose and in intensive care most of the time. Actually he came out of the coma when he first entered Cedars Sinai Hospital.

Q: With all the human drama of the situation, how was the Pogo *strip maintained?*

SELBY KELLY: The syndicate had gone back to publishing reprints of *Pogo*. I gave Don Morgan some of the stories that Kelly had written for him. Then Don started drawing *Pogo* and we started sending them back to the syndicate.

Q: Did Don Morgan then actually draw the complete strip?

SELBY KELLY: Yes, he did. It's Kelly's story-line and Morgan's drawing. I'm not sure when they were published, but Don Morgan started drawing *Pogo* while Kelly was still in the hospital. This was most likely in September 1973.

Q: During the period from Kelly's funeral until all the family matters were settled, was it Morgan's stuff that carried Pogo *over the rough times?*

SELBY KELLY: Yes, but then Morgan suddenly had domestic troubles. There was an unexpected divorce. Apparently neither he nor his wife expected it would happen. He just wasn't prepared for the crisis and he was so upset he couldn't do the strip. So he got Willy Ito, who's a good animation person, to do two week's work. Believe me, it was like nothing you ever saw.

Q: Was it published?

SELBY KELLY: We had to. We had a deadline. It featured the funeral-director kind of guy, Sarcophagus McAbre, and Grundoon as the little baby in a diaper. But the strip was drawn too Japanesey. But then, Willy Ito *was* Japanese. To give him credit, he's a good artist, but he didn't have a *Pogo* model sheet and he didn't have time to practice doing the characters. However, as *Pogo* art it was unacceptable, but we had to use it.

I told Don Morgan that since he couldn't do *Pogo* I'd have to make other plans.

Q: That was when you began drawing Pogo?

SELBY KELLY: I began drawing *Pogo* using photostats. Henry Shikuma had been lettering and he continued to do so. I began doing everything, the dailies and the Sundays. Then Steve Kelly got involved helping me with it.

I told Steve that I thought there should be only one boss of anything. He immediately thought I meant myself. But I finished my sentence and said I wanted him to take total charge of the dailies and offered to help him anytime he wanted me to. I told him the daily strip was his baby and that I'd do the Sundays.

So Henry Shikuma drew the dailies and did the lettering on all the strips. They did the same thing I did on the Sundays, partially using photostats of Kelly's work because of the time element. They did get to a point where they were doing totally new artwork by Henry. Steve did the writing. That's how it went until *Pogo* was taken out of syndication. I did all of the writing and drawing, except for Henry's lettering on Sundays.

Steve became very tired of it after awhile and wanted to quit. I said okay, I'd find somebody to replace him—but of course I couldn't.

Once in awhile I would do a daily. Sometimes they'd have trouble with a deadline or I'd get an idea and work it up and ask if they minded using it. So I did help them some.

Q: Henry Shikuma must have enjoyed his relationship with Steve, as he spoke very highly of him in the interview published in Outrageously Pogo.

SELBY KELLY: Yes, I think so. Kelly used to say Henry was like an uncle to the boys.

Q: When you ended the syndication of Pogo *in July 1975, you still had enough newspapers on line for* Pogo *to be profitable?*

SELBY KELLY: Yes. I ended it because we'd paid all our bills, because I didn't like having Kelly look over my shoulder. Figuratively, I was doing his thing. I have no regrets about ending *Pogo* when I did.

A Christmas card created by Selby Kelly for Simon & Schuster in 1975.
The following year *Pogo: Bats and the Belles Free* **and** *Pogo's Body Politic* **were published.**

These are the last three Sunday pages written and drawn by Selby Kelly in July 1975. On Sunday July 20, 1975, Pogo Possum and his pals were officially "between engagements" on a daily basis. This circumstance ceased on January 8, 1989.

GORK!

.... THIS IS THE WEEK OF FRIDAY, THE THIRTEENTH ... OF PROFESSIONAL PEOPLE ... 50% BELIEVE IT'S SATURDAY ... 50% ARE OF THE OPINION IT'S MONDAY ... IT'S SOMEWHERES INBETWEEN .... ALONG ABOUT SUNDAY?

THAT'S THE OLD WAY ... VERY UNSOPHISTKATED.

REMEMBER WHEN KELLY HAD ROOM FOR HORIZONS?

THE LOST GENERATION?

POGO

THIS WORLD GOT ONE PROBLEM! TOO MANY FOR ME. FRIDAY-THE-THIRTEENTHS SHOULD COME ON A YESTERDAY.

WE'LL SHOW 'EM WHAT KIND OF STUFF WE'RE MADE OF ... AN INFURIATED MOB OF HUMORISTS ... OF HONEST, UNBIASED, OPEN-MINDED MEN ... PROFESSIONALS!

MILLIONS ... MAYBE EVEN HUNDREDS INTERVIEWED SAID THEY GOTTA CUT DOWN IN THE FULSOMENESS OF QUITE A FEW DEPARTMINTS.

ALL US COMEDIANS WILL BE OUT OF WORK!

WHICH, AS YOU CAN READILY SEE, IS A DEPLORABLE CONDITION ....

THAT'S WHAT'S WRONG WITH THE NEWSPAPER BUSINESS! PEOPLE!

7-13

..... IT'LL BE A LONG TIME AFORE THEY GET ALL THE BUGS OUT OF THE GUMMINT ... A MAN'S WORK REMAINS TO BE DONE.

I THINK RIGHT THERE YOU IS PUT YOUR FINGER ON A NATIONAL DISASTER ...

Field Enterprises, Inc. 1975

—224—

Pogo ceased his first run of syndication with this Sunday page, July 22, 1975.

Publishers-Hall Syndicate

401 NORTH WABASH AVE.
CHICAGO, ILL. 60611
TELEPHONE (312) 321-2795

November 8, 1973

FIRST GLIMPSE OF NEW (?)

POGO CREATIVE TEAM. . .

We asked Don Morgan, Walt Kelly's handpicked artist, to draw portraits of the new creative team which will be producing POGO from now on.

The enclosed art work is the result. If some of the faces look familiar, it may be because the new team has worked and lived so closely with Walt and his characters, they've begun to take on a resemblance.

Their names are clearly spelled out on the side of the boat (Kelly-style) just to help you identify them.

Bill Vaughan, associate editor of the Kansas City Star, is editor of the strip. Selby Kelly is Walt's widow, Steve and Andrew are his sons, Scott Daley is a writer, and Ol' Don Morgan you already know. As for the city of Saugus, it's just one of those delightful POGO mysteries.

PUBLISHERS-HALL SYNDICATE

30 EAST 42ND STREET, NEW YORK, N. Y. 10017 • TELEPHONE (212) 682-5560

This drawing by Don Morgan and the news release printed with it went out to *Pogo* subscribing newspapers on Nov. 8, 1973, shortly after Kelly's death on Oct. 18, 1973. The news release is incorrect in that Bill never edited *Pogo* after Kelly's death. Scott Daley is Selby's son from a previous marriage.

Starbeams

A Gentle Man—and a Genius

By Bill Vaughan

ASSOCIATE EDITOR

Herblock the cartoonist called me at home in the morning and I knew that the news was that Walt Kelly was dead. He had been terribly ill for a long time, but still he talked about getting back to work and had, indeed, drawn some "Pogo" strips recently.

Even with what I knew of his physical condition it seemed preposterous for Walt to die. He never took kindly to the departure of his friends, perhaps because he cared so deeply about them.

I remember when John Lardner died. He and Kelly had been planning a trip to Florida. Walt sat for two hours at Frank Campbell's in a solitary wake.

"I could almost imagine," he wrote me, "that we were on the train going to Florida. I was sitting there reading the paper and he was lying on the berth not saying anything. That's the way it would have been."

Those weren't the exact words, but pretty close. Kelly and Lardner were the heart of the Formerly Club, which met every Saturday at the Artist and Writers Restaurant, better known as Bleeck's, convenient to the back door of the Herald Tribune. It must be remembered that the name is Artist and Writers. Why the artist was singular and the writers plural has never been explained. The place's subtitle, as a reminder of the speakeasy days, was "Formerly Club." Hence the name of the loose organization of newspapermen, press agents, writers and cartoonists who gathered every week to play the match game.

It is a civilized game, possibly because it is so designed that nobody ever wins. It was played with great solemnity at Bleeck's.

Kelly loved bars and conversation and cigars with companions who shared his appreciation of the sort of tavern lifestyle that one must assume goes back at least to Shakespeare and Co. at the Mermaid. And, of course, there was the whiskey, too.

If his friendships were steadfast so were his enmities. He refused to believe that any friend of his could write or draw a bad line, or that anyone he disliked could produce a good one. Further than that, anybody that any of his friends didn't care for automatically appeared upon his list of incompetents.

But above all was his loyalty to "Pogo" and the other people of the Okefenokee. For all his delight in taking his ease in a tavern, no one ever worked more prodigiously than Walt Kelly. He was in every way a professional and a perfectionist.

He was, simply, a genius. The only one I have ever known, in contrast to many merely talented men.

His drawing skill was largely a product of his Disney years, but the ideas, the words, the wonderfully playful approach to the English language came from the unique brain of the Irishman from Bridgeport.

There have been many people who professed not to understand "Pogo" and others who objected to the political opinions that came through, particularly in the McCarthy days. But once you were hooked on "Pogo" you stayed that way.

Perhaps Pogo's best known line is, "We have met the enemy and he is us." Although, interestingly enough, it is difficult to pinpoint its first appearance in the strip.

Well, Walt is dead. In California, an unlikely place for him. He was a warm and sunny man whose life passed through many dark patches of personal tragedy.

I think he saw Pogo as the symbol of ordinary, decent, gentle people. What he wrote of the possum might well have been about himself:

"This is his home country. He knows it and he loves it. He has never had to join anything except the United States of America . . . And here he will stay, out on a limb a good part of the time, looking innocent and surviving."

Pogo is immortal. Walt lived only 60 years.

Bill Vaughan's obituary of Walt Kelly that appeared in the *Kansas City Star*.

The Pogo Special Birthday Special

As the interview with Selby Kelly in part concerns the production of the MGM/Walt Kelly/Chuck Jones animated television show, it is proper that the publicity campaign for the film be presented.

Phenomenal Pogophile Steve Thompson of Minnesota has alerted us that a video cassette of The Pogo Special Birthday Special *is available from MGM/UA Home Video, #MV-200704. Enjoy.*

Kelly wrote the "twinkling world of stage" news release. A photocopy of his handwritten rough draft survives.

Paul S. Hirt, promotion manager of the Chicago Sun-Times, *Pogo's home in Chicago in 1969, sent a letter to Dick Sherry of Publishers-Hall Syndicate in June 1969 to tell him of the positive ratings the show received.*

The show had a rating of 11.0. The typical four-week average for NBC at 8:30 P.M. had been 10.0. However, the firm Needham, Harper and Steers said the Pogo Special ranked third from the top among network shows as follows: Ed Sullivan (CBS) 20.0; FBI (ABC) 13.0; and the Pogo Special (NBC) 11.0.

The Nielson ratings for the two-week period ending May 25, 1969, showed the Pogo Special placing 12th with a 19.8 rating or a 33 percent share of the audience watching TV at 8:30 P.M., Eastern Time, May 18, 1969. Nielson estimated 11,290,000 homes were watching Pogo, approximately 15,000,000 people.

Those programs which placed ahead of Pogo *in that two-week period were: (in order)* Miss U.S.A. Beauty Contest, Family Affair, Lucy, Bonanza, Mayberry R.F.D., Gunsmoke, Green Acres, Dean Martin, Bewitched, Charlie Brown Special, *and* Gomer Pyle.

Kelly wrote and illustrated a special piece for Jack and Jill *magazine's May 1969 issue, including a special full-color cover. The May 17, 1969, issue of* TV Guide *contained the piece "Television Is Discovered in Okefenokee Swamp—And Vice Versa."*

Chuck Jones put out a news release declaring the week of May 18 to be National Porkypine Week, "an annual salute to a long-ignored but lovable native American creature."

"In taking the step of initiating National Porkypine Week, Jones is responding to a complaint made by Porkypine in the Special that there is 'No National Porkypine Week. . . . No, nor no Porkypine Day . . . or hour . . . or minute . . . or second, even.' "

The Pogo Special *centers on the fact that Porkypine is "a norphan" coming from a long line of "norphans,"* so all his friends in the swamp band together to throw him a surprise party.

In the cover letter of the Pogo Special *press package, Barrie Richardson, MGM Television's Director, Publicity & Exploitation, writes:*

"Because Pogo has been doing his own publicity for some 26 years now, we are happily spared the task of trying to persuade you that this newcomer to television is a personage to be reckoned with and worthy of your time and attention, not to mention space in your newspaper. Pogo and his happy Okefenokee band appear daily and/or Sundays in newspapers read by 43 million readers."

Chuck Jones, the film's co-producer with Walt Kelly, director and three of the voices in the animated special was head of the MGM Animation/Visual Arts Division. At the time Jones had been nominated 14 times for the Academy Award and was a three-time winner.

Jones came to MGM after 25 years with Warner Brothers, where he created cartoon characters, directed animated films, and was importantly involved in the evolution of many well-known folk, including The Road Runner and Wilie E. Coyote, Pepe Le Pew, Henery Hawk, Daffy Duck, Porky Pig, and the one and only Bugs Bunny.

For television, in addition to The Pogo Special Birthday Special, *he was producer-director of the* Bugs Bunny Show, Tom and Jerry, How the Grinch Stole Christmas, *and working on a feature film, both live action and animation, called* The Phantom Tollbooth. *Jones was also involved with* Horton Hears a Who *during the production of the Pogo Special.*

The studio biography on Chuck Jones noted he spent a great deal of time painting and that his work was exhibited in fine art galleries. His most recent collection at the time of the Pogo Special was a black-and-white series of the children of Biafra.

The Pogo Special also heralded the plastic Oxydol giveaway figures that Selby discusses in her interview. Each figure had a moveable part and the set included: Pogo (4 1/8" tall), Albert (5 3/8" tall), Beauregard (5 1/8" tall), Churchy (4 5/8" tall), Howland (4 1/2" tall), and Porkypine (4 3/4" tall).

The actual studio news releases are now reprinted beginning with "The Twinkling World" written by Walt Kelly. The illustrations intermingled are from model sheets of the film.

Pogo Promotion Written by Walt Kelly
for TV Special in May 1969

FOR IMMEDIATE RELEASE

The twinkling world of stage, screen and TV will be enlivened imminently with a *Pogo* film made entirely of old newspapers. The event comes twenty years to the day since *Pogo* started as a national strip.

From clips and snips and puppy dog tales distributed by Publishers-Hall Syndicate and appearing in this newspaper and five hundred or more other daily journals, *The Pogo Special Birthday Special* has been spawned. It is a half-hour animated cartoon show on NBC-TV, May 18, 1969, 8:30 P.M. E.D.T. (General audiences).

Walt Kelly, resident proprietor of the strip *Pogo*, was asked how it differed, working for films rather than newspapers. "Beneath the steely eyeglasses and attorneys of producers and/or editors beat the golden hearts of men endowed with plain humane kindliness," said Kelly, lighting a friend's cigar and smoking it with relish. "That is, those who are not afraid of animals. And who isn't? We all have families."

Working in Hollywood ("nervously"), Kelly did the story and character development for the film. "My character was developed an hundred fold," observes Kelly. "I learned how to swear in Mexican and how to hold my peace, otherwise it would have been filched."

Metro-Goldwyn-Mayer's Chuck Jones, a prize-winning director of shorts (Polka-Dot Bermuda's, 1946), read a few of the *Pogo* books collected from newspapers since 1951. In the first was *Porkypine*, a steady grump of a philosopher. Unknown to him, a party was being planned for him by the animals of the Okefenokee Swamp. His reaction to this, fraught with frustration, forms the basic story line of the film.

Mr. Jones also ran into *Bun Rabbit*, a drum-playing character who enjoyed celebrating all holidays at once or even twice in another book. His drumming ties the line together. Mr. Jones finally had Mr. Kelly seeing eye to eye with him and tooth to tooth with the Legal Department. After eighteen months of Kelly vs. lawyers and six months with Jones, a half-hour special was put together, a soap opera, courtesy of Proctor and Gamble.

A good deal of trouble was experienced at first when Mrs. Kelly, who threw out all references to blood, violence, bad words, guns, nude people and uncivil rights. "I have enough of that jazz at home," said Mrs. Kelly. Trimmed of these modern standard paraphernalia, the film stood at two frames of footage for quite a while but "was padded later," to quote Mrs. Kelly again.

In the past quarter-century, Kelly, when he is awake, figures that he has drawn 46,720 *Pogo* drawings, give or take a couple of discards, and that if he had to do it all over again he would have to give it careful thought.

To gather strength for all this, he was born early in the century. The year following this event, World War I started; in five years Prohibition had been passed, and the young artist, cut off, as it were, was busily scribbling on paper bags in a kitchen in Bridgeport, Connecticut.

Later, after keeping a careful eye in high school on the French language ("It is apt to sneak up on one"), and the French teacher, he prepared for a life of newspaper reporting by taking a job as a floor sweeper in a ladies' underwear factory. After serving the *Bridgeport Post and Telegram* as a police reporter, feature writer, artist and bon vivant for a few blameless years, the young man escaped to California and the W. E. Disney Animation Studios.

There he participated as a story man and animator in the creation of such epics as *Snow White, Fantasia, Pinocchio, Dumbo, The Reluctant Dragon,* a number of shorts, and something called *Baby Weems*. After a showing of this last, Kelly disappeared and next showed up in the Mojave Desert trudging east.

It was while working with the Foreign Language Unit of the Armed Services Institute in World War II that Kelly became fascinated by the dialects employed in the southeastern United States and evolved a feature about Okefenokee Swamp animals for a comic book in 1943. This graduated into a newspaper feature for Robert Hall of the Hall Syndicate in 1949. In May 1949 the feature called *Pogo* became nationally syndicated.

The *Pogo* comic strip now has upwards of 45,000,000 circulation daily and, using the large-sized rule of thumb employed by many magazines to estimate readership, may uncertainly convulse about a half billion readers per day, or somewhat more people than are currently present and breathing in the United States and Canada.

The dubious balance may be made up of readers of papers around the world. Certainly the Russians read it. In Japan one time the Soviet Embassy requested the Asahi Evening News (The Morning Evening News) to drop the strip because it was being unkind to a pig. The pig was said to resemble Premier Khrushchev.

Pogo, as a strip, is usually in some political trouble or other. "Why not?" asks Kelly. "Politics is a goldmine of comic material. Recall the shuttlecock shenanigans of the 1968 Presidential campaigns? They should be recalled."

The feature *Albert & Pogo* started in a comic book. It folded. The first newspaper to publish *Pogo* as a strip folded. Now numerous papers are in danger. Today TV trembles. *Pogo* will appear on NBC. NBC squirms.

Why didn't *Pogo* take up with TV before? In the early fifties the Disney Studio considered *Pogo*. Kelly, in turn, considered the Disney Studio. The possibility of *Walt Disney's Walt Kelly's Pogo* was a glum prospect.

Other talks with other producers convinced Kelly that it all would be a lot of work in the first place. MGM made its brave and noble offer two years ago. Working a year and a half vs. theatrical lawyers and six months with Chuck Jones, the director, Kelly, in the last place is convinced he was right in the first place.

"So much for history" sighs the oldest boy cartoonist in the world. "The rest is fantasy."

THE POGO SPECIAL BIRTHDAY SPECIAL

POGO TO END 26-YEAR SILENCE

SUNDAY, MAY 18 (8:30-9:00 PM, EDT) ON NBC-TV

Like the good child of old, Pogo has been seen but not heard. No less than 43 million newspaper readers in this country alone can see him daily and/or Sundays but the shy possum has yet to utter a sound.

Now, after twenty-six years of silence Pogo and ten of his highly unusual friends from the Okefenokee Swamp will burst forth not only in full voice but in song as well when they make their television debuts in "The Pogo Special Birthday Special," an animated musical in color on the NBC Television Network Sunday, May 18 (8:30-9:00 PM, EDT).

For co-producers Chuck Jones and Walt Kelly the situation will be exactly the reverse. Jones, head of the MGM Animation/ Visual Arts department, and Kelly, Pogo's creator, will each be heard but not seen as voices of several of the Okefenokee denizens.

Kelly is the voice of P.T. Bridgeport (a bear) who opens

MGM TELEVISION · 1350 AVENUE OF THE AMERICAS · NEW YORK, NEW YORK 10019

►

the show with the strains of an original song, "Go Go Pogo" With slight variations of voice, he is also the sound of Albert, the Alligator, and Howland Owl (a hot firecracker salesman).

Chuck Jones, who has three Academy Awards for his animation work, also is trying his hand as a member of the performing arts. His voice will be heard as Basil (an apprentice butterfly), Porkᵢpine and Bun Rab (a one-man celebration).

The voice of Pogo is a combination light tenor, low soprano, neither masculine nor feminine, and is provided by a veteran of animated voices, June Foray. She also provides the very womanly tones of the sophisticated vamp of the Okefenckee, Miss Mam'selle Hepzibah (a French skunk), and the motherly concerned voice of Mizz Boog (a bug).

Another veteran of voices for animation, Les Tremayne, will speak the words of Churchy La Femme (a madcap turtle) and Beauregard (a hound dog). Churchy also sings one of the numbers from the Pogo Song Book with music by Norman Monath and lyrics by Walt Kelly, "The Keen and the Quing". A chorus of butterflies will render "Happily Birthly Day" and "Truly True".

Eugene Poddany, who has composed much of the music for the "Tom and Jerry" cartoon series, as well as "Dr. Seuss' How the

Grinch Stole Christmas", has written additional music for "The Pogo Special Birthday Special" and conducts the orchestra.

All of these sounds will be combined with the finest artistry of animation to bring out the story of how wrong the forgotten man can be.

Porkypine, who doesn't have any family, gets the surprise of his life when Pogo invents a holiday for him, The Family Birthday, and all the folk of the Okefenokee join in the celebration. This all comes about while the others are trying to decide on their favorite holidays, and it is discovered that Porkypine doesn't celebrate any because he doesn't have anyone to celebrate with.

"The Keen and the Quing"??? A chorus of butterflies??? Look out, world. Here comes Pogo.

MODEL SHEET: CHURCHY AND HOWLAND

MODEL SHEET: PORKYPINE, MAM'SELLE HEPZIBAH AND POGO.

THE POGO SPECIAL BIRTHDAY SPECIAL

Storyline: - "THE POGO SPECIAL BIRTHDAY SPECIAL."

Everybody has a favorite holiday, so why not celebrate any time you choose? Christmas spirit the year around, Fourth of July patriotism in January, Easter eggs in September. "Why not?" reason the folk of Okefenokee Swamp. "Actually the year is so cluttered up with holidays now there isn't room for vacations."

Unfortunately one person in the swamp, Porkypine, doesn't celebrate any holidays on account of he is a "norphan" and doesn't have anybody to celebrate with.

Pogo and Mlle. Hepzibah, the petite French skunk, decide to right this great wrong by designating a particular day as Porky's birthday, so the entire swamp turns its considerable talents to planning a great surprise birthday party for Porky. Only thing is Porky becomes aware that a party is being planned -- but that HE hasn't been invited. When Porky finally does reach the party he is almost overcome when he learns that this is not only a birthday party but a "family" birthday party, an old traditional holiday just invented by Pogo. Porky is adopted by everybody

MGM TELEVISION · 1350 AVENUE OF THE AMERICAS · NEW YORK, NEW YORK 10019

▶

and now has a huge family, including alligators (Albert), dogs (Beauregard), owls (Howland), turtles (Churchy La Femme), apprentice butterflies (Basil and Bugs Fremont). The final song ends "Happily birthday birthday, dear Porklypine, Happily Family Birthday to you!"

###

CHARACTERS PROM MODEL SHEETS

THE POGO SPECIAL BIRTHDAY SPECIAL

ANIMATION: THE ART OF THE IMPOSSIBLE --- IN QUANTITY

"We engrave the Gettysburg address on the head of a pin, but on a production line basis."

This is the way Chuck Jones, head of MGM's Animation/Visual Arts department and three-time Oscar winner, describes his calling. "It is," Jones says, "the art of the impossible," but he says he loves it. He must; he's been doing it for more than twenty-five years.

That he loves his work is apparent, not only to audiences, but also to people like "Pogo's" creator, Walt Kelly, and famed children's book author, Dr. Seuss. Dr. Seuss wouldn't let anyone touch his characters until Jones asked to do an animated special, and now "Pogo" will come to life on television screens for the first time because Walt Kelly has implicit faith in Jones' taste and creative talents in animation.

As Kelly puts it, "Jones is a man who really knows what he's doing. That's why I said 'yes' when he approached me about doing a special with 'Pogo.'"

MGM TELEVISION · 1350 AVENUE OF THE AMERICAS · NEW YORK, NEW YORK 10019

▶

On Sunday, May 18 on NBC-TV, "The Pogo Special Birthday Special," starring the world famous possum and ten other characters from the Okefenokee Swamp, will have its premiere airing at 8:30-9:00 PM EDT. The thirty-minute program will be the culmination of nearly two years work for MGM's Animation/Visual Arts department headed by Jones and cartoonist Kelly.

Why does Jones call animation the art of the impossible? As he explains it, "It's taking something that doesn't exist and making it real, making it believable, bringing it to life on the screen."

During the past quarter of a century, Jones has not only made something real of things that didn't exist before, but some of his characters have become worldwide film stars. Besides Pepe Le Pew and the Road Runner, both of which he originated, he collaborated on "Daffy Duck", "Porky Pig", "Henry Hawk", "Elmer Fudd" and possibly the most successful and enduring character ever drawn, "Bugs Bunny".

More recently, Jones is noted for his collaboration with Dr. Seuss on "How the Grinch Stole Christmas" which has already become a Yuletide television tradition in only three years. Another book, "The Dot and the Line" by Norton Juster, became an animated short under Jones' direction winning him his third

▶

Academy Award.

"In some ways, these recent projects have been more difficult," says Jones. "At least they've required more discipline, because we're taking characters that already have identity, and bringing them to life. People know what they look like in a still form, so when they get up and move and talk they must be logical extensions of what has gone before."

"That's particularly true," he went on, "when you're dealing with Dr. Seuss characters from best-selling books, and the whole Pogo world which reaches perhaps 43 million readers every day in over 500 papers across the country. We must stick with the characters already developed, but bring them to life, otherwise no one would believe them."

Believability is not easy to come by when animating for motion pictures or television. There are short cuts, which some producers use, sacrificing believability, but Jones will have none of that. "The Pogo Special Birthday Special" for example, will require from 12-16 drawings per foot of film, and there are close to 2500 feet of film in the half-hour show, making a total of approximately 40,000 finished drawings, which have to be inked and painted as well, before they are filmed in full color.

"The average animator can do about three seconds of film a day in drawings," says Jones, "so you see what I mean about the head of a pin. And of course, I haven't even mentioned the hundreds and even thousands of preliminary sketches that we do in laying out a show. Those are all discarded as we do the finish drawings for film."

Nor did he mention the background paintings that must be done for every scene, just as a live action film must have sets. But the details of getting an animated special on the air are so infinite that Jones hesitates to try to describe everything. One of his favorite answers to people who ask him what he does is, "I produce whimsy by the yard."

MODEL SHEET: P. T. BRIDGEPORT

This poignant page was published on December 23, 1973, the Sunday closest to Christmas the year Kelly died.

Walt Kelly's Pogo — A New Engagement for the Okefenokee Players

In the report on Waycross's first Pogofest of July 1987, Selby Kelly is quoted about her interest in seeing *Pogo* and his pals resyndicated. That dream came to fruition on January 8, 1989.

One theory claims that culture, especially popular culture, goes in cycles. It's interesting that not only is *Pogo*, an icon of the 1950s, being rejuvenated, but also *Davy Crockett*, another mid-1950s hero is back.

Timing is so important when launching a comic strip. It would appear *Pogo*'s time is now. The Los Angeles *Times* Syndicate will begin syndication of *Walt Kelly's Pogo* with well over 250 newspapers.

For a while in the mid-1980s, the Walt Kelly Estate considered working with Flicky Ford, a retired Time-Life executive and friend of Walt Kelly. Although things didn't work out, Flicky Ford is the person who first made contact with writer Larry

Doyle and artist Neal Sternecky, the creative team on *Walt Kelly's Pogo*. Larry and Neal in turn now work closely with Selby Kelly to ensure *Pogo* continues in the Walt Kelly tradition.

The Los Angeles Times Syndicate sent out about two thousand promotional folders. Each was size 9 x 12 inches of heavy white uncoated stock with a 7½-inch picture of Pogo blind embossed on the cover and a three-color "I Go Pogo" button pinned to Pogo's shirt. Inside, two pockets contained six weeks of sample dailies and a number of full-color Sundays all printed on glossy stock.

The artwork on this page surrounded "Our Cheerful SALES STAFF." The balance of the enclosures are reprinted here; the only difference is that the originals were printed in black and gray.

In December 1988, the syndicate mailed out "house ads" to newspapers subscribing to *Walt Kelly's Pogo* so they could have a program to promo the strip prior to January 8, 1989.

It's a poo-rade!

Forty years after first delighting our child hearts, Pogo is back, backed by the rest of the Okefenokee irregulars, back with fresh mirth, relevant irreverence and new insouciance. It's a joyous homecoming, and well worth singing about.

Who go Pogo? *Los Angeles Times • Chicago Tribune • The Detroit News • Newsday • The Boston Globe The Philadelphia Inquirer • Newark Star-Ledger • Cleveland Plain Dealer • Miami Herald • Houston Chronicle Minneapolis Star Tribune • The Oregonian • St. Louis Post-Dispatch • Milwaukee Journal • The Arizona Republic San Jose Mercury News • Dallas Times Herald • The San Diego Union • The Sacramento Bee • The Pittsburgh Press • Louisville Courier-Journal • Seattle Times • The Indianapolis Star • Denver Post • The Hartford Courant The Baltimore Sun • Dayton Daily News • The Cincinnati Enquirer • Austin American-Statesman • The Birmingham News • San Antonio Express-News • The Record (NJ) • San Francisco Examiner • Tulsa World • The Salt Lake Tribune Tacoma Morning News Tribune • Albuquerque Journal • Syracuse Herald-Journal • Peoria Journal Star • Atlantic City Press • The Honolulu Advertiser • Baton Rouge Morning Advocate • Arkansas Democrat • Times Herald-Record (NY) Wisconsin State Journal • The Arizona Daily Star • Rockford Register Star • The Trentonian • Bridgeport Post-Telegram The Evansville Courier • Las Vegas Sun • Fort Wayne Journal-Gazette • New Brunswick Home News • Quad City Times North Jersey Herald and News • Santa Barbara News Press • The York Dispatch (PA) • San Mateo Times • Champaign-Urbana News-Gazette • Lorain Journal • Erie Morning News • Escondido Times-Advocate • Scrantonian Tribune The Anchorage Times • Centre Daily Times (PA) • Farmington Daily Times (NM) • Logan Herald Journal The Oak Ridger (TN) • Kearney Hub (NE) • Milford Citizen (CT) • San Clemente Daily Sun-Post • The Dalles Chronicle (OR) • Toronto Globe and Mail • Calgary Herald • Winnipeg Free Press • Halifax Daily News The Fort Mudge Most, and more...*

Go Pogo!

Beginning January 8

LOS ANGELES TIMES SYNDICATE ● TIMES MIRROR SQUARE ● LOS ANGELES, CALIFORNIA 90053 ● (213) 237-7987 ● TELEX 194308 ● FAX (213) 237-3698
LOS ANGELES TIMES SYNDICATE INTERNATIONAL ● 145 E. 49TH ST. ● NEW YORK, NY 10017 ● (212) 644-3355 ● TELEX 177145 ● FAX (212) 644-3359

Full page ad in *Editor and Publisher* magazine.

Possum and the Bunny

Pogo Possum
Swamp Yankee Studio
Box 2311
Bridgeport, CT 06608

For Immediate Release, 12-3-86

(Please let us know if you
want to receive a free
''Deck Us All with Boston
Charlie'' carol sing.)

PRESS RELEASE

Playboy Magazine Honors *Pogo*'s Papa for Lifetime Achievement

A holiday tradition for many American males and marsupials is to peruse the January edition of *Playboy* magazine which is published in early December. And in the current *Playboy* Walt Kelly's comic strip ''Pogo Possum'' is listed in an article on the best, as ''all-time best comic strip.'' The section of the compendium of ''bests'' that Pogo was selected in was for lifetime achievements. Pogo shared honors with such giants of American pop culture as the Oreo cookie, baseball, the Rolodex, pinball machine, and Jockey shorts.

Upon hearing this good news, Albert the Alligator asked, ''What are Jockey shorts?''

Playboy cited Walt Kelly's comic strip for being ''a world far hipper than Disney's ever was, and more nervy about taking on current idiocies.''

The piece was illustrated with a full-color reproduction of Pogo's famous Earth Day statement, ''We Have Met the Enemy and He Is Us.''

This is a busy time in the Okefenokee Swamp as Pogo Possum, Albert Alligator, Porkypine, Howland Owl and the others practice the famous Christmas carol ''Deck Us All with Boston Charlie'' for their annual concert in newspapers around the country.

''Tell all our fans we're doing fine,'' said Pogo on behalf of all the swamp critters. ''We're not syndicated but Tim Frew and our pals at Simon & Schuster are keeping a steady flow of new Pogo books available. Merry Christmas.''

A caption found with this photo identifies it as a party for the National Cartoonists Society's Ace Award held in the New York City Playboy Club about 1961. Seated (left to right) are race-car driver Sterling Moss, with cigarette; Hugh Hefner, publisher of *Playboy*; and with the eyeglasses and the back of his head, Ken Purdy, *Playboy*'s automobile editor.

Standing (left to right) are Irwin (''Dondi'') Hasen, Bill (''Smokey Stover'') Holman, a *Playboy* bunny, magazine cartoonist Dick Ericson, and Walt (''Pogo'') Kelly.

Hugh Hefner had just received the Ace Award as Amateur Cartoonist Extraordinaire.

Have you ever seen a group of talented men so intrigued by the mystery and incredible intricacies of ordering a round of drinks?

Turning the Pages on Walt Kelly

by Peter Schwed

Peter Schwed, former chairman emeritus of Simon & Schuster's editorial board, was associated with the publishing firm from 1945 until 1984. He was Walt Kelly's second editor following the untimely death in his 40s of Jack Goodman who was Kelly's first editor. While these excerpts from Peter Schwed's book, Turning the Pages: An Insider's Story of Simon & Schuster 1924–1984, *have been plunked down in the middle of the* Pogo Christmas *section of this book, there is a method to this seeming madness.*

The theory is presented that Kelly wrote "Deck Us All with Boston Charlie" for prisoners. This information was given to Peter Schwed by Bill Eveland, a close Kelly friend since the two met in Beirut, Lebanon, in 1956. The same information was given to Bill Crouch, Jr., in a phone call from Bill Eveland in August 1988. Mr. Eveland is mentioned on page 196 of Ten Ever-Lovin' Blue-Eyed Years With Pogo. *An interview with this gentleman, a retired career operative with the C.I.A., is hoped for in the future. Let it never be said that Walt Kelly didn't have a wide circle of friends.*

Our thanks go to Peter Schwed for allowing us to share with you the segments of Turning the Pages *on Kelly.*

Finally it should be mentioned that besides Pogo *books, Simon & Schuster's longest running cartoon series, the publishing house also presented Al Capp's* Li'l Abner *and* The Shmoo, *George Baker's World War II classic* Sad Sack, *and cartoon collections by* New Yorker *magazine stars Charles Addams; Peter Arno; Whitney Darrow, Jr.; and George Price.*

So outstanding was Essandess's reputation for publishing humor at this middle period of its history that an extraordinary number of submissions of a comic nature came its way, and two of them won such affection and success that each became for a time a substitute for or an embellishment to the Simon and Schuster colophon of the Sower. They were Walt

Kelly's *Pogo* books and Kay Thompson and Hilary Knight's *Eloise*. Here is a sampling of how Essandess adapted the first of its two pet characters for use on books, stationery, Christmas cards, sales letters, and ads, which was a good idea because there have been mighty few cartoon characters so universally beloved

as Pogo. Eloise was another, and you'll learn about her a few pages on.

The first collection of *Pogo* comic strips burst upon the world in 1951 as the result of Jack Goodman's insistence that there should be such a book for those who could not afford a daily newspaper, particularly since it was the only thing in the newspapers worth reading. As Walt Kelly wrote in a reissue of the original book in 1963, according to wall scratchings in the caves of Simon and Schuster, the daily strip in 1951 had 205 newspapers and 26,000,000 readers; subsequently those figures tripled or quadrupled, and over the years Essandess issued about thirty more *Pogo* books. *Pogo* was *the* comic strip of the nation and the many books that were published before Walt died each sold in the hundreds of thousands of copies. Several of them are still going strong, although of course not to that extent. *Pogo*, through the 1950s and 1960s, had the sort of unstinted popularity with fanatics that *Peanuts* enjoys today.

Pogo was more than a funny comic strip, and Walt Kelly was much more than a brilliant cartoonist. He was an engaging writer as well, and both in accompanying text and in the words in the balloons that issued from the lips of Pogo Possum—and the other denizens of the Okefenokee swamp, Albert Alligator, Howlan' Owl, Churchy Turtle, and others—Kelly turned out some of the most biting and effective satire against political evil of anyone in the nation. Senator Joseph McCarthy and Richard M. Nixon were particular targets, and readers, while constantly laughing at the humor, were at the same time getting punchy social commentary. Kelly had a powerful effect upon the entire nation but, since we all knew him so well on

almost a daily basis, he had a particularly strong one on his worshippers at Simon and Schuster. He was the only author whose advertising copy for his own books was so marvelous that the S & S professionals took the day off.

When Pogo was out on the swamp in his flatboat, Walt would letter a pal's name on the side of the boat, thus immortalizing that person in several hundred newspapers. It is one of my proudest publishing boasts that he did that twice with me in his full-color Sunday strips, and a black-and-white reproduction of one of them appears on the next page.

A collateral effect that *Pogo* worked upon millions of Americans ranging from schoolchildren to stockbrockers took place each Christmas in homes all over the country, when the words to the traditional carol, ''Deck the Hall with Boughs of Holly,'' suffered a deep sea change. People instead were singing the lyrics that the *Pogo* ensemble was chanting on those occasions,''Deck Us All with Boston Charlie.'' They didn't have the slightest idea of what the apparently nonsensical words meant either in that first line or the following ones, like ''Nora's freezin' on the trolley,'' or why strange towns like Kalamazoo, Walla Walla, Pensacola, and Louisville suddenly popped up in a verse, but they didn't care. The parody was fun to sing, forming a sort of brotherhood for *Pogo* fans among the carolers.

Walt Kelly went for years without ever revealing the secret of what inspired his catchy but incomprehensible lyrics. Now, in what is probably the biggest news scoop in this book, I am privileged to unveil it. Wilbur Crane Eveland, who along with Bill Vaughan of the *Kansas City Star* was probably Walt's closest

friend, had been saving it for a biography of Kelly that he had planned to write, but since he has now discarded that idea, he has graciously given me the story to use.

At one time Walt held something of a record for making speeches all over what *Pogo* fans know as the U. S. and A. He made no distinctions with respect to his audiences: the staff of the Harvard *Crimson* was no more attractive to him than an assemblage of convicts. It was for those convicts, for many of whom he had sympathy, that Kelly wrote "Deck Us All with Boston Charlie." There is an explanation for every unfathomable reference, but just a few are all that are needed here.

Walla Walla, Kalamazoo, Pensacola, and Louisville are the sites of state prisons. "Boston Charlie" was the name given to all guards in prisons—you can look up "Charlie" in Eric Partridge's *Dictionary of Slang* and you will find that he is the man with the stick, the prison guard. Why "Boston"? A throwback, in all probability, to the days of the original Colonies.

Why is Nora "freezin' on the trolley"? "Nora" is the cognomen given to sexual partners of male prison inmates, and the answer to her/his cold condition comes in two parts. The trolley is the wire that inmates string between cells for use in passing notes to one another. Thus, Nora was not communicating via the trolley. The second aspect of the line is that a person in the "freezer" is in solitary confinement, so Nora was not only not communicating, he/she had been slapped into solitary.

You may wonder why Kelly, a law-abiding citizen, had enough empathy for his convict audiences to write a special, secret Christmas song for them. I suspect it was because that good man felt, along with Pogo, that we are all God's Screechers.

A BEAR TALE

"MANY CENTURIES AGO IN THE LAND OF WEST BOUNDBUSSES THERE WAS A HANDSOME PRINCE.

"NOT ONLY WAS HE HANDSOME, HE WAS BRAVE. HE RODE A FIERCE STALLION, NO SADDLE AND NO REINS.

"HE WAS THE DARLING OF THE COUNTRY, ESPECIALLY BELOVED BY THE CHILDREN.

"HE WAS ALSO KNOWED FAR AND WIDE AS A REMARKABLE SINGER... HIS VOICE WAS LIKE NO OTHER.

"ONE DAY OUR HANDSOME PRINCE BEHELD A BEAUTIFUL PRINCESS. HE IMMEDIATELY GOT A PAIN IN HIS STOMACH.

"HE DECIDED IT WAS LOVE AND NOT BREAKFAST AND OFFERED TO FIGHT ONE AND ALL FOR HER HAND...

"HOWEVER, BEING A MAN OF TRUE COMPASSION, THE PRINCE KNEW THAT SOMETHING MORE GENTEEL WAS NEEDED.

"THE FERTILE BRAIN OF THE PRINCE STRAIGHTWAY SPUN OUT A MASTERLY PLAN···"

"HE CALLED THE ROYAL POET AND HAD HIM DICTATE A SERENADE FOR THE LOVELY PRINCESS.

"HOWEVER, THO' THE PRINCE WAS A MAN OF MANY TALENTS, HE COULD WRITE BUT COULD NOT READ··· SO, HE CALLED THE POET AGAIN···"

"HE LEARNED THE POET HAD READ WHAT HE'D WRITTEN, EATEN THE MANUSCRIPT AND JUMPED OUT OF THE WINDOW···"

"COURAGEOUSLY, THE PRINCE SANG THE SERENADE AS HE RE-MEMBERED IT ··· A SMALL BOY HURRIED UP WITH DIRE TIDINGS···

"THE PRINCE LEARNED THAT HIS LOVELY PRINCESS HAD BEEN INCARCERATED BY HER EVIL DADDY··· THE PRINCE SWORE A MIGHTY OATH!

"HE RUSHED BRAVELY AT HER DOOR··· HE WOULD TEAR HER OUT OF HER PRISON BY BRUTE STRENGTH!

"FROM WITHIN THERE WAS A MIGHTY RESISTANCE··· THE PRINCESS COULD BE HEARD SCREAMING.

"WHEN THE PRINCE FINALLY BROKE THE DOOR DOWN, THE PRINCESS WAS OUT OF HER MIND WITH FEAR.

"EVIDENTLY SHE HAD BEEN GIVEN A VANISHING POWDER BY HER EVIL DADDY. SHE DISAPPEARED!

"AT ANY RATE, NO ONE WAS HOME. THE PRINCE TOOK HIS MEMORIES, SUCH AS THEY WERE, WENT HOME ALONE AND LIVED HAPPILY EVER AFTER."

A VISIT FROM ST. NICHOLAS

(To the Moon)

Pogo's best splash of publicity during the 1987 holiday season was a reprinting of "A Visit From St. Nicholas" in full glorious color in the Sunday New York News Magazine, December 20, 1987. It included the cover and ten pages inside.

The magazine's editor, Jay Maeder, is a foot-stomping, hard-drinking, rantin'-and-ravin' Pogophile. Alleluia. The cover reprinted the Kelly cover for Newsweek of December 26, 1955.

While the years rolled on and Pogo was not in national syndiction, fewer and fewer newspapers seemed to answer the call to publish Pogo at Christmas. Always some major paper, in this case the largest-circulation tabloid daily in the nation, would come through splendidly.

In 1822, the Episcopal priest Clement Moore wrote "A visit from St. Nicholas" solely to amuse his six small children. It was published the following year in only one newspaper. As Kelly loved Christmas and children, it's most fitting we reprint his version of this classic poem.

The children were nestled
All snug in their beds

While visions of sugar plums
Danced in their heads;

When out on the lawn
There arose such a clatter.

I sprang from the bed
To see what was the matter.

Away to the window
I flew like a flash,

Tore open the shutters
And threw up the sash.

When, what to my wondering
Eyes should appear,

But a miniature sleigh,
And eight tiny reindeer,

With a little old driver,
So lively and quick.

I knew in a moment
It must be St. Nick.

More rapid than eagles
His coursers they came,

And he whistled and shouted
And called them by name:

"Now, Dasher! Now, Dancer!
Now, Prancer and Vixen!

"On, Comet! On, Cupid!
On, Donder and Blitzen!

"To the top of the porch!
To the top of the wall!

"Now dash away! Dash away!
Dash away all!"

As dry leaves that before
The wild hurricane fly.

When they meet with an obstacle,
Mount to the sky.

So up to the house-top
The coursers they flew,

With a sleigh full of toys,
And St. Nicholas, too.

And then in a twinkling,
I heard on the roof

The prancing and pawing
Of each tiny hoof.

As I drew in my head,
And was turning around,

Down the chimney
St. Nicholas came with a bound.

His eyes, how they twinkled!
His dimples how merry!

His cheeks were like roses!
His nose like a cherry!

He had a broad face
And a little round belly

That shook, when he laughed,
Like a bowl full of jelly.

He spoke not a word
But went straight to his work.

And filled all the stockings:
Then turned with a jerk,

And laying a finger
Aside of his nose,

And giving a nod
Up the chimney he rose;

He sprang to his sleigh,
To his team gave a whistle,

And away they all flew
Like the down of a thistle.

But I heard him exclaim,
Ere he drove out of sight,

"Happy Christmas to all,
And to all a goodnight!"

A PAGE OF THANKS

The Okefenokee Star and these anthologies would not be so enjoyable or so packed full of information if we didn't have many wonderful Pogophile friends. The editors would like to thank:

Bill Watterson
Edward Mendelson
Thomas Andrae
Geoffrey Blum
Ward Kimball
Jud Hurd
Malaika Adero
George J. Lockwood
Nancy Beiman
Peter Schwed

Bill Maher
Helen Barrow
Milton Caniff
Stan Drake
Jimmy Walker and staff
Bart Thigpen
Iris Hitt
Steve Thompson
Lucy Caswell
Luther Boren

and the countless Pogophiles who send suggestions in the mail. These should be sent to: *The Okefenokee Star*, Swamp Yankee Studios, P.O. Box 2311, Bridgeport, CT 06608.

Since the last volume was published (*Pluperfect Pogo*), the family of Walt Kelly has authorized the formation of an official Pogo Fan Club. Those interested in keeping up to date on the possum's progress should write to: Pogo Fan Club, c/o Steve Thompson, 6908 Wentworth Avenue South, Richfield, MN 55423.

Jud Hurd, publisher and editor of the quarterly magazine *Cartoonist PROfiles*, was extremely generous in letting *The Okefenokee Star* reprint a number of interviews. *Cartoonist PROfiles* is one of the premier magazines published on cartooning. For more information write to: Jud Hurd, P.O. Box 325, Fairfield, CT 06430.

Best of luck to *Walt Kelly's Pogo's* creative team and the Los Angeles *Times* Syndicate for many, many happy years of syndication.

Chronological List of Pogo Books
Published by Simon & Schuster/Fireside Books

Many new Pogophiles are surprised to discover the extensive list of Pogo books. *Phi Beta Pogo* is the 45th Pogo book published. To assist those who enjoy browsing in second-hand bookstores, here is a list of the books.

1. Pogo (1951)
2. I Go Pogo (1952)
3. Uncle Pogo So-So Stories (1953)
4. The Pogo Papers (1953)
5. The Pogo Stepmother Goose (1954)
6. The Incompleat Pogo (1954)
7. Pogo Peek-a-Book (1955)
8. Potluck Pogo (1955)
9. The Pogo Sunday Book (1956)
10. The Pogo Party (1956)
11. Songs of the Pogo (1956)
12. Pogo's Sunday Punch (1957)
13. Positively Pogo (1957)
14. The Pogo Sunday Parade (1958)
15. G. O. Fizzickle Pogo (1958)
16. The Pogo Sunday Brunch (1959)
17. Ten Ever-Lovin' Blue Eyed Years With Pogo (1959)
18. Beau Pogo (1960)
19. Pogo (Election) Extra (1960)
20. Pogo a la Sundae (1961)
21. Gone Pogo (1961)
22. Jack Acid Society Black Book (1962)
23. Instant Pogo (1962)
24. Pogo Puce Stamp Catalog (1963)
25. Deck Us All with Boston Charlie (1963)
26. The Return of Pogo (1965)
27. The Pogo Poop Book (1966)
28. Prehysterical Pogo in Pandemonia (1967)
29. Equal Time for Pogo (1968)
30. Pogo: Prisoner of Love (1969)
31. Impollutable Pogo (1970)
32. Pogo: We Have Met the Enemy and He Is Us (1972)
33. Pogo Revisted (1974) *Reprints*: The Pogo Poop Book, Instant Pogo, The Jack Acid Society Black Book
34. Pogo Re-Runs (1974) *Reprints*: I Go Pogo, The Pogo Party, Pogo (Election) Extra
35. Pogo Romances Recaptured (1975) *Reprints*: Pogo: Prisoner of Love, The Incompleat Pogo
36. Pogo's Body Politic (1976)
37. Pogo: Bats and the Belles Free (1976)
38. Pogo Panorama (1977) *Reprints*: The Pogo Stepmother Goose, Pogo Peek-a-Book, Uncle Pogo So-So Stories
39. Pogo's Double Sundae (1978) *Reprints*: The Pogo Sunday Parade, The Pogo Sunday Brunch
40. Pogo's Will Be That Was (1979) *Reprints*: Positively Pogo, G. O. Fizzickle Pogo
41. The Best of Pogo (1982)
42. Pogo Even Better (1984)
43. Outrageously Pogo (1985)
44. Pluperfect Pogo (1987)
45. Phi Beta Pogo (1989)

IN ADDITION

Pogomobile (1954) *This was not a book, but a mobile, packaged in its own decorated envelope with a picture on the front and instructions on the back.*